Regional Italian Cookery

THE INTERNATIONAL WINE AND FOOD SOCIETY'S GUIDE TO

Regional Italian Cookery

Robin Howe

COLOUR PHOTOGRAPHY BY KENNETH SWAIN

DRAKE PUBLISHERS INC
New York

First published in the United States of America in
1972 by Drake Publishers Inc.,
381 Park Avenue South, New York, 10016, U.S.A.

Published under the auspices of
The International Wine and Food Society Ltd,
Marble Arch House, 44 Edgware Road, London, w2.

© Robin Howe 1972

This book was designed and produced by
Rainbird Reference Books Ltd,
Marble Arch House, 44 Edgware Road, London, w2.

Printed in Great Britain by
A. Wheaton & Co, Exeter, Devon

Editor: Susan Standen

Indexer: Dorothy Frame

Library of Congress Catalog Number 72-4329
ISBN 87749-321-9

For George Rainbird, in the hope that this book
will help him to enjoy Italian food and wines with the same
pleasure as he does the French

Also by the author

Balkan Cooking

Cooking from the Commonwealth

A Cook's Tour

A Dictionary of Gastronomy (with André L. Simon)

Far Eastern Cookery

French Cooking

German Cooking

Greek Cooking

Italian Cooking

Making your own Preserves

Poultry and Game

Rice Cooking

Russian Cooking

Soups

Sultan's Pleasure (with Pauline Espir)

contents

 # list of color plates

# acknowledgments

Over the past twenty years I have been a fairly regular visitor to Italy and this year, in order to write this book, I stayed for several months in different places, keeping house in the Italian fashion but also traveling a great deal. At all times and in all places I seemed to be talking about food; asking a great many questions and receiving long and detailed replies.

There is no doubt therefore that I owe a 'thank you' to the many Italian men and women, in the markets, restaurants, shops and even on the streets. I remember coming out of a butcher's shop in Diamante, Calabria, clutching a leg of lamb and being instructed by a passer-by on just how she would roast her lamb—with potatoes and rosemary—and to make sure that I at least added the rosemary she pulled me off a sprig from her own bunch.

However, apart from the mass of people who have generally helped me there are those who have assisted in a more definite manner: the Contessa Salvatori of Perugia, Ruth Fricker of Lucca, the late Nancy Catheron-Cogan whose guest I was for so long in Sicily, Signor Pasquale, as D. P. Vuilleumier of Ravello is affectionately known, Eva Agnesi of Imperia, Luciano Draghetti of Bologna, Scoditti Pirro of Brindisi, Vernon Jarratt of Rome, and the several Marinas, Ginas, Pinas and Marias: the cooks of friends who never minded my coming into their kitchens to watch and who cheerfully gave me cooking 'lessons'. I should also like to thank Rosemary Wadey who prepared the food for photography and finally my husband for appreciating my enthusiasm for Italy and sharing the eating, drinking and driving all over the country.

Perugia, 1971

# introduction

Italian cooking reflects the character of the Italian people, it is imaginative, with infinite variety, uncomplicated, sometimes elegant and at other times earthy; in other words, it is Mediterranean cooking at its best. Dr Gino Tani, of the Academy of Italian Cuisine, wrote of his country's cooking: 'In every region the cuisine strikes a profound harmony with the climate, with the beauties of the landscape. It varies from city to country and from town to town, just as does the mercurial Italian temperament.'

The history of food and eating in Italy is ancient and fascinating. While other Europeans were still gnawing at bones and eating messily with their fingers from a communal bowl, the Italians were using forks, which they invented, and had place settings. Their condiment sets were fashioned in silver and gold and designed by well-known artists, like the great Benvenuto Cellini, who created the famous salt cellar of Francis I, now at Vienna. By the fifteenth century the Italians were printing books with advice on cooking, on table manners, and with emphasis on the presentation of dishes in an orderly sequence: some to be carried in from the kitchen, others to be served from the *credènza*, sideboard.

The earliest cook book is generally accepted to be that supposedly written by the Roman gourmet Apicius in the first century A.D., which abounds in recipes for sausages, meat loaves and vegetables. There are also many recipes for sweet-sour dishes which combine meat, honey, vinegar and syrups; these provided the origins of many present-day sweet and sour combinations.

To compare the Italian and French cuisines is as useless an exercise as comparing their wines. Nor should it be thought that Italian cooking is an imitation of the French. Quite the contrary. Catherine de Medici (heiress of one of the richest and proudest families in the then divided Italy) on leaving her native country in 1533 to become the bride of the second son of Francis I of France (himself an admirer of the Italian cuisine), took with her as part of her dowry a small army of Italian pastry cooks and chefs. This culinary entourage caused something of a stir in France, for these Italian *maîtres queux* (head chefs) soon became fashionable and introduced to French tables artichokes, truffles, quennelles, a liking for veal, grated Parmesan cheese, sweetbreads, liver etc.

This fashion in Italian chefs lasted until the time of Henry IV of France for, as

Larousse Gastronomique states: 'At that time the Italian *maîtres queux* were considered the best in the world. These Italian cooks, against whose instruction the French practitioners had the good sense not to revolt, taught them a great many recipes which have since remained in the French repertoire.'

Undoubtedly the apex of Italian cooking was reached in the sixteenth century, with the finishing touches of elegance and refinement given in the seventeenth century. In the nineteenth century came the great restaurants where the *bourgeoisie* could enjoy the culinary pleasures that had hitherto been the privilege of the princes and the aristocracy.

There are two great zones of cooking in Italy, the wine-and-olive zone, and the milk-and-butter zone. Emilia-Romagna, Lombardy and Veneto are cattle country where the olive tree does not flourish, hence the milk and butter industry; while in Umbria, Liguria and the South, where olive trees cover vast areas of the country, cooks use olive oil, and are exceedingly particular about quality and flavour. Tuscany is probably one of the few areas where both butter and oil are used in cooking, mainly because both cattle and olive trees are plentiful. Lucca, an ancient town near Florence, is well known for its olive oil.

The hitherto rigid regional aspect of Italian cooking is breaking down slowly over the years mainly because of better transport, the introduction of supermarkets, and the mobility of Italian workers who take with them their own methods of cooking. Rome itself is a great collector of regional dishes, later slyly claiming them as its own.

It is a standard pattern throughout the country for Italians to start with a first course before the main course. This first course might well be the antipasto, designed to whet the appetite, not to dull it, or, as in Piedmont, soup. 'Even a condemned man is entitled to a bowl of soup', is a local saying. Pasta starts the southerners' meal, while rice in a variety of forms, but mainly as a risotto, begins the meal eaten in the North.

Another fairly standard pattern of living throughout Italy is the absence of breakfast, even the light continental variety. Most Italian men and women on their way to work, stop off at the nearest cafe to drink a coffee and eat a sweet bun. Others will stop at the local delicatessen and have a sandwich made up for them, usually of thick warm bread enclosing ham, salami, mortadella etc.

THE REGIONS

PIEDMONT

The name means 'at the foot of the mountain'. The Alps slope down laying out forests and grazing meadows through which flow rivers and streams, thus providing the materials for a cuisine of heavy stews, thick soups, meat roasts and sauces, as well as fish from the rivers and lakes. It is substantial peasant food, married to the more subtle dishes of the Court, dating from the days when Piedmont was a kingdom. It was Piedmont's King Victor Emmanuel who became the first ruler of united Italy in 1861, thus causing a Piedmont writer to declare that 'Piedmont gave birth to gastronomic Italy'.

Without doubt the most important single item of food in Piedmont is the fragrant white Alba truffle which, finely flaked, is dispensed with regal largesse and provides the dominant note to the cooking of the region. It is sprinkled over meat, turkey breasts and ragouts, over rice dishes, cheese and even salads. It 'makes' the Piedmont *fonduta* and the region's equally famous *bagna cauda*. When you see *alla piemontese* on the menu this usually implies that the dish is truffled.

Here, perhaps more than anywhere else in the country, it is believed that good cooking begins in the market, although this is the universal belief of all Italians. Markets from the Alps to Sicily are filled with eager customers picking over and choosing their produce, demanding the freshest and discarding the wilted. Not for the Italians that forbidding 'please do not touch' sign.

The irrigation by alpine streams makes Piedmont's soil a fine producer of vegetables which are often served raw with a sauce for dunking, *bagna cauda* is an example. The most important of their meat dishes is *bollito variato*, served in a splendid frame of vegetables and pickles, an exception to the Italian rule of serving only a few potatoes and salad with the meat, plus *salsa verde*, *salsa di pomodoro* or other local sauces. There is game in plenty in the heart of the Italian Valtournanche where you can sample wild boar, goat and chamois cooked in rich spicy sauces. Especially good is *camoscio in salmi*, chamois braised in red wine with garlic, herbs and anchovies and flavoured with *grappa* or brandy. Other delights are a haunch of venison roasted over hot coals; *finanziera di pollo*, chicken giblets with sweetbreads, mushrooms and truffles cooked in a *ragù* or tomato sauce; *pernici allo zabaione*, partridge with zabaione sauce; and finally *tortino di tartufi alla piemontese*, layers of game meat and sliced truffles served on toast with a wine and game sauce.

The Piedmontese are also rice and polenta eaters and serve these as a first course when not serving soup. But if a pasta is served it will be a local speciality such as *agnolotti* with its minced beef and vegetable stuffing and a rich meat sauce, or potato or semolina gnocchi served with melted Fontina cheese, *gnocchi alla fontina*.

The flooding of the rice fields brings frogs which are made into a stew, *pane alla piemontese*, or soups, or the legs are fried in a batter, *rane dorate*. Other attractions of the local cuisine are pheasant stuffed with truffles, *fagiano tartufato*, or cooked with mushrooms, *fagiano con funghi*; or *lepre alla piemontese*, hare cooked in a sauce which includes brandy, sugar and bitter chocolate. Maybe because of the Bonapartist influence, there are a number of dishes labelled *alla marengo*, all slightly different, hardly surprising if one considers the odd combination of ingredients that were said to have gone into the original dish created for Napoleon after the battle in which he defeated the Austrians at Marengo in 1800.

Turin, the capital of Piedmont, is credited with having invented *grissini*, bread sticks, Napoleon called them *les petits bâtons de Turin*, as well as most of the sweet dishes of the region which are as much appreciated outside of Piedmont as locally. King Emmanuel Filiberto introduced cocoa into the city, thus there are many chocolate confections, such as *gianduiotti*, nut chocolates, for which Turin is famed. Other Piedmont sweet dishes are the *marrons glacés*, candied chestnuts of Chiusa di Pesio; Pecetto cherries simmered in Barolo wine; the *caramelle* or *diablottini* of Turin; the *dolce torinese*, a light chocolate cake; and the *nocciolini*, macaroons, of Chivasso.

Of the Piedmont cheeses, the three best are Fontina, Robiola and Tome, and it is the first which goes into many local dishes.

LOMBARDY

When we think of Milan, the busy capital of Lombardy, the first image that comes to our mind is that of the cathedral, followed by thoughts of risotto and *panettone*, or so one reads in the guide book. This interest in food was probably always there. A Milanese artist, Giuseppe Arcimboldo, made a name for himself in the sixteenth century by painting human likenesses from a fantastic combination of vegetables and fruit; while Bergamo, also in Lombardy, devoted a school of painting to the subject of food.

Veal dishes are the speciality of Lombardy, the modest but good shin of stewed veal called *ossobuco*, the more sophisticated *vitello tonnato*, are two examples. There is *annegati*, roast veal flavoured with white wine, and the breadcrumbed cutlet, *costoletta alla milanese*. Beef is simmered for hours in red wine or thick sauces to make a succulent beef stew, *stufato di manzo*. Pork comes into its own in the *cassoeula*, a dish of pork and vegetables, so does *busecca*, tripe cooked in broth with onions and other vegetables. The *fritto misto alla milanese* when in full flight, is probably one of the dishes of which the Milanese are most proud. Snails, frogs and game are popular, and guinea fowl, *faraona alla creta*, a legacy from the Romans, is baked in clay to retain its natural flavours. A speciality of lovely Bergamo is *polenta e osei*, spit-roasted small birds served in a rich sauce on top of a mound of polenta. Another favourite but heavy winter dish is *polenta pasticciata*, baked polenta in alternate layers with onions, mushrooms, salami and a sauce, and occasionally flavoured with truffles.

The lakes, especially Lake Como, supply fish: perch, shad, pike and carp. Specialities are *tinca carpionata*, fried fish marinated in wine and spices and small dried shad, *agoni seccati in graticola*, also called *missoltitt*.

Although the Lombardians consume vast quantities of rice and polenta, they have their pasta favourites. Bergamo has *casonsei*, ravioli with a spiced minced beef stuffing dressed with butter and grated cheese; *pizzoccheri*, a casserole of noodles and mixed vegetables; and *tortelli di zucca* from San Lorenzo, ravioli with a sweet pumpkin and Cremona *mostarda* filling, served sprinkled with grated Parmesan cheese. (*Mostarda de Cremona* is a mixture of candied fruits with mustard in a sweet syrup.) One of the best-known vegetable dishes is *peperonata*, peppers, tomatoes and onions cooked together in oil and butter.

The most popular of the sweet breads in Lombardy is *panettone*, originally eaten only at Christmas. It is a type of fruit *brioche* and comes in every size from a bun to an immense loaf, and has its full share of local legends. It is distributed throughout the country as is its rival *colomba pasquale*, the Easter bun or 'dove' cake. The dove is a reminder of a battle fought in 1176 when two doves landed close to the Milanese army just before they went into battle against Frederick Barbarossa of the Holy Roman Empire. The doves were a sign, thought the Milanese, of divine protection.

Macaroons, *amaretti*, are reputedly an invention of the Italians, so perhaps it is not remarkable that we hear so much of them. In Lombardy the best are the almond macaroons, *amaretti di Saronno*. There are bite-size buns, aniseed-flavoured *pan de mej*, and the spicy *cos di mord* (the name means to bite) which are hard and dry. In the autumn *busecchina*, chestnuts simmered in wine, is served, and *torrone di Cremona*, a honey and almond-flavoured nougat. Finally there is a vast array of macaroon-like biscuits with such names as *fave dei morti*, beans of the dead.

TRENTINO-ALTO ADIGE

Although these two zones have been united to form this region, there is considerable difference between them. Trentino, correctly speaking, is the region which occupies the central part of the Adige valley into which run other lovely valleys and above which towers the massif of the Dolomites and the Adamello group. This is a region of strong Germanic or, if preferred, Austro-Hungarian culinary influences, for it was for many years under foreign domination. This shows itself particularly in the wines, of which there are twenty different varieties, and most of these excellent wines are produced on the German pattern. There are also numerous Austrian and German fruit drinks which are popular in Italy, such as *Himbeersaft*, raspberry juice, known in Italian as *sciroppo di lamponi*. Then there are the various liqueurs with their Austro-Slav influence, for example, *Slivovitz*, *Aquavit*, *Kümmel*, and *Enzian*, gentian liqueur, as well as several aniseed-flavoured drinks. Especially popular is the German wine bowl, *Waldmeister Bowle*, which in Italian becomes *asperula odorata*, and in English simply woodruff wine bowl. But maybe woodruff is as foreign to English ears these days as either of the foreign names.

Probably the most interesting aspect of the cooking of this region is its split personality quality. There is a mixing of style and considerable assimilation of one cooking school with another, rather than one style conquering another. Menus have a tendency to reveal a delightful combination of Italian and Austrian names. Examples of the oddity of naming dishes are frequent. For example, we have *crauti* or *cavoli acidi* which is Sauerkraut; *saure Suppe*, or a tripe soup flavoured with vinegar is *zuppa acida*. The milky *Tschottnudeln*, vermicelli cooked in milk and variously flavoured, becomes *vermicelli al latte*, and is considered a speciality of the Val Venosta. Both Italians and Austrians have a great love for dumplings of all possible flavours and types. Those who favour gnocchi may well find a favourite under the Austrian name of *Knödl*. In the Isarco valley *gnocchi agli spinaci* becomes *schwarze Knödl*, or black dumplings. Large ravioli stuffed with spinach and Ricotta cheese, are *ravioli pusteresi* or *Pustertaler Törtln*. *Frittelle* are also *Riebln*; the familiar Italian *frittata di patate e carne* is the equally familiar Austrian *Gröstl*. Among the sweet dishes perhaps the Austrians win. There is *alte Weiber* or *vecchine*, a plum pastry or pasty cooked in wine, another of the Puster valley specialities; the *pane-tyrolese* or *Zelten*, which is the local variant of *panettone*; and strudel, surely Austrian but also appearing under the pseudonym *torta di frutta*.

VENETO

This north-eastern corner of Italy with Venice as its main tourist attraction followed closely by romantic Verona where Romeo and Juliet are supposed to have loved and died, and Padua with probably one of the loveliest markets in the world (looking more like an opera house), and pretty Treviso, with a market that roams through the town, is also a rich agricultural region which produces plenty of fruit, vegetables and grapes, and is an important area for fish.

The cooking of this region is straightforward and dominated by the cooking of Venice. Vegetables, superb salads, and spicy sauces are much in evidence, so is polenta . . . oh how much polenta these people of Veneto manage to consume . . . served with numerous meat and fish dishes but more often with *stoccafisso*, salt fish, a local passion.

Being a seaport and a city of canals, the Venetians have a special predilection for fish dishes, and the windows of typical Venetian restaurants are filled with fresh fish: sturgeon, scampi, sole, mullet, lobster and other crustaceans, mussels (*peoci* in Venice), squid and cuttlefish. Fish salads are served as antipasto, so is *bottarga*, a hard roe served with a lemon and oil dressing; and the eels of nearby Comacchio are roasted or grilled and served with a sauce. There is traditional *minestra*, soup, the *risi e bisi*, and *pasta e fagioli*, a heavy winter soup of pasta and beans, sprinkled with grated cheese. Among many rice dishes there are *risotto di scampi*, a risotto with a rich small prawn or shrimp sauce; *risi e peoci*, rice with mussels; and *risi e luganega*, rice with sausages. Tripe lovers enjoy *zuppa di trippa*, rich and sustaining with tomatoes, potatoes and fat bacon.

Finally there are some small dry biscuits, *baicoli*, flavoured with orange, a local speciality; and an almond tart, *torta di mandorle*.

FRIULI VENEZIA GIULIA

Thanks to the lush pasture of the alpine slopes, this is beef and dairy-farming country, and the home of the smoked San Daniele ham of Udine, good enough to assure the region of a gastronomic star.

As befitting a mountain region, the food is plain, albeit of gourmet quality. Trieste, its best-known city and one subjected to many outside culinary influences from Austria, Hungary and the Balkans generally, claims a goulash soup in no way inferior to that of Hungary. There are also fish soups, including the inevitable *brodetto*. What Italian coastal city could be without a *brodetto*? The Friuli version of the *Schnitzel*, *costoletta alla viennese*, is fried in oil instead of the more usual lard or butter. Fritters, *Krapfen*, are widely popular in this area, and local specialities are *struffoli*, a pastry of sweet leavened dough with onion and a bay leaf, deep fried in olive oil; *pane di fichi*, dried figs with raisins and bay leaves; *favette*, rum-flavoured fritters; and *gubana*, sweet pastries with nuts, candied fruit and chocolate.

LIGURIA

It has been written that it is safer to face an angry grizzly bear than to argue with the Genoese on the quality and origin of their local dishes. There can be no better dish of pasta, they insist, than *trenette al pesto*; or *gnocchi al pesto*; no finer fish soup than their *buridda or ciuppin*; no better salad than the monumental *cappon magro*; and no finer pie than *torta pasqualina* (Easter cake) which is flaky pastry stuffed with spinach, artichokes, eggs and cheese. Along the famous Italian riviera coast are numerous *trattorie* which specialize in fish dishes, for the sea provides Ligurians with much of their food, while the olive trees produce the medium for cooking.

Three seasonings typify dishes *alla genovese*; *il pesto*, a sauce with a basis of basil, cheese and walnuts; *il tocco*, a meat sauce flavoured with tomatoes, celery, onion and mushrooms, and cooked in wine; and *l'agliata*, garlic pounded in a mortar with vinegar and breadcrumbs.

Among the best-known dishes, there are *cima alla genovese*, a round of beef stuffed with sweetbreads, pork, peas, onions and garlic, and eaten both hot and cold; *fricassea di pollo*, chicken simmered in butter and served with an egg, lemon and parsley sauce;

fritto allo stecco, a mixture of cubed veal, brains and mushrooms all rolled in egg and breadcrumbs and spit-roasted on a skewer, i.e. *stecco*, and served with *pesto*; *imbrogliata di uovo con pomodoro*, scrambled eggs with tomatoes and chopped bacon; *vitello all' uccelletto*, cubed veal seasoned with sage, to give the veal a flavour of game; and *anitra all' olivo*, casserole of duck in a thick sauce with chopped and whole olives.

Probably the lightest of the many fish soups is the *zuppa di datteri* (a soup made of date-shaped shellfish), and one of the best is the *zuppa di pesce* of La Spezia with its mixture of fish cooked in *zimino*, a sauce of white wine, tomatoes, mushrooms and rosemary.

A favourite Ligurian sweet dish is the *pan dolce*, a type of raisin *brioche* flavoured with candied peel, but there are others: *pizza di noci e canditi*, a walnut and candied peel pie; large Ligurian peaches stuffed with chopped pumpkin and baked in wine, *pesche ripiene*; snow dumplings (egg white) simmered in milk and served with a rich pistachio sauce; and a large variety of biscuits.

EMILIA-ROMAGNA

Gastronomically this is a special region of Italy, where there is an abundance of everything: great juicy tomatoes, sugar beet, garden produce, and a large production of wines to wash it all down. The people are positively addicted to good eating and nowhere is this more striking than in Bologna, a city affectionately called 'the learned' (for its ancient university), 'the fat' (for its food), and 'the turreted' (for its turrets or towers). It is no wonder that Rossini, who loved food as he loved music, lived in this city, or that the great Italian culinary writer, Pellegrino Artusi, wrote: 'When you hear mention made of Bologna cooking, drop a little curtsy, for it deserves it. It is a rather heavy cuisine, if you like, because the climate requires it; but how succulent it is, and what good taste it displays. It is wholesome too and, in fact, octogenarians and nonagenarians abound here as nowhere else.'

Strolling through this fine city of arcades one is almost overwhelmed with the bewildering range of foods: smoked meats and hams, sausages of all kinds, a dozen varieties of mortadella each labelled 'our own make' and made from a 'secret' recipe. Delicatessen stores have kitchens where customers can watch the cooking and stand ecstatic in front of a spit on which is speared a piglet, several chickens, a roast of beef at either end, all turning gently over lapping flames.

Apart from the butchers' astonishing range of beautifully prepared meats, the pastry shops display a mouth-watering range of cakes and pastries which make home baking seem small beer.

But not only does Bologna feed itself well, so too does its neighbouring culinary rival Modena, and lovely Parma with its delightful market full of Parmesan cheese and great hides of smoked bacon and excellent *salami di Felino*. A *costoletta alla modenese* is veal fried as the Milanese version and served with a meat sauce. Modena has its *zampone*, stuffed pigs' feet, and *cotechino*, which has the same filling as *zampone* but is stuffed into a sausage skin, both important for the Emilia-Romagna *bollito misto*, mixed boiled meats. (Cabbage is cooked in the broth in which these are cooked to become *crauti alla modenese*.) Ravenna boasts a sausage, locally called *gentile*, which can be translated as kind, delicate, etc; Busseto produces *culatello*, a rump of pork cured as ham, a village production with a carefully guarded 'secret' recipe reputedly handed down since the twelfth century. Everyone in Emilia-Romagna eats *tortellini*, each town or village claiming the 'best' and 'secret' recipe. In this province *filetti di tacchino*, sliced turkey breasts covered with Fontina cheese and ham and sprinkled with white wine, and *costoletta alla bolognese*, veal cutlets, are popular specialities which become masterpieces when sprinkled with truffle.

It is easy to discourse on food in this area: to drool over *lasagne al forno* and *involtini*, similar to *saltimbocca*; or to remember *fritto misto di pesce*, mixed fish fry and the *anguilla carpionata*, or fried and marinated fresh-water eel; or to think back on rice cooked with wild duck, *riso con l'anitra*, or superbly cooked capon, or chunks of fresh Parmesan cheese. Bologna has a school of cooking which even the Italians of other regions recognize. It is said of the Bolognese that they come to the table not just to eat but with the intention of enjoying fine food. When Emilians are accused of loving a heavy diet, they reply: 'Food in this area is a hymn to the taste, a triumph of the palate and a sublimation of the best man has been able to achieve in the field of gastronomy.' And in Bologna, they add: 'thank heaven in this well-fed Bologna one can still find ineffable delights of the palate.' Which all adds up to the fact that cooking and eating here is almost a religion.

TUSCANY

The Tuscans share the same pride in cooking and eating as the Emilians; it has been written of them, 'the fact of living in the midst of beauty and history has kept the Tuscans to the straight and narrow path in the aesthetics of cooking.' But it is not all aestheticism, the Tuscans are a pleasure-loving people and renowned for their lusty appetites. Tuscany has a coastal region which provides an abundant supply of fish, its hills are cloaked in vineyards, and the fertile plains are cultivated like gardens. So altogether the basic cooking materials are incomparable, as the Tuscans say, second to none in the country.

It is true too that where there is good eating in this area there are no class barriers, *conte* and *contadino* sit together. Almost the first question Tuscans ask one another when they get together is 'have you found any good places in which to eat lately?' A true Tuscan luncheon for the faint hearted can be almost an ordeal and will include antipasto, *pasta in brodo, fritto misto di verdura*, maybe a rabbit cooked in wine, roast beef or veal, or *bollito misto* with both a *salsa verde* and a red sauce made from chilli pepper and tomatoes, plus seasonings; or an *arista alla fiorentina*, a saddle of pork flavoured with cloves, garlic and rosemary.

If there is one dish of which the Tuscans are particularly proud, it is their *costata alla fiorentina*, charcoal grilled steak. There is plenty of game in the region and the Tuscans have evolved such dishes as *pappardelle alla cacciatora*, noodles hunter's style, or *alla lepre*, with hare, or *coll'anitra*, with wild duck.

Dishes popular in the area are tripe cooked in a thick tomato sauce, heavily spiced and sprinkled with Parmesan cheese, *trippa alla fiorentina*, and those labelled *spezzato di muscolo*, lean beef gently stewed with onions and tomatoes. Although a region of good beef, the Tuscans have a fondness for pig's liver and there are numerous recipes for spit-roasting, grilling and frying it.

Along the Tuscany coast we find *cacciucco livornese* and *triglie alla livornese*, as well as *baccalà alla livornese*, stewed salt fish cooked with potatoes and tomatoes, like a chowder.

Tuscans have so many bean dishes, they are dubbed the 'bean eaters'. One favourite is *fagioli all'uccelletto*, beans cooked with sage, garlic and tomatoes, 'once tasted never forgotten', say the Tuscans.

Although on French menus any dish labelled *à la florentine* means with spinach and a bechamel sauce, this is not so in Italy. Florentine dishes are varied: *funghi alla Toscana*, mushrooms in a tomato sauce with garlic and oregano; *tortina d'uova alla fiorentina*, eggs beaten with milk and butter and baked; *tortina di carciofi*, or fried sliced artichokes; *piselli alla fiorentina*, peas cooked with oil, garlic, ham, and seasonings; hare in a sweet-sour sauce, *lepre in agrodolce*; and finally some aromatic dishes of game, including wild boar from Maremma, roasted and served in a sauce, all come under this heading, as are beans cooked in the same manner, *fave in stufa*.

Sweet dishes are many. There are various interesting *torta*, and *buccellato* from Lucca, is an aniseed-flavoured bread which, when stale, is dunked in red wine. In Siena there are almond paste macaroons, *ricciarelli di Siena*; *brigidini*, aniseed-flavoured wafers sold at festival times on the streets; and the famous *panforte*, a candied fruit cake with an almost nougat texture. In Florence *castagnaccio*, a chestnut flour cake, is sold throughout the city, while everywhere in Tuscany during winter a sweet chestnut polenta is served, but considered a Sienese dish.

UMBRIA AND THE MARCHES

These are neighbouring regions often with similar recipes, the former high-lighting pork dishes, the latter its fish stews and soups. But the roasting of pork has spread throughout the entire area, and also into nearby Lazio.

Umbrian cooking is characterized by the almost exclusive use of local products: olive oil, pork and lamb, veal and small game. There are trout, perch, grey mullet and eel in Lake Trasimeno. (In Perugia they bake a traditional fruit cake in the shape of an eel.) Typical is *regina in porchetta*, carp dressed with minced ham, garlic, salt and pepper, sprinkled with rosemary, olive oil and lemon juice and spit-roasted. Mountain lamb is grilled, basted with oil and sprinkled with salt, pepper and vinegar, *agnello all'arrabbiata*, and the Perugians take particular pride in a tender veal steak called *mongana*. Chopped cardoon is boiled, dipped in batter and fried in oil, *cardi alla perugina*, and pigeons are seasoned and spit-roasted until a golden brown, *palombacce allo spiedo*.

There are black truffles from Norcia which make a black truffle sauce, *salsa di tartufi neri*, a true Umbrian speciality; so is *spaghetti ai tartufi neri*, and *frittata di tartufi neri*. So too is *salsa ghiotta*, sauce gourmet, which is a mixture of minced mountain ham, red and white wine, sliced lemon and olive oil, served with spit-roasted small game.

At the time of the olive harvest, olive pickers eat *bruschetta*, toasted country bread rubbed with garlic, sprinkled with salt and freshly pressed oil. It is best, caution the Umbrians, 'to avoid an amorous meeting after eating *bruschetta*.' A similar midday snack is *la panzanella*, country bread, sliced, and sprinkled with water, olive oil, vinegar, salt, chopped basil and onion. Another powerful dish is *le ciriole* made in Terni, a pasta cut in uneven lengths and served with a garlic and tomato sauce. Once a week Umbrians will eat *la polenta con salsicce*, polenta with sausages. Throughout the region *la pizza al testo* is served hot and sliced with smoked mountain ham. In Trevi they serve white celery cooked in a tomato sauce, and a popular and quickly prepared dish is *spaghetti ad aglio ed olio*, spaghetti with oil flavoured with garlic and ginger.

However, not all Umbrian dishes are *rustico*. There are turkey breasts cooked with the sweet, so-called white olives, *olive bianche*, and truffle and asparagus *frittata*.

From Norcia come all the products of the pig: the best sausages, salami, smoked hams and probably the best *porchetta*, spit-roasted sucking pig, although all Umbrian butchers excel in roast pork.

The Umbrians manage to consume vast quantities of pastries, cakes and buns. I was gravely informed that 'not to taste these delicacies constitutes a big mistake.' Perugian chocolates are world famous.

By combining most of the above dishes with those inspired by the fish which come from the ports and harbours along the coast of the Marches (the name means frontier province), one has a fair idea of the cooking of this region.

Other specialities are meat stewed in sauces; huge pies; pasta dishes such as *calcioni*, baked meat-stuffed ravioli; *pasticciata*, pasta filled with *ragù* and Mozzarella cheese and baked; and *vincisgrassi*, a variety of lasagne which one finds all along the Adriatic coast, baked with meat balls, *ragù* and bechamel. There is a good reason for the many dishes labelled *alla Rossini*. The composer was born in Pescara and, being a gourmet as well as a musician, many local dishes were honoured with his name. *Tournedos alla Rossini* is claimed as a local Marches speciality.

LAZIO

Until the Reformation, Rome was the centre of Christendom. Always a meeting place for many people, it became, gastronomically, the focus point for specialities from all parts of Italy. Despite this, Lazio cooking is generally plain but well seasoned and aromatic, with vigorous sauces, and meats cooked in their own gravy. Much of the aroma comes from the *battuto*, a mixture of butter, oil and pork fat, *strutto*, which starts the cooking of most Lazio dishes. Garlic, wine, vinegar, herbs and spices are all used in the cooking of this region.

Lamb, *abbacchio*, and goat, *capretto*, have been and still are traditional Easter fare in many parts of the world, so it seems natural that the Romans have made a speciality of both at Eastertide. Whole-roasted unweaned lamb is one of the masterpieces of Roman cooking. When Romans are not proving their culinary abilities with lamb, they are doing so with baby artichokes which, in their hands, become like tiny, crisp cooked roses, *carciofi alla giudia*, or with large artichokes which are stuffed and cooked in oil over a slow fire, *carciofi alla romana*. Equally important are dishes of vegetables such as *cipolline in agrodolce*, small, new onions cooked in sweet-sour sauce; *piselli al prosciutto* new peas with ham (probably 'annexed' from Modena); and large mushrooms rubbed with garlic and oil and grilled in hot embers, *funghi arrosto*. Oxtail becomes a first-rate dish cooked in tomato sauce, *coda alla vaccinara*, as are beans cooked in a tomato sauce with thick chunks of pork crackling, *fagioli con le cotiche*, and butter beans cooked with onions and fat bacon *fave al guanciale*.

The Roman approaches food with gusto. He positively gloats over the specialities of his forefathers, which no doubt is the reason that, despite the number of *haute cuisine* restaurants, most of the favourite dishes are best sampled in the *osterie* and *trattorie* of the city. He will eat *gnocchi alla romana*, potato dumplings, *fettuccine al burro*, or the Roman cannelloni, and the many spaghetti and macaroni dishes, such as *spaghetti all'arrabbiata* with a sauce which has a basis of hot peppers, or *spaghetti al cacio e pepe*, i.e. with strongly-flavoured goat cheese and freshly-ground pepper. One could continue almost endlessly. There are Roman dishes such as *filetti di baccalà*, strips of salt fish dipped in batter and fried in oil; broccoli simmered in white wine; *pollo alla diavola*, chicken flattened and grilled on a hot plate and served with lemon juice; *saltimbocca*, of Lombard origin now acclimatized in Rome, and other veal dishes; and stuffed, spit-roasted pigs, which are eaten *ad nauseam* during the Festa di Noantri (festival 'for the rest of us') for the residents of the Trastevere quarter of Rome. On midsummer night, June 24, the Romans eat snails, *lumache*, cooked in a garlic, tomato, anchovy and mint sauce, or with ginger and tomatoes. Christmas brings eels and stuffed capon. Every festival has its gastronomic accompaniment.

Rome, like every large Italian city, has a pastry shop on every street—often more than one—and the choice of sweet dishes, cakes, pastries etc. is mouth-watering, bewildering and fascinating.

ABRUZZI AND MOLISE

This is a divided region, an interior of broken mountains interspersed by rivers, with high plateaux, dense forests, and a coastal plain. This division is reflected in the foods produced: the green oases of fertile valleys grow good garden produce but little grain, and rear cattle herds to produce plenty of fresh cheese. Fishing is the main source of food along the coast. But it is only in the lowlands where the land is flat enough that vines grow; also a little grain is produced.

The people of the region are deeply traditional and their cooking reflects the landscape. Local mountain hams, cheeses, mainly from sheeps' milk, plenty of fresh Ricotta and sausages heavily garlicked, are used. Two interesting sausages are the *salsicce di fegato*, made from pigs' liver, seasoned with garlic, salt and pepper and a pinch of grated orange peel, which is dried and then fried, and *mortadella di Campotosto*, which is like the Bologna variety but drier and with plenty of garlic.

Reclaimed land has become a productive area for floury potatoes. Aquila produces excellent white celery, and elsewhere in the province grows the ubiquitous aubergine (eggplant) with which a sophisticated dish, *timballo di melanzane*, is made.

The local *brodetto* is flavoured with a sprinkling of white vinegar; excellent too is *scapece*, fish fried and marinated in vinegar, from a recipe said to be two hundred years old. Spit-roasted mullet is served in a sauce; trout is available almost everywhere; and cuttlefish and octopus cooked in a red, hot chilli sauce, has earned for itself the name *polpi in purgatorio*.

Perhaps because life is austere, sweets are popular in this region. The sugared almonds of Sulmona; *zeppole*, ring doughnuts served throughout northern Italy on St Joseph's Day; *taralli*, which are biscuits of varying size and texture; *torrone di fichi secchi*, dried fig confections with almonds, cinnamon and lemon from Chieti, made from the small floury Abruzzi figs; soft chocolate nougat; sweet chestnut-stuffed ravioli, *calcioni del*

Molise; and a cake with almond paste and chocolate icing, a speciality of Pescara, all bring a touch of sweetness to life.

CAMPANIA

This is a region of 'boasts' and 'bests' with a cuisine influenced by the ebullient Neapolitans. It is full of flavour, derived from the plentiful use of olive oil, garlic, tomatoes, herbs, anchovies, cheese, olives and fish of all kinds. Pasta dishes are a prominent part of Neapolitan cooking and macaroni and spaghetti are what 'God has provided as a basis for an entire meal', as a nineteenth-century writer put it. The favourite Neapolitan dish of pasta is *spaghetti al pomodoro*, spaghetti with a tomato sauce; varieties of this dish are *pommarola 'n coppa*, a tomato sauce with bacon and garlic, and *al sugo*, with a thick meat sauce. This dish has provided for a long time the dominant note to the cooking of Naples and the southern regions. Capri, across the water from Naples, makes a *spaghetti ai totani*, a pasta with a cuttlefish sauce.

At one time spaghetti was sold on the streets in Naples, naturally served with *pommarola*, and Neapolitans are proud to say that, lowly though the pasta origin may have been, it is an Italian speciality that has conquered the world.

After pasta, Naples is synonymous with pizza. Pizza is always available throughout southern Italy and nowadays has invaded the North, as well as cities in other countries. It was described in the *Moretum*, a work attributed to Virgil, as 'a half-baked disc of unleavened dough sprinkled with herbs'. Apart from the *pizzerie*, there are street sellers who produce a *libretti*, a type of folded pizza, to munch as one strolls the streets. No time is wasted in busy Naples, from the pan to the mouth is the watchword. Those hungry but in a hurry can buy bite-sized appetizers from the *passatempo* man, miniature *pizze*, oysters-on-the-shell, and other types of fish cooked and uncooked.

As only to be expected, there are many fish dishes. The *fritto misto* here consists of fish plus a mixture of vegetables, sweetbreads and other offal, with Ricotta. The *fritto di pesce* is made of mixed fish, the type and variety depending on the day's catch. Cuttlefish lovers enjoy *polpi alla luciana*, cuttlefish which is simmered until tender in a sauce of olive oil, parsley and ginger. The marriage of fish with pasta is to be found with spaghetti or vermicelli with clams, *vongole*, and there are many good fish stews usually highly seasoned.

Among the best-known local meat dishes are *costolette*, cutlets, or *bistecca alla pizzaiola*, with a hot, herb-flavoured sauce.

Vegetables grow prolifically in this province, and often to an enormous size, especially aubergines (egg plants) and sweet peppers, and considerable culinary play is made with them. Two excellent vegetable dishes are *parmigiana di melanzane*, fried sliced aubergine baked in layers alternating with tomato sauce, Parmesan cheese and minced basil, and *peperoni gratinati*, sweet peppers stuffed with tomato, anchovies, Mozzarella cheese and breadcrumbs, then baked.

Campania still has buffaloes from which the best Mozzarella cheese is made; elsewhere in Italy this is now being made from cows' milk. A useful local dish is *mozzarella in carrozza*.

Other local specialities are *sartu*; *calzoni alla napoletana*, pasties stuffed with Mozzarella, anchovies and tomatoes, and fried or baked; smoked meats from Secondigliano, and Neapolitan sausages; and a large range of table fruits.

Campanians enjoy pastries and a host of sweet dishes are made in this region. Thin slices of flaky pastry stuffed with Ricotta and candied peel or a rich custard sauce, something like a *millefeuille* and known as *sfogliatelle*, are popular, as are *pastiera*, short pastry with Ricotta and a candied fruit stuffing. But, in general, a meal is finished with a bowl of mixed fruits or a *macedonia*, a fruit salad that is always seasonal and well doused with wine or liqueur.

APULIA

Sometimes called Puglia, this heel of Italy is often thought of as the 'poor relation' of neighbouring Campania, a situation perhaps encouraged by the latter. But on the cooking map it boasts many robust dishes in which the main ingredients are vegetables, flanked by the inevitable pasta dishes, for the Apulians are said to be the champion pasta eaters of Italy, and with a great many pasta dishes of their own invention. There are the 'little ears' of pasta always made at home and variously named *orecchiette*, *recchietelle* and *stacchiodde* which are served with a tomato sauce and sprinkled with cheese; small pasta spirals called *turcinielli*, also served with a tomato sauce; *maccheroni al forno*, baked macaroni with Mozzarella cheese; and savoury ravioli, *panzarotti*, stuffed with Mozzarella cheese, anchovies and eggs.

But all is not pasta. There are lamb roasts and stews, such as *agnello al forno con patate e pomodori*, a typical dish of cubed lamb baked in the oven with onions, rosemary, tomatoes, tiny new potatoes and white wine. Also *capretto ripieno*, kid stuffed with herbs and spices and roasted; and there is leg of veal stuffed with ham, salami, anchovies and garlic. A speciality of the Cisternino district is *gnumariedde*, lambs' or kids' intestines, rolled round a skewer and spit-roasted. Vegetables are cooked and made into moulds; potatoes and beans are baked together in the oven with black olives and cardoons. The local form of pizza is *calzoni*, trousers, stuffed with onions, black olives and anchovies. Lecce is locally noted for the variety of its *pizze*. This is mushroom country and pizza, smothered with fried mushrooms and tomatoes, is not be missed.

Along the Apulian coastline there are fish as exotic in flavour as they are in colour. Taranto has its oyster and mussel beds. Bari has a favourite dish of curled octopus called *arricciati*, and Brindisi is noted for its shellfish. Its fish market is open at night, and for those on their way to the motor car ferry I would recommend a short stop. A favourite dish along the coast is *risotto alla marinara*, which consists of prawns, mussels, herbs, tomatoes etc., and white wine.

There is an abundance of fresh fruit but particularly good is the Brindisi melon, *popone*, sweet, perfumed and flamboyant; and *fichi d'India*, prickly pear or cactus fruit, in all its colours and varieties. Taranto has incredibly sweet and juicy figs, both green and purple, many of which are dried and stuffed with almonds.

BASILICATA

It has been said that the cooking of Basilicata 'is always a pleasant surprise'. No explanation was offered as to why this should be, but perhaps one answer is the Lucanians' reputation for frugality, which might hinder any attempt at gastronomic finesse.

This is sheep-farming country populated by shepherds and, until fairly recently, by brigands, perhaps not the best people to lay down a tradition of fine eating. It is also a mountainous region with hardly a square inch of flat earth. However, potent wines are produced on the steep slopes to accompany the robust food of the countryside which largely consists of substantial *minestre*, soup, home-made pasta, lamb, pork, game, and abundant dairy produce. The products of the pig are prepared and smoked as they have been for a century or more. There are local sausages, *sopressate*, smoked, then preserved in olive oil; the salami of Stigliano; and everywhere mountain hams and fat bacon. Lamb in this province takes on the flavour of the herbs and grasses on which it feeds. Local specialities are cubed lamb cooked with onions, celery and rosemary, *i cutturiddi*; pork ribs with black olives, *costatine*; salt cod with giant sweet pepper; hunter's hare, *lepre alla cacciatora*, cooked with tomatoes and flavoured with sage, garlic and rosemary; woodcock in salmi; and wild boar cooked in various ways. *Pollo alla lucania* is chicken stuffed with Pecorino cheese, chopped chicken livers and eggs, and another dish is chicken cooked in oil and white wine, together with onion, red pepper, fresh tomatoes and basil. Two other specialities are *gnommerielli di animelle*, sweetbreads on skewers, and *capuzzadde*, spit-roasted lamb's or kid's head.

Ginger, simply called 'strong' is present in every dish from a fried egg to the sauces. It is there, say the locals, to promote thirst.

Even in southern Italy it can be cold, especially in the mountains, thus we find thick winter soups, in particular *minestra di cavolo*, made from cabbage, fat bacon and chilli peppers.

Turning to fish: there are eels from Lake Monticchio which are roasted and heavily garlicked and trout from Lake Sirino served grilled or *in carpione*, that is, fried and then marinated in vinegar flavoured with onion and local herbs. Snails and mussels are cooked in rich aromatic sauces.

Pasta dishes in this region are pretty robust, especially those from Matera where unleavened bread, *panalle*, is still made. There is *maccheroni alla trainiera* or *alla carrettiera*, which is noodles served with a sauce of olives, spices, olive oil, capers and the inevitable ginger. *Pizza rustica*, eaten hot, is made from flaky pastry, stuffed with hard-boiled eggs, Ricotta cheese and a so-called sweet salami.

In this region there are the usual cheeses, including a mild but hard Caciocavallo, a strong Provolone, a buttery cream cheese called Manteche, and Casiddi, hard, small cheeses. And finally there are plenty of fruits and vegetables of all kinds which flourish in the luxuriant Metaponto plain.

CALABRIA

Locally they boast that Calabria's cooking is the mother of good Italian cooking, needless to say, a sentiment not shared elsewhere. This is a region of acres of fragrant orange and lemon groves, endless vistas of olive trees, and vineyards which produce robust and generous wines in great quantity.

Of the vegetables which grow profusely, the most widely used is the aubergine (eggplant) which provides the basis for many local dishes. It is served fried in oil, grilled, boiled, puréed, pickled in a sweet-sour sauce, in stews and soups, or *al funghetto*, which means cut into small pieces, with the skin still on, flavoured with minced garlic, chilli peppers and oregano, and baked with cheese. Another important local vegetable is *peperoni*, a giant sweet pepper which, combined with aubergines, onions, potatoes and courgettes (zucchini), make a type of *ratatouille* called here *ciambotta*.

Calabria produces good soups: *zuppa alla pasqualina*, Easter or onion soup flavoured with local brandy; the so-called *pancotto alla calabrese*, or bread cooked in broth with tomatoes, celery, garlic, parsley, bay leaves and chilli pepper to liven it up; and a number of fish soups, the ingredients varying according to the latest catch. A favourite fish along the Calabrian coast is the swordfish which, cut into thick steaks, is baked, grilled or poached. Other fish specialities include the Calabrian, *fritto misto*, which uses boiled tunny fish; *sarde alla cetrarese*, fresh sardines cooked in oil and flavoured with oregano; *merluzzo*, cod and clams; *fritto dello stretto*, a fish fry from the Straits of Messina; baby fish fritters; *stoccofisso* or dried salt cod; and *tortiera di alici*, fresh anchovy pie.

Although the quality of meat is not good, Calabrian cooks are inventive with what they have. Veal is cooked in the usual ways typical of southern Italian cooking: it is roasted in huge stone fireplaces, and thick veal steaks are grilled directly on hot juniper embers which give the meat an unusual flavour. Local cooks make succulent dishes from lamb, goat and kid; also with chicken, rabbit and hare, and in particular with guinea fowl which is roasted in olive oil and served with roasted or baked potatoes and fresh figs. An unusual dish is *capretto ripieno al forno*, or kid stuffed with cooked spaghetti and *ragù*, surrounded by potatoes and onions and baked. Red wine is used to cook rabbit and hare, and offal of all kinds is also cooked in wine. Lamb kidneys are flavoured with juniper berries; in Catanzaro lamb and pork offal, *morseddu*, is cooked in a tomato sauce, sprinkled with chilli pepper and served on bread or stuffed into *pitta*, a type of pie made from a bread dough. Calabrians have a whole range of these *pitte*, the recipe and name being of ancient origin and meaning painted or coloured. The *pitta* dough is 'coloured' by its accompanying ingedients. Pizza too is a traditional Calabrian dish and some of the best of these are the *pizza di pesce* which are prepared with fish of various kinds.

Mushrooms grow well in Calabria and it is a very poor peasant indeed who cannot have a dish of mushrooms from time to time. Salads from large, raw mushrooms in an oil and lemon dressing are a special feature of this province, so are mushrooms grilled and served in red wine, or puréed and served with roast meat.

In Calabria pasta is made into the oddest shapes and given quaint names; it is said this is to hide the fact that the pasta is made of only flour and water. They have *capiddi d'angilu*, angel's hair, *filatelli*, strands, *nocchetedde*, rectangles, *stivaletti*, little boots, *ricchie i prieviti*, priests' ears, and *ricci di donna*, ladies' curls. A formidable dish of wide noodles is *chine sagne*, baby artichokes, meat and tomato sauce, eggs, ground pork, three kinds of cheese, and mixed vegetables. All this is served with red Calabrian wine to make a main course; so is *maccheroni alla calabrese*, wide noodles with smoked ham, chilli peppers, Pecorino cheese and garlic.

Like most southern Italians, the Calabrians are sweet-toothed and the number of sweet dishes, although often of Sicilian origin but given local dialect names, is enormous. Every festival brings its own specialities: St Joseph's Day means doughnuts, *zeppole*, and shortbread biscuits (cookies); Christmas brings *crespelle*, another type of doughnut, and the Sicilian *susumelle*, small cakes flavoured with almond and caramelized sugar, or *turdilli*, honey-flavoured biscuits sprinkled with powdered cinnamon and musk. St Martin's Day produces a sweet pizza and *pezzotta*, a honey cake coated with chocolate.

Typical sweets are *crocette* of Cosenza, stuffed, dried and baked figs; *pastiera*, an elaborate cheesecake; *taralli* and *mustazzole*, ground almond and honey biscuits baked in odd shapes—hearts, animals, fish, horses etc.—and *mostaccioli*, hard little biscuits of Arab origin made from flour, honey and white wine, and seasoned with spices, often aniseed. All are equally popular in Basilicata.

SICILY

Food and cooking in Sicily is a matter for lively discussion. Everything has a special and local character and the cuisine is no exception. Outside influences over the centuries have been many and brought changes to the Sicilian way of life and the kitchen. The Greeks, Spaniards and Arabs have made their culinary mark.

Sicily is the largest island in the Mediterranean. It has a generous fish harvest; specialized land crops, such as citrons, oranges, lemons and mandarins; luscious almonds and prickly pears, *fichi d'India*. The island is described as a paradise for wine growers and is 'celebrated for its output of generous wines, while the Sicilian cooking is in no way inferior to the wines which accompany the food.'

Rice is seldom served, although the Arabs introduced this cereal into Italy via Sicily; probably the only typical Sicilian dish of rice is *arancine di riso*.

Sicilian cooking is based on fish and vegetables. Some of the fish dishes are considered among the finest in Italy. Apart from fish salads and stews, or such delicacies as *anelletti gratinati*, rings of cuttlefish dipped in egg and breadcrumbs and deep fried, there are interesting fish and vegetable combinations. Dressed tunny fish roe, *bottarga*, is served with an oil and lemon dressing; mussels appear in every guise, and the Sicilian mixed fry of small fish, *frittura di sciabacheddu*, is particularly good, as are all the many ways in which swordfish is cooked.

Meat is not generally good. As a result it is used in meat loaves and rissoles, and dishes such as *farsumagru*, breast of veal stuffed with eggs, minced meat, cheese, spices etc., and simmered in a tomato sauce. When the Sicilians do get a good piece of meat, they like to treat it regally and cook it in a dry Marsala or other local wine. Game, and there is plenty, is often cooked in a sweet-sour sauce with black olives or other local vegetables.

The Sicilians pay great attention to their pasta dishes, serving them with rich and unusual sauces. For example, there is *pasta con le sarde*, spaghetti with a sauce of fresh sardines; *vermicelli alla siciliana*, vermicelli with a sauce that includes aubergines (eggplants), garlic, tomatoes, sweet peppers, salted anchovies, black olives, capers, basil and olive oil. Then there is the excellent *pasta 'ncaciata*, or macaroni baked in layers with *ragù*, grated cheese, ground pork, sliced hard-boiled eggs, seasonings and herbs etc. Messina claims the best Arab food, but the best-known Sicilian Arab dish is the *cuscusu*, couscous, from Trapani, prepared with coarse semolina in the traditional manner but, contrary to the North African couscous, which is served with lamb or chicken, the Sicilian version is served with mixed fish: shellfish, shallow-water fish, eel, etc.

Most Italians would probably agree that the Sicilians excel in the making of sweet dishes. Three of their best-known sweets are the *cannoli alla siciliana*, at its best in Catania where I am assured the Ricotta is the finest in all Italy. *Cannoli* are flaky pastry tubes stuffed with Ricotta, flavoured with candied peel, sweet Marsala, coffee or bitter chocolate (sometimes both), sugar and *glacé* cherries. The others are the *cassata alla siciliana* (*dolce*), a spongecake stuffed with Ricotta cheese and candied fruit, and the *cassata alla siciliana* (*gelato*), an ice-cream made in different coloured layers with candied fruit and almonds. Ice-creams, sorbets, *granite*, are excellent, so is the *frutta candita*, candied fruit, and other cakes and pastries too numerous to mention.

Sicilian bread too is excellent; it comes hot from the oven with a crisp brown crust and vast quantities are consumed. A favourite snack is bread direct from the oven, spread with oil, rubbed with garlic and sprinkled with finely-chopped green herbs.

Sicilians, while making *pizze* in the established Naples fashion, also have their own versions, made with flaky pastry and covered with tomatoes, anchovies and cheese. Local cheeses are sharp and often salty. In Santa Lucia there is smoked Ricotta as well as the fresh, and a pepper-studded Pecorino type of cheese is made in the hills.

Mushrooms are excellent and some of the best are the *funghi di castagno* which are the size of a saucer and grow under chestnut trees. They are particularly good eaten raw, thinly sliced with an oil and lemon dressing.

Palermo is locally noted for its cooking, and the narrow streets are made narrower by the many stalls selling cooked fish, octopus, mackerel, sliced fried aubergine (egg plant), and local sheeps' and goats' cheeses.

SARDINIA

The main characteristic of Sardinian cooking is spit-roasting or, as they say locally, *a furria-furria*. The island does not produce much in the way of *haute cuisine*, but its charm lies in the cooking of shepherds who spend months away with their flocks of sheep, or of their wives who stay at home and make the strange snowy-white Sardinian bread called *carasau* or *carta da musica*, which is as thin as music paper and has extraordinary keeping qualities. To the Sardinians this bread is a symbol of family unity, and the sheets are stored in damp cloths and have to be softened in boiling water before they can be eaten.

There is plenty of game on the island and the shepherds live on this while they are away from their families. They have learned to catch the wild suckling pig and other small game, such as goats, which they roast on a spit over aromatic wood taken from the thickets. (The moufflon, which they have almost hunted out of existence, is now protected.) Spit-roasting is a primitive method of cooking but in the right atmosphere it cannot be bettered. Another traditional method of cooking whole animals, particularly pig, is to wrap them in aromatic leaves and bury them in a deep hole in the ground, *carne a carrargiu*, in which a fire has been allowed to die out, they are then covered with earth and on the top is spread a slow-burning fire. It is a ritual dish and never served without traditional ceremony.

But, as in Sicily, it is with the fish dishes that Sardinian cooking comes into its own, dishes which include tunny, lobster, mussels, eels etc. There is *cassola*, a spiced fish stew; *zuppa di arselle*, or clam soup; *buridda*, made with dogfish and skate; and local dishes of cuttlefish, and octopus. Trout is cooked in Vernaccia wine, *trota alla vernaccia*; and snails, called *monzette*, are a speciality of Sassari. *Buttàriga* or *bottarga*, the compressed and dried eggs of the grey mullet, is served as an appetizer.

One ancient Sardinian dish, *porceddu*, roast pig, has become something of a tourist attraction; it is roasted in a deep pit on hot stones, or on a spit from a recipe two thousand years old, it is claimed. A dish of small birds, *tacculas*, blackbirds, partridges and thrush wrapped in myrtle leaves is baked as the *porceddu* is spit-roasted. Spit-roasted partridges are served with a caper sauce and plaited intestines of lamb or goat are spit-roasted and served with a tomato sauce and peas, *corda*. Another popular dish is *favata*, a classical recipe from the mountains in which beans are cooked with fat pork and bones, mountain sausage, fennel, sage and other aromatic herbs. There is *malloreddus*, a small cornflour gnocchi or dumpling flavoured with saffron, served with a spicy sauce and sprinkled with the sharp Sardinian Pecorino cheese. Very similar are *ciciones* from Sassari.

The local sweet dishes are numerous and often extremely delicate: *suspirus* or 'sighs' made from almonds and egg white, a variety of macaroon; *pardulas*, fritters made from mixed Ricotta and crushed macaroons; *pabassinas*, fruit and nut biscuits; *gueffus*, almond sweets; *aranciata*, a type of nougat, *torrone*, with orange peel. Finally there is fruit of almost every kind.

 # a few general hints

1. Unless otherwise specified, flour in the following recipes always means plain or all-purpose flour.

2. In Italy it is usual to peel and gently squeeze out the seeds of tomatoes before cooking them.

3. Onions and other vegetables should be peeled unless otherwise stated.

4. In general Italians use unsalted (sweet) butter in cooking when not using olive oil.

5. Olive oil varies considerably in flavour both from region to region and country to country. When cooking *alla italiana*, it is best to use Italian olive oil to obtain the correct Italian flavour.

6. Generally freshly-milled pepper and freshly-grated nutmeg are used in Italian kitchens, and sea salt in preference to highly-refined salt.

7. The grill should always be heated before being used.

8. Italian tomatoes and tomato paste are canned in three sizes, large, medium and small:

	Large	*Medium*	*Small*
WHOLE TOMATOES	1 lb. 12 oz.	14 oz.	6 oz.
TOMATO PASTE	1 lb. 12 oz.	14 oz.	$5\frac{1}{2}$ oz.

hors d'oeuvre  *antipasto*

The word antipasto means before the main course and what is served may be either simple and inexpensive, or elaborate and expensive; but no important Italian meal omits this course. Many Italians will not decide on the main course until they have settled the antipasto.

In general the antipasto is a combination of many things and can be anything which fits into the meal as a first course. It should never be overpowering in flavour, or so plentiful that it ruins the appetite for the next course. On the whole it should be slight, good to look at, and sharpen the appetite, not dull it. The antipasto is both regional and seasonal, and hot or cold as the weather and occasion demands.

What then constitutes a typical antipasto? The list is endless and generally divided into three groups: meat, fish and vegetables. For a start, there are cold meats: rare roast beef, roasted chicken or turkey (breasts only), ham, tongue, pork and veal, all thinly sliced, neatly arranged and generously garnished with aspic. Possibly there will also be chicken or turkey galantine, and a brawn, *coppa di testa*. Venice offers *coppa Veneta*, a type of meat loaf made with tongue, ham and mortadella, and Modena has stuffed pigs' feet, *zampone*, rich but excellent, and *cotechino*, the same stuffing in a thin sausage skin.

Also under cold meats come the great hams of Italy, invariably sliced paper-thin. Of these the best known is the Parma ham, *prosciutto di Parma*, a pale red colour and delicate in flavour. But there are other equally interesting hams. Worth trying is *prosciutto di cinghiale* or wild boar ham, and the smoked hams from the mountain areas—*prosciutto di montagna*, which always comes on the bone and is therefore hand cut, is sweeter and cheaper than most other hams. Two particularly fine hams are *San Daniele* from Udine in Friuli, pink, slightly sweet and fragrant, and the Norcia ham. These hams are served alone or with butter, or with melon and figs. Then there is *coppa vera Parma*, a salted and seasoned fat ham, or *culatello*, a ham of fine quality, boned and without rind. Extremely good is the *giambonetta*, a boned ham hock from Parma.

Also listed among the cold meat is mortadella, a Bolognese speciality—but of what quality and variety. It is a type of pressed pork from selected meat, dotted with bits of fat, necessary for its flavour, and has been produced in the city since the Middle Ages. It is pale pink, always tender, light and appetizing. Then comes salami in enormous variety: the best known among foreigners is the Milanese type, small-grained and made from a mixture of beef, pork and pork fat. But there are hundreds even thousands of salami. Many Italians consider *crespone extra*, very lean but studded with fat, the finest of the salami. Genoa produces, among others, salami made from pork, veal, and pork fat; Tuscany has its fennel-spiced salami, *finocchiona*, and its *fiorentina*, a pure pork salami; a fine salami in the South is made from wild boar and pork meat; while from the Po valley comes *bondiola*, a wine-flavoured pork salami, greatly prized. Apart from the well-known salami, there are those made in every town and village, each proclaimed with pride as 'the best' or *nostrale*, local. Then there are cooked aromatic salami, *salame cotto pressato*, or cooked pressed salami, somewhat coarser than the regular quality salami but very good.

Calabria has a variety of highly seasoned, chilli-hot smoked sausages. Among these is the pure pork sausage, *luganega*, known to Cicero and to the Romans as *lucanica*; the *sopressata*, made from lean pork and lard and packed into a pig's intestines and smoked in the hearth; and the *capocollo*, again pork, from the neck and shoulder of the animal, minced and stuffed into its bladder and then smoked. But there are many others; they start in the North and continue south to the heel and toe of Italy.

Numerous vegetables find themselves on the antipasto list: mushrooms, breaded and fried, raw in a salad or marinated or pickled; tomato salads; sweet peppers, grilled and served with a dressing, or pickled and garnished with fillets of anchovies; courgettes (zucchini) pickled or fried; gherkins; pearl onions; carrots and aubergines (eggplants); mixed pickles and baby artichokes preserved in oil. The Sicilian salad, *caponata*, is a popular cold antipasto in the South. There are olives, black or green, and the so-called white olives of Ascoli; they come large or small, plain or stuffed, or rolled in egg and breadcrumbs and fried in oil. There are radishes, both red and white, served with butter; tiny young turnips and crisp celery; asparagus, the cultivated and the wild; and fennel, thinly sliced and served with a dressing.

Eggs are cooked until hard and stuffed with chopped capers or anchovies and chopped olives.

But not all antipasto is cold. There are rice croquettes filled with Mozzarella cheese known as *supplì di riso* or *al telefono* (telephone croquettes, because the Mozzarella when cooked spins long threads like wires); spinach and Ricotta croquettes, and several others. Italians use a lot of Mozzarella in their cooking and included among antipasto is *mozzarella in carrozza*. There are various *crostini*, toasts, some are good, others admittedly a little dull. But one of the best is *crostini alla fiorentina*, a mixture of chicken livers, minced onion, chopped anchovy fillets and finely-chopped parsley, cooked gently in butter and wine and spread on toast. Bel Paese and Mozzarella cheeses are dipped in egg and bread-crumbs and fried. Fontina cheese is fried together with chopped black olives, or melted and served with truffles to make Piedmont's *fonduta*. A more simple dish is sliced stale white bread soaked in red wine or milk, sprinkled with salt and black pepper, and gener-ously coated with grated Parmesan cheese, then fried in hot butter or oil. In Naples and further south pizza is regarded as a starter to a meal; while in due season Rome delights in serving snails.

But a great many of the antipasto dishes are *magri assortiti* or *misti*, which means they are without meat and will often be simply fish of all kinds. In the South and along the coasts they favour cold fish combinations, *antipasto di pesce*, made from cuttlefish, inkfish and octopus, which can be very good. There are the familiar prawns in a mayonnaise, sardines in oil, and smoked trout, and tunny (tuna) salad, for the Italians eat as much tunny preserved in oil as they do fresh. Fresh sardines are marinated, and in Venice they make a pleasing dish with canned sardines and a tomato sauce. Naples serves uncooked small sweet mussels with chunks of lemon and garnished with parsley. Excellent are the *riccio di mare* or sea urchins, red-brown or purple. These are cut open, and the flesh which is served raw on the two halves of its prickly shell, is sprinkled with lemon and scooped out with a spoon. They call *riccio di mare* the caviar of Sicily but it takes a lot of them to make a pleasing quantity to eat. Another crustacean is a pale blue mother-of-pearl shellfish, they are like tiny oysters, and also eaten raw. In Sardinia and elsewhere in the South, they serve dried and salted fish roe, *uova di tonno*, or *di cefalo*, a little like *bottarga* as prepared in Turkey and Greece. Thick slices of cooked carp, served with mayonnaise, form another typical fish antipasto.

One could continue, but the above is enough to indicate that almost anything which is good to eat and can precede a main course is, as far as the Italians are concerned, antipasto.

ARTICHOKE HEARTS IN SAUCE (*Fondi di carciofi in salsa*)

4–6 servings:

12 small artichoke hearts, canned, bottled or frozen
4 tablespoons (5) olive oil
2 tablespoons (2½) lemon juice

finely-chopped oregano or marjoram to taste
salt, pepper to taste

Put the artichoke hearts into a bowl. Mix the remaining ingredients to make a dressing. Pour this over the artichokes, then carefully mix and chill for several hours, turning occasionally to ensure all are coated with the dressing.

AUBERGINE SWEET-SOUR SALAD (*Caponata alla siciliana*)   *Sicily*

4 servings:

3 medium-sized aubergines (eggplants)
salt, pepper
olive oil
1 head white celery
3 tablespoons (3¾) grated bitter chocolate

2 tablespoons (2½) sugar
1 tablespoon (1¼) capers
12 green olives, pitted and chopped
¼ cup (⅓) wine vinegar

Peel the aubergines and cut into 1-inch cubes. Sprinkle with salt and leave between 2 plates for 1 hour. Wash well to remove all the salt, then pat dry. Heat plenty of oil (aubergines absorb oil) and fry the aubergines until brown and soft. Drain. Slice the celery into small rounds and fry in the same oil until a golden colour. Drain and mix with the aubergines. Add the remaining ingredients with salt and pepper to taste and leave to settle. Turn into a bowl, mix well and serve cold.

This is one version of this famous Sicilian salad. Some recipes omit the chocolate but add green tomatoes, onions, pine nuts and black olives. If using onion, it must be fried slowly until mushy but not brown. The celery is as important an ingredient as the aubergine.

A *caponata* will keep for several days in a refrigerator. It is served with cold sliced chicken, cooked octopus and hard-boiled eggs.

FRIED COURGETTES (*Zucchini dorati*) *Sicily*

6 servings:

2 lb. small courgettes (zucchini)	2 eggs, well beaten
2 tablespoons (2½) grated Pecorino or Parmesan cheese	flour
	1 cup (1¼) olive oil

Wash the courgettes and without peeling them cut into ½-inch lengths. Mix the cheese into the eggs. Roll the courgettes first in flour and then in the egg-cheese mixture. Heat the oil and fry the courgettes until brown.

BREADED MUSHROOMS (*Funghi impanati*) *Lombardy*

3–4 servings:

12 large firm mushroom caps	2 eggs, beaten
salt	fine breadcrumbs
½ lemon	4 oz. (8 tablespoons) butter
2 tablespoons (2½) flour	

Wipe the mushrooms with a damp cloth, sprinkle with salt and squeeze lemon juice over them. Toss them lightly in flour, drop into the eggs and coat with breadcrumbs.

Heat the butter and fry the mushrooms until they are tender, turning them from time to time. Extra hot butter may well be required as both mushrooms and breadcrumbs soak up a great deal of fat. Serve hot.

MARINATED MUSHROOMS (*Funghi marinati*)

4–6 servings:

1 lb. small fresh mushrooms	6 tablespoons (7½) olive oil
½ cup (⅔) wine vinegar	4 tablespoons (5) water
6 peppercorns	1 teaspoon (1¼) salt
2 cloves garlic, crushed	1 bay leaf (optional)

Clean the mushrooms and remove the stems. Mix the remaining ingredients, put them into a pan and bring to a gentle boil. Reduce the heat, cover and simmer for 15 minutes. Add the mushrooms and simmer for 5 minutes, stirring occasionally. Take from the stove but let the mushrooms cool in the marinade. The mushrooms can be chilled and served at once (strained from the marinade), or they will keep for 2 days in the marinade in the refrigerator. Serve as part of an antipasto.

SWEET PEPPERS IN OIL (*Peperoni all'olio*) *Calabria*

6 servings:

**6 sweet peppers, preferably mixed
  colours**
¼ cup (⅓) olive oil

2–3 sprigs parsley, finely chopped
salt, pepper

Cut the peppers into halves or quarters and discard the stems, cores and seeds. Grill the flesh until it chars and blisters. Cool and pull off the outer skin. Cut the flesh into strips. Combine the remaining ingredients. Arrange the strips of sweet peppers on a plate, add the dressing and stir lightly.

SWEET PEPPERS WITH BAGNA CAUDA SAUCE *Piedmont*
(*Peperoni alla bagna cauda*)

6 servings:

6 sweet peppers
**4 large ripe tomatoes, peeled and
  sliced**

4 anchovy fillets, chopped
2 cloves garlic, finely chopped
bagna cauda sauce (see page 161)

Prepare the peppers as in the previous recipe. Arrange the strips in a salad bowl, cover with tomatoes and anchovies, sprinkle with garlic and pour the sauce over the top.

SMOKED HAM WITH MELON (*Prosciutto e melone*)

This is served in two ways. Either a thick slice of melon (any kind except water melon) is wrapped in a slice of *prosciutto*, or the *prosciutto* is placed at the side of the melon.

SMOKED HAM WITH FIGS (*Prosciutto con fichi*)

Serve thinly-sliced *prosciutto* on a dish with fresh ripe green or purple figs, peeled or unpeeled but cut open to show their insides.

MARINATED SARDINES (*Sarde fresche in escabecio*) *Sicily*

4–6 servings:

**2 lb. fresh sardines (or smelts or other
  small fish)**
flour
olive oil
**1 each small onion and carrot, thinly
  sliced**

4 cloves garlic, chopped
½ cup (⅔) wine vinegar
2 tablespoons (2½) warm water
salt, pepper
1 bay leaf
a little chopped parsley

Clean the sardines without removing the heads or tails, pat them dry and roll lightly in flour. Heat ¾–1 cup of oil and fry the sardines, a few at a time, until brown. Drain, then put on to a flat dish. Fry the onion, carrot and garlic until brown. Add the vinegar and water, stir the mixture well, and add salt, pepper, bay leaf and parsley. Bring to a gentle boil and boil gently for 20 minutes. Strain the marinade over the sardines and leave in a cold place for 2–3 days, by which time the sardine bones will have dissolved. Take the sardines from the marinade and drain before serving.

SARDINES IN A TOMATO SAUCE (*Sardine sott'olio alla veneta*) *Veneto*

4 servings:

2 cans large sardines
lemon juice
1 oz. (2 tablespoons) butter
3–4 ripe tomatoes, chopped
1 clove garlic, crushed

2–3 sage leaves
pinch sugar
salt, pepper to taste
2 hard-boiled eggs
1 sweet pepper to garnish (optional)

Drain the oil from the sardines, and carefully skin and bone them. Arrange them on a plate, sprinkle lightly with lemon juice and chill.

Heat the butter, add the tomatoes, garlic, sage, salt and pepper and cook over a moderate heat until the tomatoes are soft. Cool, then rub through a sieve. Spread this over the sardines. Chop the egg whites and yolks separately and sprinkle over the sauce. If using sweet pepper, it must be grilled until it blisters, the thin outer skin removed, and cut into strips.

TUNNY FISH WITH ONION (*Tonno sott'olio con cipolle*) *Sicily*

3 servings:

1 medium-sized can Italian tunny
   (tuna) fish
black pepper

1 teaspoon (1¼) capers
1 small mild onion, sliced

Drain the tunny and crumble it coarsely. Arrange it on a small salad dish, and sprinkle with pepper, capers, a little of the tunny oil, and the onion. Serve chilled.

DEEP FRIED CHEESE SANDWICHES (*Mozzarella in carrozza*) *Campania*

2–4 servings:

4 slices Mozzarella cheese, about 7 oz.
2 eggs
salt, pepper
¾ cup (1) milk

8 slices 2-day-old white bread (French
   or Italian style)
flour or fine breadcrumbs
oil for deep frying

Beat the eggs, adding salt, pepper and 2 tablespoons (2½) of milk. Pour the rest of the milk into a shallow dish. Cut the bread into rounds just slightly larger than the Mozzarella slices, trimming off the crusts. Make 4 Mozzarella sandwiches. Dip them into the milk, press them down all round the edges to ensure they do not come apart when cooking, then dip into the beaten egg and milk mixture, and roll in flour or breadcrumbs. Heat the oil until it begins to smoke, and fry the sandwiches until brown on both sides, then drain quickly and serve hot.

FONDUE PIEDMONT STYLE (*Fonduta*) *Piedmont*

This is Piedmont's most famous dish, available from September into December. It can ONLY be made with Fontina cheese. Even if the truffles are omitted, it is still a *fonduta*, but not if it is prepared with any other type of cheese.

4 servings:

¾ lb. Fontina cheese	pinch pepper
milk	4 slices fried or toasted bread
4 egg yolks	1 white truffle, sliced paper-thin
1 oz. (2 tablespoons) butter	

Trim off the rind and cut the cheese into small pieces. Put them into a shallow bowl and cover with milk. Leave for several hours or overnight.

To make the *fonduta*, thoroughly beat the egg yolks and JUST melt the butter. Pour the cheese with the milk into the top of a double boiler over simmering but NOT boiling water. Add the egg yolks, butter, pepper but no salt, since Fontina cheese is sufficiently salty, and cook over a low heat until the mixture is creamy and smooth, stirring with a wooden spoon all the time. Pour the *fonduta* over toast and sprinkle with finely-sliced truffle. Or, if preferred, pour the *fonduta* into deep bowls, sprinkle with truffle and serve with fingers of toast.

MEAT STUFFED RICE CROQUETTES (*Arancine di riso*) *Sicily*

6 servings:

1 lb. (2½ cups) short grain Italian rice	½ lb. ground meat (see below)
1½ cups (2) each milk and water	½ cup (⅔) white wine
4 eggs, beaten	salt, pepper
3 tablespoons (3¾) grated Parmesan or Pecorino cheese	1 tablespoon (1¼) flour
nutmeg	1 tablespoon (1¼) tomato paste
1½ oz. (3 tablespoons) lard	fine breadcrumbs
1 small onion, minced	olive oil for deep frying

Cook the rice in the milk and water until tender and all the liquid has been absorbed. Take from the heat, beat in 2 eggs, the grated cheese and a sprinkling of nutmeg. Spread the mixture out on to a plate and leave until cold.

Heat the lard, fry the onion until soft, and brown the meat; add the wine, salt and pepper. Cook until the wine is absorbed, mix the flour into the tomato paste, stir this into the meat, add ½ cup (⅔) of water, cover and simmer for 40 minutes. When the meat is quite tender and the sauce thick, take from the heat and cool.

With moistened hands, make golf-sized balls with the rice, push a fairly deep hole in the middle of each and fill it with the stuffing. Close over the hole. Repeat until all the rice balls are stuffed. Dip in the remaining beaten eggs and roll in breadcrumbs. Leave in the refrigerator for 1 hour. Heat plenty of oil and fry the croquettes until a golden brown. Drain and serve hot. The type of meat used is generally a mixture of veal, liver, sweetbreads, giblets etc., but it can also be all veal or other chosen meat.

RICE CROQUETTES WITH HAM ('*Suppli*' *al telefono*) *Lazio*

6 servings:

1 lb. (2½ cups) Italian short grain rice
3 oz. (1 cup) grated Parmesan cheese
3 eggs, beaten separately
2 oz. (4 tablespoons) butter
1 onion, chopped
1 slice smoked ham (prosciutto)

2 mushrooms, chopped
6 oz. (½ cup) ground meat
salt, pepper, nutmeg
6 oz. Mozzarella cheese, diced
flour, breadcrumbs
oil for frying

Cook the rice either in plenty of boiling, salted water until tender or as for risotto (see page 101). Drain and mix with half the Parmesan cheese and 1 egg. Spread out on a flat dish and leave to cool.

Heat the butter and fry the onion until soft. Add the ham, mushrooms and meat. Cook the meat until brown and mix the whole to a paste. Take from the pan, add the second egg and the rest of the Parmesan, salt, pepper and nutmeg. Put 1 good tablespoonful of rice into the palm of your hand and smooth it out with the back of a wooden spoon. Place a portion of the filling in the centre, add 2–3 dice of Mozzarella and close your hand in such a manner that the rice envelopes the filling. Shape into small balls, roll in flour, then in the remaining beaten egg, and breadcrumbs. Leave to rest for 15 minutes. In the meantime heat plenty of oil for deep frying and fry the croquettes, a few at a time, until a golden brown. (Two pans of oil can be heated at once so that all the croquettes can be cooked together.) Drain and keep hot until all the croquettes are ready. Serve hot.

MORTADELLA AND CHEESE CUTLETS *Emilia-Romagna*
(*Cotolette di mortadella*)

4 servings:

4 thick slices mortadella
8 slices Mozzarella or Bel Paese cheese
oil for deep frying

1 cup (1¼) bechamel sauce (see page 159)

Cut each slice of mortadella into half. Cover each piece with a slice of cheese. Press down firmly. Have the oil very hot, dip the mortadella and cheese into the bechamel sauce and then fry until a golden brown. Serve hot.

Instead of a bechamel sauce, an egg, flour and water batter may be used.

pizzas  *pizze*

The word pizza in Italian means pie in its widest sense, although the international popularity of the Naples-style pizza has led foreigners to believe that this is the only kind of pizza in Italy, which is by no means the case. Pies of all kinds are called pizza in this country, some of which resemble the Naples pizza—these usually in the South—but a great many which are distinctly different.

One striking example of the difference between the Naples pizza and other varieties is the *pizza di noci e canditi* from Liguria which is more like a cake about half an inch thick and flavoured with walnuts and candied peel. The Umbrian pizza is made with bread dough and mixed with three kinds of cheeses, and at Easter garnished with sliced salami, hard-boiled eggs, black olives and sometimes black truffle. Umbria also has a *pizza dolce*, which is flavoured with lemon rind and sweet white wine, and another which looks like flaky pastry stuffed with bacon.

There are the many *pizze rustiche* with a stuffing of country cheeses or crumbled pork sausages. Lecce in Apulia has a *pizza rustica* which is made with two layers of bread dough filled with a mixture of cooked onions, anchovies, and pitted and chopped black olives. Also from Apulia comes *torta tarantina di patate* made with a potato dough, and *pizza con uova e cipolle*, egg and onion pie.

However, it is undoubtedly the Naples pizza which is universally popular with its traditional garnish of tomatoes, Mozzarella cheese and olives, although this too has its variations according to the imagination of the cook. To watch the expert pizza cook at work is like watching an actor. Like an actor, he requires a stage and an audience. His set is his igloo-shaped oven, his fire of faggots, a baker's shovel with a long handle, and his risen bread dough. This last he works with deft hands, pulling small lumps of dough into rounds or oblongs, quickly smearing them with his chosen garnish, loading them on his shovel and putting them into the hot oven. In no time at all it seems that they are ready and his customers—at the same time his appreciative audience—eat them hot, crisp and appetizing.

Garnishes for *pizze* are many. In the South there is fish pizza with a garnish of fish so tiny and delicate that they do not require pre-cooking before being spread over the dough. They are then sprinkled with olive oil, oregano, garlic, salt and black pepper.

Another garnish is of fresh mushrooms cooked until soft in olive oil and flavoured with garlic. In Calabria they cook a mixture of tomatoes, canned tunny (tuna), anchovies, black olives and capers to a thick sauce as a pizza garnish.

PIZZA (*Pizza alla napoletana*) *Campania*
ILLUSTRATED PAGE 57

2–4 servings (makes $1\frac{1}{4}$–$1\frac{1}{2}$ lb. of dough):

1 oz. ($1\frac{1}{2}$ cakes compressed) fresh yeast
$\frac{1}{2}$ pint ($1\frac{1}{4}$ cups) warm water
1 lb. (4 cups) flour
1 teaspoon ($1\frac{1}{4}$) salt
olive oil

1 lb. fresh ripe or canned peeled
  tomatoes
$\frac{1}{2}$ lb. Mozzarella cheese, sliced
anchovy fillets
finely-chopped oregano to taste

Stir the yeast in a bowl with the water until it is dissolved. Add enough of the flour to make a soft, smooth dough. Cover the bowl and leave it in a warm place to rise, approximately 30 minutes. Sift the remaining flour and salt together. Make a well in the middle, fill this with the risen yeast mixture and mix together. When the mixture can be gathered into a rough ball of dough, put it on a floured board and knead it vigorously with the ball of the hand, first in one direction and then in the other, for at least 15 minutes or until the dough is smooth and elastic. (Or mix and knead in an electric mixer.) Roll it into a ball, put into a bowl, cover with a damp cloth and leave in a warm place until the dough has doubled in bulk. This will make 1 large pizza; to make 2–3 smaller *pizze*, the dough should be broken into 2–3 pieces, each piece rising separately.

Heat the oven to 475°F. (mark 9) or higher. When the dough has risen, flatten it down lightly with a rolling pin and place it on a well-oiled rectangular baking pan about 12 × 14 inches in size. Stretch and push the dough evenly with the fingers until it has stretched to the size of the pan. (If making *pizze* in smaller pans, work in the same manner.) The edges of the dough should be a little thicker than the middle but no part should be more than $\frac{1}{4}$-inch thick. Make small depressions on the dough, brush with oil and spread with tomatoes (sliced or squashed according to whether canned or fresh). Spread over the top the Mozzarella cheese and anchovy fillets, and sprinkle with oregano and a little oil. Bake in the hottest part of the hot oven (475°F., mark 9) for 10–15 minutes. Reduce the heat to 350°F. (mark 4) and bake for 5–10 minutes longer. When brown and crisp, take from the oven and serve at once. The following 4 recipes are prepared in exactly the same manner.

ROMAN-STYLE PIZZA (*Pizza alla romana*) *Lazio*

2–4 servings:

pizza dough (see above)
$\frac{1}{2}$ lb. Mozzarella cheese, cut into strips
$\frac{1}{2}$ cup (5 tablespoons) grated Parmesan
  cheese

$\frac{1}{4}$ cup ($\frac{2}{3}$) olive oil
finely-chopped basil to taste (optional)

Spread the prepared dough with the Mozzarella cheese, and sprinkle with Parmesan cheese, oil and basil.

SICILIAN-STYLE PIZZA   (*Pizza alla siciliana*)   *Sicily*

2–4 servings:

pizza dough (see page 39)
1 large can Italian peeled tomatoes
6 anchovy fillets

¼ cup (⅓) olive oil
18 black olives, pitted and coarsely chopped

Drain and coarsely chop the tomatoes and spread them over the prepared dough. Garnish with the remaining ingredients.

PIZZA WITH GARLIC   (*Pizza all'aglio*)   *Calabria*

2–4 servings:

pizza dough (see page 39)
3–4 sprigs parsley, oregano or marjoram, finely chopped

6 cloves garlic, finely chopped
8 tablespoons (10) olive oil

Mix the herbs with the garlic and oil and carefully spread this over the prepared dough. A pizza only for those who like their flavours stark.

PIZZA WITH CLAMS OR MUSSELS   (*Pizza con le vongole o cozze*)   *Southern Italy*

2–4 servings:

pizza dough (see page 39)
2 lb. clams or mussels
6 tablespoons (7½) olive oil
4 cloves garlic, finely chopped
parsley to taste, finely chopped

1 large can peeled Italian tomatoes
salt, pepper
finely-chopped oregano or marjoram to taste

Thoroughly clean the clams (or mussels) and put them into a pan with the oil, garlic and parsley. Cook over a moderate heat until they open, shaking the pan from time to time. Take the fish from the shells and keep them warm in their own liquid. Carefully drain the tomatoes, chop them coarsely and spread them evenly over the prepared dough. Sprinkle lightly with salt, pepper and oregano. Bake in a hot oven. As soon as the pizza comes from the oven, spread it evenly with the shellfish and sprinkle with black pepper.

CHEESE PIZZA   (*Pizza al formaggio*)   *Umbria*

4–6 servings:

pizza dough (see page 39)
3 oz. (1 cup) Parmesan cheese, grated
1½ oz. (scant ½ cup) Pecorino cheese, grated

2 oz. (½ cup) Provolone cheese, diced
2 eggs, well beaten
olive oil

Combine the cheeses and beat this mixture into the eggs. Punch down the risen dough, knead it, adding 2 tablespoons (2½) of oil as you work. Continue kneading until the oil is completely absorbed into the dough. Make a well in the centre, pour in the egg and cheese mixture, carefully fold over the dough and knead until the eggs and cheese are absorbed. Roll this into a smooth ball.

Brush a round, shallow baking pan generously with oil. Add the dough, spread out to the size of the pan, brush with oil, let it rise a little, then bake in a moderate oven (350°F., mark 4) until it is a golden brown and has completely risen, 25–30 minutes.

Provolone cheese is usually available in Italian shops anywhere, but not always Pecorino for which Cheddar can be substituted.

POTATO PIZZA WITH CHEESE (*Torta tarantina di patate*) *Apulia*

6 servings:

3 lb. floury potatoes
1 lb. large ripe tomatoes
olive oil
salt, black pepper
flour

½ lb. Mozzarella cheese, diced
10–12 black olives, pitted and chopped
finely-chopped oregano to taste
2 oz. (⅔ cup) grated Parmesan cheese

Peel and slice the tomatoes, discarding the seeds. Wash the potatoes and cook them, without peeling, in boiling water until tender. Drain, cool and peel. Mash or put them through a ricer and add about ¼ cup (4–5 tablespoons) of oil. Beat until smooth, adding salt to taste.

Brush the bottom of a large, shallow baking dish with oil, sprinkle lightly with flour, add the mashed potato and spread it evenly. Cover with the Mozzarella, olives, tomatoes, and sprinkle with salt, pepper, oregano and finally with Parmesan. Trickle 2–3 table-spoons of oil over the top and bake in a hot oven (400°F., mark 7) until a golden brown, 15–20 minutes.

CALZONI (*Calzoni*) *Apulia*

There is no real translation for *calzoni*, which vary from district to district. Some are like turn-overs or pasties, as in Apulia; some are baked in flat rounds, like a pizza, and indented to hold a filling; while others are deep fried.

6 servings:

Prepare a pizza dough (see page 39). When it has risen, divide it into 6 portions. Roll these out into paper-thin circles 8–10 inches in diameter. Brush lightly with oil and on one side put the chosen filling—any of the pizza fillings can be used. Moisten the edges with water, fold over the dough to make envelopes or half-moon shapes and seal the edges well. Arrange the *calzoni* on an oiled baking sheet, cover with a dry, warmed cloth, and leave for 1 hour or until the dough has risen. Bake in a hot oven (425°F., mark 7) for about 10 minutes or until the *calzoni* are a golden brown. Serve them as soon as they are taken from the oven.

salads  *insalate*

The Italian approach to salads is more akin to that of the French than either the British or American, and one of the most popular is the simple green salad, *insalata verde*, or lettuce with an oil and vinegar dressing. What the Italian does not do is to add ripe tomatoes to a green salad, these are for sauces and considered too rich for salads. Green tomatoes are for salads.

In the South, in spring, almost the only salad offered is one of thinly-sliced fennel for, as with all Italian dishes, salads are strictly seasonal.

ITALIAN SALAD DRESSING (1)   (*Vinaigrette*)

4 servings:

6 tablespoons (7½) olive oil
salt, pepper

2 tablespoons (2½) red or white wine
vinegar
finely-chopped herbs to taste (optional)

Mix the oil, salt and pepper, add the vinegar and mix well. If adding herbs, do so at this stage. Stir or shake the dressing before using.

Sometimes garlic, tarragon and continental mustard are added.

ITALIAN SALAD DRESSING (2)   (*Salsa al limone*)

4 servings:

6 tablespoons (7½) olive oil
salt, pepper

2 tablespoons (2½) strained lemon
juice

Prepare as for vinaigrette (see above).

ASPARAGUS TIP SALAD   (*Insalata di punte d'asparagi*)   *Emilia-Romagna*

4–6 servings:

2 lb. fresh green or canned asparagus
salt
dressing No. 2 (see page 42)

parsley to taste, finely chopped
2–3 hard-boiled egg yolks, finely chopped

If using fresh asparagus cook it in lightly-salted boiling water until tender. Cut off the spears and put these on a salad plate. Add the dressing, toss lightly and sprinkle with parsley and egg yolks.

GREEN BEAN SALAD   (*Insalata di fagiolini*)   *Tuscany*

2–3 servings:

1 lb. French (snap) beans
salt

dressing No. 2 (see page 42)

Trim the beans and cook them in salted boiling water until tender. Drain, cool, then chill before adding the dressing. Toss the beans lightly in the dressing.

CAULIFLOWER SALAD   (*Insalata di cavolfiore*)   *Calabria*

4 servings:

1 large cauliflower
salt
dressing No. 2 (see page 42)
3 anchovy fillets

finely-chopped parsley to taste
a few pitted and chopped black olives
2 tablespoons (2½) capers

Cook the cauliflower in boiling, salted water until tender. Take from the pan, drain well and cool. Separate the flowerets and arrange them in a shallow salad bowl. Pour the dressing over the cauliflower, carefully tossing so that each floweret is well covered. Garnish with the anchovies, parsley, olives and capers.

FONTINA CHEESE SALAD   (*Insalata di fontina*)   *Piedmont*

6 servings:

½ lb. Fontina cheese, diced
3 yellow sweet peppers
6 green olives, pitted and chopped
1 teaspoon (1¼) continental mustard

salt, pepper
2–3 tablespoons (2½–3¾) olive oil
2–3 tablespoons (2½–3¾) cream

Cut the peppers into halves, discard the seeds and cores and grill until the skins blister. Cool, pull off the thin outer skin. Cut the flesh into strips. Put the peppers, cheese and olives into a bowl. Combine the remaining ingredients and pour them over the top of the mixture. Stir gently, leave for 2–3 hours and stir again just before serving.

CELERY SALAD   (*Insalata di sedani*)   *Umbria*

3–4 servings:

1 head crisp celery   **dressing No. 1** (see page 42)

Thoroughly wash a head of white, crisp celery and cut into thin rounds, discarding any coarse stalks and the leaves. Mix with the salad dressing and toss lightly.

In Piedmont they prefer a dressing of mayonnaise and grated white truffle over the top.

CHICORY SALAD   (*Insalata di cicoria*)   *Veneto*

4 servings:

2 heads crisp chicory   **1 small mild onion, minced**
2 cloves garlic, minced   **dressing No. 1** (see page 42)

Wash and dry the chicory discarding any coarse leaves. Pull the leaves apart and drop them into a salad bowl. Add the garlic and salad dressing and toss until all the chicory is coated with the dressing.

Escarole is prepared in the same manner.

FENNEL SALAD   (*Insalata di finocchi*)   *Southern Italy*

6 servings:

2 fennel bulbs   **dressing No. 2** (see page 42)

Thinly slice the fennel, discarding the leaves and tough outer skin, and put in a salad bowl. Add the dressing and lightly toss.

GREEN OR LETTUCE SALAD   (*Insalata verde o di lattuga*)
ILLUSTRATED PAGE 118

6 servings:

3–4 lettuces   **dressing No. 1** (see page 42)

Thoroughly wash the lettuces, pull the leaves apart, and discard the thick stalks and the bruised leaves. Dry them in a salad basket or wrap them in a towel and keep in a refrigerator for 1 hour. This procedure will also help to crisp even wilted leaves. Do not put the dressing on wet leaves as the flavour is wasted.

Often Italians will mix varieties of lettuces together or perhaps other green salad ingredients such as chicory, escarole, dandelion leaves, or field chicory, will be added and other green leaves, often quite bitter, which the Italians like to collect on their Sunday outings in the country.

ONION SALAD   (*Insalata di cipolle*)   *Southern Italy*

6 servings:

3 large mild onions, peeled and thinly   **8 anchovy fillets, chopped**
    sliced   **black olives, pitted and sliced**
dressing No. 1 (see page 42)

Drop the onions into iced water and leave for 30 minutes. Drain, pat the onions dry, put them into a salad bowl, add the dressing and mix well. Serve garnished with anchovies and olives.

GREEN TOMATO SALAD   (*Insalata di pomodori*)

Peel and coarsely chop green or just ripening tomatoes, discarding the seeds. Place them in a salad bowl, sprinkle with finely-chopped garlic, basil or continental parsley, salt, a little sugar and black pepper, and coat with olive oil. Toss and chill.

GENOESE FISH SALAD   (*Cappon magro*)   *Liguria*

There is no satisfactory English translation for this salad which is the pride of Genoese cooking. It is not a dish to be undertaken lightly, the list of ingredients runs to about two dozen and its success depends on the variety of both fish and vegetables, plus a careful hand in its arranging.

The base of the salad is a large, garlic-smeared ship's biscuit lightly soaked in a mixture of vinegar and water and placed in a round dish, rubbed with garlic. On top are placed layers of ingredients arranged pyramid-style, tier upon tier. First comes a layer of dried dolphin meat, *musciame*; then one of sauce (a mixture of pine nuts, chopped garlic, parsley, gherkins, pickled mushrooms, hard-boiled eggs etc.); then mixed vegetables such as artichoke hearts, cooked carrots, green or snap beans, scorzonera, celery and potatoes, all cut into small pieces. The vegetables are spread with the sauce and these two layers repeated several times. Next the fish such as cooked bass or local sole, *orata* (red snapper), lobster, shrimps, crawfish etc., and at least a dozen crabs are added. Finally comes a layer of chopped hard-boiled eggs, black olives, pickled salted anchovies, capers, pickled mushrooms and possibly a handful of oysters.

A dish which takes a long time to prepare and which can lay heavily upon the stomach; indeed a salad only for the strong.

vegetables  verdure

The quality and the flavour of Italian vegetables are excellent. Many are the reasons given for this: some declare it is because the sea mists carry salt and other minerals which are deposited on the land; and others that it is because farmers still use natural fertilizers. Then there is the difference of climate and soil, and of course the manner in which the land is husbanded. Whatever it is, Italians throughout the year have some of the finest vegetables in the world. In southern regions, for example in Calabria, where the meat is of poor quality, housewives have learned to embellish their vegetables in a remarkable manner.

Italians boil, fry and stuff vegetables or serve them raw, but they never cook them alone in water. They will add herbs, seasoning in plenty, a dash of freshly-grated nutmeg (especially with mushrooms), and all without ruining the flavour of the vegetables.

Vegetables are not usually served with a main dish, they are a course on their own and served as often tepid as hot, or even cold.

Vegetables are seasonal and localized. Italians wait for the first asparagus, artichokes and sun-ripened tomatoes to appear and eat them daily until the season is finished. In a country with such a varied climate as Italy's, almost all known vegetables can be grown. The cold climate of Trentino, for example, produces white cabbages (Umbria and Tuscany also grow a true black cabbage), potatoes, turnips and other similar vegetables. The Tuscans produce so many beans they are dubbed *mangiafagioli*, bean-eaters. But Venezia is a close second in bean growing, and onions there are much in evidence. Umbria is rich in vegetables; the town of Bassano in Venezia claims the best white asparagus in Italy, a claim disputed by Ravenna in Emilia-Romagna which points out that its fame as an asparagus producing town was already known in Roman days. Trevi, in Umbria, is locally famed for its celery, and throughout this central part of Italy *cardi* or *cardone*, cardoon, a member of the thistle family which resembles celery and grows to a height of three to four feet, is much used.

It is in the South that we find scarlet, almost over-ripe and mis-shapen tomatoes, full of the tangy flavour of sun-ripened fruit. Curiously, although it is difficult to think of Italian cooking without tomatoes, they were only introduced into Italy in the sixteenth century. Red plum-shaped tomatoes are used for sauces etc., and green tomatoes for

46

salads. When cooking Italian dishes outside of Italy, it helps to achieve the authentic flavour by using Italian canned tomatoes.

Also in the South are aubergines (eggplants), sweet peppers and courgettes (zucchini), all of which grow to an enormous size, and are therefore easy to stuff and turn into main dishes. Fennel also grows in abundance. Italy is believed to be the original home of broccoli and cauliflower which, botanically, are varieties of the same species. The common name broccoli is Italian and derived from *brocco*, a shoot, the earliest form of the vegetable being loose spikes.

Potatoes are not a great feature of Italian cooking; they do not grow too well in this country and many are imported. But apart from the usual ways of cooking potatoes, there are many interesting and unusual Italian potato dishes.

Much of the culinary genius of the modern Roman cook goes into artichoke dishes, one of the most popular Italian vegetables. Throughout the country they are cooked in every possible way but they reach the peak of their perfection in Rome. No one who is in Rome at Eastertime should fail to eat a dish of *carciofi alla giudia*, young artichokes deep fried in olive oil until crisp, then flattened to reach the table looking like a rose. Another Roman speciality is *carciofi al tegame alla romana*, large artichokes stuffed with breadcrumbs, mint, garlic etc., and cooked in oil. Tiny chokeless artichokes are used for pickling and served as an antipasto or used to fill a *frittata*, and are a main ingredient in the Genoese Easter pie, *torta pasqualina*. Larger artichokes are boiled and served with a butter sauce, extra large ones are usually stuffed.

Asparagus, both white and green, is another fine Italian vegetable. It appears in the markets in April and continues for two months or so. This too is cooked in a variety of ways. Particularly good is a wild, bright green asparagus with tender spears full of flavour. Industrious families spend their weekend gathering wild asparagus in the woods and fields as they do wild chicory and herbs.

Mushrooms in Italy are important both as a food and as a flavouring, and there is considerable variety. There are so-called flap mushrooms, large and succulent; honey mushrooms; the delicious *porcini* so tender they literally melt in the mouth; and a host of others, for in Italy people understand their mushrooms. Equally popular are dried mushrooms, sold either strung on a string or in plastic bags; those on the string have a finer flavour. Italian dried mushrooms have quite a different flavour to those of other countries. When only cultivated mushrooms are available, Italians will add some dried mushrooms to them, this considerably livens up their otherwise too bland flavour.

Universally, a favourite vegetable is the delicately-flavoured courgette (zucchini). They are not peeled, the ends are trimmed and the courgettes are cooked whole, if they are small enough, or if larger sliced lengthwise or in rounds, and cooked in oil or butter or a mixture of both. Care must be taken not to over-cook them. The orange courgette blossoms are dipped in batter and fried.

Another interesting Italian vegetable is the so-called oyster plant or salsify, scorzonera, which comes in two forms, white and black; the Italians prefer the black. Both root and leaf are eaten. Finally there are onions, strong, mild or sweet in flavour, red, white, yellow, or mauve in colour. There are pumpkins in the South, all colours, shapes and sizes which are cooked in numerous ways: fried, puréed, and made into soups. Their yellow blossoms too are made into fritters.

Truffles, the fruit of a fungus growing one to two feet below the ground, can hardly be called a vegetable. The best known types of truffle are the Italian white truffle, and the French black. Both are extremely expensive, even on their home ground. The Italian white truffle area is Alba, south-east of Turin, but they are also found in the foothills of the ranges that border the Lombardy plain, and the north side of the Apennines as far as Modena. Their season begins in October with a 'truffle fair' and continues until the snows put an end to it. White truffles look like chunky, yellow, mis-shapen potatoes and are usually the same size, although giant truffles are found from time to time. They have a strong perfume, quite unique, which I am not able to describe. In Italy truffles are usually grated with a special knife or grater into razor-thin slices directly on to the dish they are to flavour. White truffles are far better eaten raw for it is their perfume which counts, not their flavour. Canned white truffles are available, but their processing results in such a loss of flavour they are hardly worth buying. One small truffle is sufficient for several people. Equally good are the black truffles of Umbria, from Norcia and Spoletto, both centres of some of the finest truffles in Europe, richer, it is considered, than those of Perigord in France. The ancient Romans were particularly appreciative of Spoletto's truffles, as indeed are the modern Romans, and the French who import them in large quantities.

ASPARAGUS AU GRATIN (*Asparagi gratinati*) *Emilia-Romagna*

6 servings:

2 lb. asparagus	salt, pepper
¼ lb. smoked raw bacon, cut into strips	1 cup (1¼) dry white wine
4 oz. (8 tablespoons) butter	3 oz. (1 cup) grated Parmesan cheese

Thinly peel the thick stalks of the asparagus stems (obviously do not touch the tips), and cook them in a flat pan or in an asparagus cooker with plenty of lightly-salted water until tender. Cooking time depends on the thickness of the stalks but usually it is 15–25 minutes. Test by piercing the bottom of a spear with a knife, when it pierces easily, it is ready.

As soon as the spears are tender, drain thoroughly and place them flat in the bottom of a large shallow baking dish. Add the bacon. Melt half the butter and sprinkle this over the top of the spears. Add salt, pepper and wine, cover with the Parmesan and dot with the remaining butter cut into slivers. Bake in a hot oven (450°F., mark 8) for about 10 minutes or until the top is a golden colour.

Serve as a main course or antipasto.

STUFFED ARTICHOKES (*Carciofi ripieni*) *Sicily*

6 servings:

6 large artichokes	2–3 sprigs parsley, finely chopped
1 lemon	4 tablespoons (5) soft breadcrumbs
salt, pepper	4 anchovies in brine, washed, boned
1 cup (1¼) olive oil	and chopped
1 small onion, chopped	3½ oz. (7 tablespoons) butter
1 clove garlic, crushed	

Pull off the outer, coarser leaves of the artichokes and cut off the stalks closely, so that the artichokes will stand upright. Cut off the tips of the leaves with scissors then wash the artichokes thoroughly in lemon-flavoured water. Drain. Open out the leaves, sprinkle them with salt and pepper and put aside.

Heat half the oil in a small pan and add the onion and garlic. When the garlic browns, discard it. Stir the parsley into the oil and remove it from the heat. Take 2 tablespoons (2½) of the hot oil and reheat it in a small pan. Add the breadcrumbs and fry them until brown. Blend the anchovies and butter. Mix together the onion (with its oil), breadcrumbs, anchovy-butter and a little salt. Push this mixture between the leaves of the artichokes. Put them in a shallow pan, just large enough to contain them close together in an upright position, sprinkle lightly with the remaining oil, cover the pan and cook over a moderate heat for 30–40 minutes, basting from time to time. To test when the artichokes are tender, pull off one leaf, if it comes away easily, the artichokes are ready. Serve either hot or cold as a main dish or as antipasto.

AUBERGINE AU GRATIN (*Parmigiana di melanzane*)   *Abruzzi-Molise*

6 servings:

6 aubergines (eggplants), about 2 lb.	tomato sauce:
salt	**2 tablespoons (2½) olive oil**
olive oil	**1 small onion, minced**
2 oz. (⅔ cup) grated Parmesan cheese	**2 lb. tomatoes, peeled, chopped and**
a leaf or so of basil, finely chopped	**seeded**
½ lb. Mozzarella cheese, thinly sliced	**2–3 basil leaves, finely chopped**
2 tablespoons (2½) breadcrumbs	**salt, pepper**

Peel the aubergines and cut them into medium-thick slices. Sprinkle with salt and leave them on a tilted plate for 1 hour to drain off their bitter liquid. Thoroughly wash off the salt and pat the slices dry.

Make the sauce: heat the oil in a large pan and fry the onion until soft but not brown. Add the tomatoes, basil, salt and pepper. Gently bring to the boil, lower the heat and cook for 30–40 minutes. Rub the mixture through a sieve.

Heat plenty of oil in a deep pan and fry the aubergine slices, a few at a time, until brown. Take out and drain. Cover the bottom of a deep casserole with a layer of fried aubergine. Sprinkle with Parmesan, add a little basil, a layer of sliced Mozzarella, and spread with the tomato sauce. Repeat this operation until the ingredients are finished. Sprinkle the top with breadcrumbs. Bake in a hot oven (450°F., mark 8) for about 30 minutes. Serve hot or cold.

In Bari a similar dish, called locally *parmeggianne*, is prepared using Pecorino instead of Parmesan cheese. If fresh basil is not available, use parsley or any favourite fresh herb.

STUFFED AUBERGINES   (*Melanzane ripiene*)   *Apulia*

6 servings:

6 medium-sized oval aubergines (egg-plants)	**2 tablespoons (2½) soft breadcrumbs**
salt, pepper	**3 tablespoons (3¾) grated Parmesan cheese**
1 oz. (1 cup) dried mushrooms, soaked in water for 30 minutes	**1 egg, lightly beaten**
2 cloves garlic, finely chopped	**4–5 leaves basil, finely chopped**
	½ cup (⅔) olive oil

Wash the aubergines and cut them in halves lengthwise; sprinkle the insides with salt and lay them, cut-side down, on a dish, leaving them to drain for at least an hour. Thoroughly wash to rid them of the salt and dry well.

Scoop out enough of their flesh to leave the aubergines boat-shaped but with fairly thick shells. Drain and chop the mushrooms. Chop the aubergine flesh and mix it with the garlic, mushrooms, breadcrumbs, Parmesan, egg, basil, salt and pepper. Fill the hollowed-out aubergines with this mixture and arrange them, spaced well apart, in a baking pan. Add the oil and the same quantity of warm water. Bake in a very hot oven (450°F., mark 8) until the aubergines are soft; do not overcook them as they will lose their shape. Serve as a main dish or as antipasto.

STUFFED SWEET PEPPERS   (*Peperoni farciti alla napoletana*)   *Campania*

6 servings:

6 large sweet peppers, preferably mixed colours	**6–8 black olives, pitted and chopped**
olive oil	**3–4 anchovy fillets, chopped**
1 clove garlic, finely chopped	**1 teaspoon (1¼) finely-chopped oregano**
3 ripe tomatoes, peeled, seeded and chopped	**pepper, salt**
1–2 tablespoons (1¼–2½) capers	**½ lb. small macaroni**

Wipe the peppers with a damp cloth and slice off the tops; retain them to use as lids. Discard the cores and seeds. Heat 4 tablespoons (5) of oil, lightly brown the garlic, add the tomatoes and cook over a good heat for 10 minutes. Take the pan from the heat and add the capers, olives, anchovies, oregano and pepper.

Bring plenty of salted water to the boil, add the macaroni and cook it until *al dente* (see page 83). Drain and mix with the tomato sauce. Fill the peppers with this mixture, cover with the tops and arrange them upright and closely packed in a baking pan. Sprinkle with ½ cup (⅔) of oil and bake in a moderate oven (350°F., mark 4) for 1–1½ hours or until the peppers are soft but still firm. Serve as a main course or as antipasto.

BROCCOLI BRAISED IN WINE   (*Broccoli 'a crudo'*)   *Lazio*

This recipe also appears as *broccoli alla romana* since it is a Roman speciality. Broccoli is one of the best of the vegetables grown around Rome and this dish is a favourite during the early days of the broccoli season when it is young and tender.

4–6 servings:

2 lb. broccoli
salt, pepper
4 tablespoons (5) olive oil

2 cloves garlic, crushed
1½–2 cups (2–2½) dry white wine

Wash the broccoli, discard any tough outer leaves and the tough ends of the stalks, and cut off the remaining stalks about 2 inches below the heads. Put the heads aside. Peel the stalks and cut the thick ones through lengthwise. Leave the heads and stalks in salted, iced water until ready to use.

Heat the oil in a large pan and fry the garlic until it is a golden colour. Add half the wine, then the stalks, sprinkle lightly with salt and pepper, cover the pan and cook gently until the stalks are tender. Lay the broccoli heads on top of the stalks, sprinkle again with salt and pepper, add the remaining wine and continue cooking, uncovered, until the heads are tender. By this time the wine should be reduced to about ½ cup (⅔). If it has not reduced sufficiently, raise the heat for a minute or so until it has. Arrange the broccoli in a hot serving dish and pour the remaining liquid over the top.

CABBAGE COOKED IN WHITE WINE (*Cavolo al vino bianco*) *Veneto*

4–6 servings:

1 large white cabbage
1 oz. (2 tablespoons) butter
1 tablespoon (1¼) olive oil
1 medium-sized onion, grated
1 cup (1¼) boiling water

1 teaspoon (1¼) salt
1 teaspoon (1¼) sugar
1 tablespoon (1¼) capers
1 cup (1¼) dry white wine

Remove any wilted leaves from the cabbage, cut it into quarters, cut out the hard stalk and leave the cabbage to soak in iced, salted water for 30 minutes. Drain well and shred.

Heat the butter and oil together in a large pan, fry the onion until brown, add the cabbage and stir well. Add the remaining ingredients. Stir, cover and bring gently to the boil, lower the heat and cook until the cabbage is tender, 20–25 minutes.

CABBAGE COOKED WITH BACON (*Cavolo alla casalinga*) *Veneto*

4–6 servings:

1 large hard white cabbage
salt, pepper
1 tablespoon (1¼) olive oil
3–4 thin strips bacon, diced

1 onion or leek, finely chopped
1 tablespoon (1¼) wine vinegar
2 cups (2½) water

Strip off any wilted leaves from the cabbage, quarter it and cut away the hard stalk. Drop the cabbage into iced, salted water and leave for 30 minutes. Drain and shred. Heat the oil in a heavy pan, add the bacon and cook until its fat runs. Fry the onion until it changes colour, add the cabbage, vinegar, water, salt and pepper. Stir well, cover the pan and cook until the cabbage is tender, 20–25 minutes. Drain off all liquid before serving.

BAKED ONIONS WITH MARSALA (*Cipolle di Napoli*) *Campania*

6 servings:

12 large mild onions, peeled	**1 sprig thyme**
12 cloves	**½ cup (⅔) Marsala**
salt, pepper	**1 tablespoon (1¼) capers**
½ cup (⅔) olive oil	

Push 1 clove into each onion, place them in 1 layer in a baking pan, and add salt, pepper, oil and thyme. Cover and bake in a moderate oven (350°F., mark 4) for 1 hour or until the onions are soft, gently shaking the pan from time to time.

Sprinkle the Marsala over the onions and cook uncovered until it has evaporated. Arrange the onions on a serving dish, discard the cloves and thyme, sprinkle with capers and serve at once.

If Marsala is not available, use a medium or sweet sherry. Serve as a main dish or as antipasto.

BEANS COOKED IN A CHIANTI FLASK (*Fagioli nel fiasco*) *Tuscany*

This is a traditional country style of cooking fresh beans, white haricot in particular, but it is not often done these days. The beans are pushed into the Chianti flasks, oil added and the flask placed on the top of smouldering charcoal embers and left until the beans are tender. But today modern gas or electric stoves are available almost everywhere and this method of cooking is dying out, except as a gimmick with some tourist restaurants. It might well even be forgotten when the Chianti flask itself is a thing of the past, for the wine makers are finding it costs more to produce these famous flasks than it does their wine.

6 servings:

1 Chianti flask of 3–4 pint	**2 leaves sage**
(7½–10 cups) capacity	**2 cloves garlic**
1 lb. fresh white beans	**salt, pepper**
½ cup (⅔) olive oil	

Remove the straw covering from the flask. Put the beans into the flask—do not fill it as the beans have to swell. Add the oil, sage and garlic, and 2 cups (2½) of water. Fill the mouth of the flask loosely with straw, leaving space for the steam to escape. If not cooking the beans over charcoal, the same result can be achieved by putting the bottle into a slow oven (325°F., mark 3) and leaving them for about 3 hours. To serve, turn them out into a bowl, sprinkle with salt, pepper and olive oil and serve hot or cold or even tepid.

I have not attempted this recipe myself and offer it more as a curiosity. However, in Tuscany it was once used regularly although often the bottles would break.

CAULIFLOWER MILANESE STYLE (*Cavolfiore alla milanese*) *Lombardy*

4–6 servings:

1 large cauliflower	**1 small onion, very thinly sliced**
salt	**1–2 sprigs parsley, chopped**
3 oz. (6 tablespoons) butter	**grated Parmesan cheese to taste**

Trim the cauliflower and wash it in cold, salted water. Put it into a pan with boiling, salted water, head uppermost, and cook until just tender. Drain and cool, then divide into flowerets.

Heat half the butter in a shallow, heavy casserole (one which can be transferred to the oven), add the onion and parsley and cook gently until the onion begins to change colour. Add the flowerets, arranging them as neatly as possible, flower portion uppermost and tightly packed. Sprinkle with plenty of Parmesan. Melt the remaining butter and sprinkle it over the top. Transfer the pan to a hot oven (450°F., mark 8) and bake for 10–15 minutes.

BOILED CARDOON (*Cardone lesso*) *Tuscany*

This is one of the best ways to cook cardoon and retain its delicate flavour. Wash it well, strip off the coarse leaves, cut it into small pieces and cook in salted water until tender. Drain, return to the pan, add a little butter, some grated Parmesan cheese, stir gently and serve hot.

BAKED CELERY WITH BACON AND TOMATO (*Sedani al forno*) *Apulia*

6 servings:

2 large heads celery	**4 slices streaky bacon, finely chopped**
½ lb. tomatoes, chopped	**salt, pepper**
juice 1 lemon	**1 cup (1¼) stock**
olive oil	**3 sprigs parsley, finely chopped**
1 onion, sliced	

Canned or fresh tomatoes may be used in this recipe. If using canned tomatoes, drain them well before chopping. The liquid is not required. If using fresh tomatoes, they must be very ripe and should be peeled, seeded and chopped.

Thoroughly wash the celery, discarding the coarse leaves and any bruised stalks. Drain and cut them into 6-inch lengths. Bring a large pan of water with the lemon juice to the boil, add the celery and boil for 5 minutes. Drain.

Heat 4 tablespoons (5) of oil in a large pan and fry the onion and half the bacon until both change colour. Add the celery and cook over a brisk heat for 5 minutes. Add salt, pepper and the stock. Cover the pan and cook over a low heat until the celery is tender.

Transfer the celery with the oil etc. to a baking dish, sprinkle the remaining bacon over the top, add the tomatoes, and sprinkle with salt, pepper, parsley and a little oil. Bake in a moderate oven (350°F., mark 4) for about 20 minutes.

CELERY COOKED IN SAUCE (*Sedani di Trevi in umido*) *Umbria*

4 servings:

2 large heads white celery
4 pints (5) water
salt, black pepper
4 strips fat bacon, diced

1 medium-sized onion, diced
1 sprig parsley, finely chopped
2 tablespoons (2½) Italian tomato paste

Wash the celery, cut off the leaves, and cut the stalks into 4-inch lengths. Put them into a pan, add the water, salt and pepper to taste and cook for 5 minutes over a brisk heat. Drain, put the celery aside but keep the liquid.

In another large pan fry the bacon until the fat runs freely, add the onion and parsley and fry until the onion changes colour. Dilute the tomato paste with some of the liquid from the celery, stir this into the bacon and onion, then add the rest of the celery liquid, salt and pepper, and cook over a moderate heat for 30 minutes or until the sauce has considerably reduced. Add the celery and cook until it is tender.

The quality of the celery in Trevi is famous in Italy and the above recipe is a local favourite.

COURGETTES IN MARSALA SAUCE (*Zucchini in salsa al marsala*) *Piedmont*

6 servings:

2 lb. courgettes (zucchini)
salt to taste

sauce:
4 egg yolks, beaten

½ cup (⅔) dry Marsala
salt
2 tablespoons (2½) water
1½ oz. (3 tablespoons) butter, chopped

Wash the courgettes, trim off both ends and cut into thick rounds. Put them into a pan, cover with cold, salted water, bring to the boil and cook until they are tender.

Beat the egg yolks with the Marsala, salt and water and pour the mixture into the top of a double boiler. Stirring constantly, cook over hot but not boiling water until the sauce is thick. Take from the heat and stir in the butter.

Drain the courgettes and put them into a hot serving dish. Pour the hot sauce over the top and serve at once.

CASSEROLE OF FENNEL (*Finocchi alla casalinga*) *Sicily*

Fennel bulbs vary considerably in size but usually 2 lb. is sufficient for 5–6 people.

5–6 servings:

2 lb. fennel
salt, pepper
6 tablespoons (7½) olive oil

2–3 cloves garlic, well crushed
½ cup (⅔) water (or white wine)

Trim off the outer leaves and ends of the fennel and cook it in lightly salted, boiling water for 15 minutes. Drain and slice it thickly. Heat the oil in a casserole on top of the stove, add the garlic, let this brown, discard it, then add the fennel, the water (or white wine), and sprinkle with salt and black pepper. Cover and cook gently for 40 minutes or until the fennel is tender. Serve in the casserole.

MUSHROOMS WITH AN ANCHOVY SAUCE (*Funghi trifolati*) *Lazio*

The correct mushrooms for this dish are the large, tender *porcini* but, failing these, any large, tender mushrooms can be used.

4 servings:

2 lb. mushrooms	6 anchovy fillets
4 tablespoons (5) olive oil	2–3 tablespoons ($2\frac{1}{2}$–$3\frac{3}{4}$) finely-chopped
2 cloves garlic, crushed	parsley
salt, pepper	juice 1 lemon
2 tablespoons ($2\frac{1}{2}$) butter	

Clean and thinly slice the mushrooms. Heat the oil over a moderate heat, brown the garlic and discard it. Add mushrooms, salt and pepper. Cover and cook for 8–10 minutes or until the liquid from the mushrooms has evaporated and they are tender. Take from the pan and put on to a hot plate. Keep hot. Add the butter and the remaining ingredients to the pan, stir well and cook for 3–4 minutes. Pour this sauce over the mushrooms.

MUSHROOMS COOKED IN CREAM (*Funghi coltivati alla crema*) *Umbria*

3–4 servings:

$1\frac{1}{2}$ lb. small white mushrooms	1 cup ($1\frac{1}{4}$) thick cream
3 oz. (6 tablespoons) butter	salt, pepper
$\frac{1}{2}$ glass dry red wine or Marsala	nutmeg

Clean the mushrooms and pull off the stems (the latter can be used in a soup or stew). Heat the butter, add the mushrooms and cook them until they brown. Add the wine and continue cooking until this has reduced by half. Add the cream, salt, pepper and a sprinkling of nutmeg and continue cooking gently until the mushrooms are tender.

Two or three tablespoonfuls of dried mushrooms, soaked for 30 minutes, dried and chopped, may also be added to the pan at the same time as the fresh mushrooms.

PEAS WITH BACON (*Piselli al prosciutto*) *Lazio*

3–4 servings:

2 lb. fresh green peas	$\frac{1}{2}$ cup ($\frac{2}{3}$) hot water or stock
2 oz. (4 tablespoons) butter	salt, pepper
1 small mild onion, finely chopped	4 oz. smoked ham or bacon, diced

Shuck the peas and put them into a pan with the remaining ingredients, except the ham, and cook until tender. Just before they are ready, add the ham and continue cooking until this is hot.

MIXED VEGETABLES (*Ciambotta*) *Calabria*

4–6 servings:

4 medium-sized aubergines (eggplants)
salt, pepper
6–8 courgettes (zucchini)
2–3 sweet peppers, according to size
½ cup (⅔) olive oil

2 large onions, thickly sliced
¾ lb. ripe tomatoes, peeled, seeded and
chopped
1–2 cloves, garlic, crushed

Peel the aubergines and cut them into 1-inch cubes. Put them into a colander, sprinkle with salt and drain for 30 minutes. Wash off the salt and wipe the aubergines dry. Wash the courgettes and cut them into medium-thick slices. Cut each pepper into 4 pieces, discarding the cores and seeds. Grill them until the outer skin is brown and blistered. Cool and pull off the outer skin.

Heat the oil, add the onions and cook until soft but not browned. Add the aubergines, courgettes, tomatoes, garlic, and salt and pepper to taste. Cook gently for 1 hour until all the vegetables are tender, stirring gently from time to time. Turn out the vegetables with their liquid into a deep dish to serve.

Sometimes cubed potatoes, fried separately, are also added to the dish, mixed in just before it is served. If potatoes are added, the vegetables must be served hot, but if not, they can be served hot or cold.

OPPOSITE *Pizza alla napoletana* (*page 39*) *one of the traditional pizzas of Naples.*

OVERLEAF AND BELOW *A selection of uncooked pasta from the many hundreds, or possibly thousands of varieties in existence.*

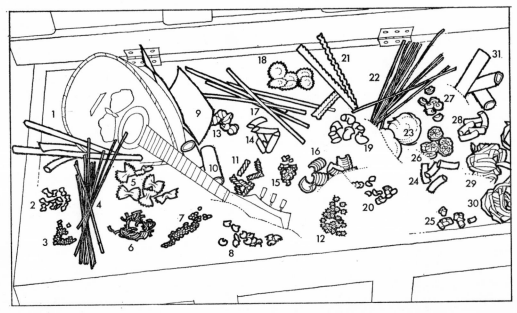

1 Maccheroncini 2 Tripolini 3 Tempestine 4 Vermicelli 5 Farfallone 6 Stortini 7 Anellini
8 Cirillini 9 Lasagne verde 10 Canelloni 11 Fusilli 12 Stelline 13 Gnocchi 14 Penne rigate
15 Corallini 16 Gnocchi sardi 17 Bucatini 18 Pagliacci 19 Pipette 20 Cinesini 21 Reginette
22 Spaghetti 23 Vermicelli a matassa 24 Tortiglioni 25 Ditalini rigati

POTATOES HUNTER'S STYLE (*Patate alla cacciatora*) *Southern Italy*

4 servings:

2 lb. potatoes, not floury
4 tablespoons (5) olive oil
1–2 cloves garlic
½ cup (⅔) dry white wine

½ lb. tomatoes, peeled, seeded and
  chopped
1 bay leaf
salt, pepper

Scrub the potatoes and cook them in their skins until almost tender. Cool, peel and cut them into cubes. Heat the oil in a deep frying pan, add the garlic, lightly brown it, add the potatoes and fry them until brown. Add the wine and continue cooking until this evaporates. Add the tomatoes, bay leaf, salt and pepper and continue cooking until the potatoes are tender. If necessary, a little more liquid may be added: stock, water or wine.

POTATOES WITH GARLIC (*Patate all'aglio*) *Calabria*

6 servings:

3 lb. potatoes
¾ cup (1) olive oil
2 cloves garlic, crushed

salt
fresh oregano to taste

Wash, peel and slice the potatoes. Heat the oil in a casserole, add the garlic and when it begins to brown add the potatoes. Sprinkle generously with salt and oregano and cook on top of the stove over a moderate heat until tender. Shake the pan from time to time to prevent the potatoes from sticking. When they are soft and a golden brown, discard the garlic and serve the potatoes in the casserole.

POTATO CAKE (*Gattò di patate*) *Campania*

6 servings:

2 lb. floury potatoes
¼ lb. salami, diced
½ lb. Mozzarella cheese (or Bel Paese),
  diced

1 cup (1¼) grated Parmesan cheese
4 eggs, hard-boiled and chopped
salt, pepper
butter, flour

Scrub the potatoes and cook them in salted water until tender. Drain, cool, then peel, and mash until smooth. Add the remaining ingredients, except the butter and flour, and beat until the mixture is well blended. Rub a round baking pan with butter and sprinkle lightly with flour. Add the potato mixture and bake in a hot oven (425°F., mark 7) for 15 minutes.

BACK *Hard polenta with its traditional board and knife* (*page 107*); CENTRE LEFT *Baked noodles with prawns* (*page 100*); CENTRE RIGHT *Cannelloni with Mozzarella cheese* (*page 91*); FRONT LEFT *Spinach and cheese dumplings* (*page 106*); FRONT RIGHT *Risotto milanese* (*page 102*)

POTATO AND RICOTTA PIE (*Torta di ricotta*) *Liguria*

4 servings:

2 lb. potatoes
½ lb. Ricotta cheese
olive oil
2–3 sprigs parsley, finely chopped

2–3 eggs, well beaten
2–3 small leeks, white part only
breadcrumbs

Cook the potatoes until tender and put them through a ricer or mash them until free of lumps. Mix with the Ricotta. Heat a little oil and gently fry the parsley until it changes colour. Mix this into the potato, then beat in the eggs. Wash the leeks and slice them, not too thinly, into strips.

Rub a round cake pan with oil and lay half the potato at the bottom, cover with the leeks, add the remaining potato and smooth it down lightly with a fork. Sprinkle the top with breadcrumbs and a liberal coating of oil. Bake in a moderate oven (350°F., mark 4) until the top is a golden brown.

This type of *torta* is served on the vigil of feast days and during Holy Week.

SPINACH CARTHUSIAN STYLE (*Spinaci alla certosina*) *Piedmont*

6 servings:

4 lb. spinach
6 tablespoons (7½) olive oil
1–2 cloves garlic, finely chopped
1 tablespoon (1¼) sultanas (white raisins)

2 teaspoons (2½) pine nuts
4 anchovy fillets, chopped
12 green olives, pitted and chopped
8 black olives, pitted and chopped
1 tablespoon (1¼) capers

Thoroughly wash the spinach and cook it for 5 minutes without adding water. Drain it well and chop. Heat the oil, brown the garlic and add the remaining ingredients. Add the spinach, stir it well into the mixture, and bring to boiling point. Serve hot.

STUFFED TOMATOES (*Pomodori al pane*) *Sardinia*

6 servings:

12 ripe tomatoes
soft breadcrumbs, white or brown
a few basil leaves, finely chopped
2–3 sprigs parsley, finely chopped

2 cloves garlic, finely chopped
salt
1 tablespoon (1¼) sugar
¼ cup (⅓) olive oil

Choose tomatoes of equal size. Wash them well, wipe dry and slice off the tops to make 'lids'. Turn the tomatoes upside down on a plate to drain, and reserve the drained-off liquid. Combine the breadcrumbs, herbs and garlic, add a little salt, sugar, a trickle of olive oil and the tomato liquid. Fill the tomatoes with this mixture, cover with the lids and arrange in a baking pan with ½ cup (⅔) of warm water. Sprinkle lightly with salt and the remaining oil. Bake in a moderate oven (350°F., mark 4) for 1 hour or until the tomatoes are soft, but do not let them collapse. Serve either hot or cold.

egg dishes  *piatti di uova*

In Italian restaurants there seems to be no set place on the menu for egg dishes. Sometimes there is a small section labelled *uova*; sometimes egg dishes come under *piatti del giorno*, today's dishes, or *piatti da farsi*, dishes to order; sometimes there is no reference at all.

EGGS FRIED ITALIAN STYLE   (*Uova fritte all'italiana o Uova fritte al bacon*)

3 servings:

6 eggs	**olive oil**
butter	**tomato sauce** (see pages 160–161)
12 thin slices pancetta (streaky bacon)	

Heat the butter and fry the bacon until it changes colour. Put aside but keep it hot. In the same pan heat a little oil and fry the eggs. As they are fried, place them on a hot, round plate leaving space between each to put 2 slices of bacon. Garnish with hot tomato sauce and serve at once.

FRIED EGGS WITH MOZZARELLA   (*Uova fritte con mozzarella*)   *Campania*

eggs	**Mozzarella cheese, thinly sliced**
butter	**salt, pepper**

Quantities are as required and the cheese and eggs should be cooked in small frying pans that can be brought to the table.

Rub as many small pans as required with butter. Add a layer of Mozzarella cheese. Cook over a moderate heat until the cheese begins to melt. Break 1–2 eggs into each pan and continue frying until the eggs are set. Sprinkle with salt and black pepper.

63

FRIED HARD-BOILED EGGS (*Uova alla torinese*) *Piedmont*

3 servings:

6 hard-boiled eggs, shelled	salt, pepper, nutmeg
2 sprigs parsley, 1 sprig rosemary, 1 sprig thyme	3 tablespoons (3¾) grated Parmesan cheese
1 oz. (2 tablespoons) butter	oil for deep frying
2 eggs	flour

Cut the eggs into halves. Finely chop the herbs. Heat the butter, add the herbs and fry for 2 minutes. Turn into a mixing bowl and leave to cool. Beat the remaining eggs with a good pinch of salt, pepper and nutmeg and stir in the Parmesan. Pour this mixture into the butter and beat with a fork until thoroughly blended.

Have ready a pan with plenty of oil for deep frying. Lightly roll the hard-boiled eggs in flour and dip them into the egg and butter mixture. Fry at once in boiling hot oil until a golden brown. Serve hot.

SCRAMBLED EGGS (*Uova strapazzate o stracciate*)

3 servings:

6 eggs	1½ oz. (3 tablespoons) butter
salt, pepper	

Lightly beat the eggs and season. Heat the butter, add the eggs and cook them slowly over a low heat; they must not coagulate too quickly. Stir them with a wooden spoon until set but still moist.

The Italians have another and unusual method of cooking eggs which is a cross between scrambling and an omelette. Lightly beat the eggs, adding seasoning. Heat the butter, add the eggs but do not stir; instead let the underneath portion of the eggs set, then carefully lift it up with a spatula and allow some of the uncooked egg from the top to run underneath. When this has set, lift it up again and continue as before until all the egg has cooked. The result is a layered mass of scrambled egg. Gently slide on to a serving plate and serve plain or with a sauce.

SCRAMBLED EGGS WITH CHICKEN LIVERS
(*Uova strapazzate con fegatini di pollo*)

2–3 servings:

6 eggs	4 tablespoons (5) dry Marsala
4 oz. (8 tablespoons) butter	salt, pepper
8 chicken livers, trimmed and chopped	

Heat 1 oz. (2 tablespoons) of the butter, add the chicken livers and *sauté* them for 3 minutes. Take them from the pan with a perforated (slotted) spoon and keep them warm. Add the Marsala, stir it into the butter and cook until it is reduced by half. Take the pan from the heat, add the chicken livers, put the pan to one side but keep it warm. Lightly beat the eggs and add salt and pepper. In another pan heat the remaining butter, add the eggs, stir with a wooden spoon and cook gently until the eggs are set. Take from the pan, quickly turn on to a serving dish, garnish with the chicken livers and sauce and serve at once.

SCRAMBLED EGGS WITH TRUFFLE (*Uova con tartufi*) *Piedmont*

2–3 servings:

6 eggs	**3 oz. (6 tablespoons) butter**
salt, pepper	**a little white truffle, grated**

Mix the eggs lightly with a fork and season with salt and pepper. Heat the butter until it is golden, add the eggs, cook over a low heat and stir constantly but gently with a wooden spoon until creamy. Serve sprinkled with truffle.

Umbria prepares a similar dish with black truffles.

POACHED EGGS WITH PINE NUT SAUCE (*Uova in salsa di pinoli*) *Liguria*

4 servings:

4 eggs	**½ teaspoon (⅔) salt**
1 tablespoon (1¼) vinegar	**1 cup (1¼) pine nut sauce** (see page 163)

Put 2 pints (5 cups) of water into a shallow pan, add the vinegar and salt, bring almost to the boil, then let it simmer. Break the eggs, one at a time, into a cup and slide them into the simmering water. Simmer for 3–4 minutes. When the eggs are cooked, remove them with a perforated (slotted) spoon, drain, and arrange on a hot serving dish. Cover with the sauce and serve at once.

If the eggs are a little ragged after poaching, trim them with kitchen scissors before adding the sauce.

EGGS HUNTER'S STYLE (*Uova alla cacciatora*) *Emilia-Romagna*

6 servings:

6 eggs	**1 cup (1¼) dry white wine**
1 oz. (2 tablespoons) butter	**rosemary, basil, thyme to taste**
1 small onion, minced	**6–8 green olives, chopped**
4 chicken livers, chopped	**salt, pepper to taste**
flour	**6 slices toast**
1 cup (1¼) tomato juice	**chicken liver pâté**

Heat the butter, add the onion and lightly fry it until soft; add the livers and when they change colour sprinkle them lightly with flour. Stir and cook gently for 5 minutes. Add the tomato juice, stir well; add the wine, herbs, olives, salt and pepper and gently mix. Add the eggs, breaking them carefully into the pan one by one. Continue to cook over a moderate heat until the eggs are set. Spread the toast with *pâté*, put an egg on each piece and cover with the sauce. Serve at once.

EGGS IN A SWEET-SOUR SAUCE (*Uova in salsa agrodolce*)   *Umbria*

3–6 servings:

6 eggs	**1 cup (1¼) hot stock**
1 oz. (2 tablespoons) butter	**2 cloves**
1 onion, finely chopped	**1 bay leaf**
1 tablespoon (1¼) flour	**1 tablespoon (1¼) sugar**
salt, pepper	**1 cup (1¼) dry white wine**

Cook the eggs for exactly 6 minutes in boiling water, then plunge them into cold water and shell them. Do this very carefully as they are still soft enough to break.

Heat the butter, add the onion and cook it gently until it is soft, but not brown. Sprinkle with flour, salt and pepper, stir until the mixture is smooth, then gradually pour in the stock. Cook gently for 5 minutes, add the cloves and bay leaf and continue another 15 minutes. Add the sugar and wine, stir well, add the eggs and continue cooking until they are hard. Serve the eggs in the sauce with crisply fried bread.

BAKED EGGS NAPLES STYLE (*Uova in tazzina alla napoletana*)   *Campania*

For this recipe ramekin dishes or small, round, fireproof dishes some three to four inches in diameter with low, straight sides and a chunky handle should be used.

6 servings:

6 eggs	**6 tablespoons (7½) tomato sauce** (see
3 oz. (6 tablespoons) butter	pages 160–161)
	salt, pepper

Heat the dishes and rub them with butter. Pour 1 tablespoon (1¼) of tomato sauce into each dish, add 1 egg, sprinkle with salt and pepper and 1–2 slivers of butter. Put the dishes into a large, medium-deep pan and pour in enough boiling water to come half-way up the outside of the dishes. Cook in a moderate oven (350°F., mark 4) for 8–10 minutes or until the eggs are set.

OMELETTES AND FRITTATE (*Omelettes e frittate*)

There is a difference between the two. A *frittata* is not an omelette and it is better not to think of it as such. It is a mass of beaten eggs with a filling cooked over a high heat until thick and set, turned out, then returned to the pan to cook on the other side until set. A *frittata* is not folded over like an omelette.

Frittate are made with a variety of fillings: fish, vegetables, cheese, ham, sausages etc.

POTATO FRITTATA (*Frittata con patate*)

2 servings:

6 eggs	**salt, pepper**
¼ lb. cooked potatoes, sliced or cubed	**2 oz. (4 tablespoons) butter**
1 tablespoon (1¼) grated Parmesan cheese	

Lightly beat the eggs. Add the potatoes, cheese, salt and pepper. Heat the butter in an omelette pan, add the eggs and, using a wooden spoon, immediately stir 3–4 times, then cook slowly until the eggs are quite firm underneath. Slide the *frittata* out on to a flat plate and return it to the pan to cook and set firmly on the other side. Serve at once.

COURGETTE FRITTATA (*Frittata di zucchini*)

2 servings:

6 eggs
½ lb. courgettes (zucchini)
2 oz. (4 tablespoons) butter
1 tablespoon (1¼) oil

1 small onion, finely chopped
salt, pepper
2–3 ripe tomatoes, peeled and chopped

Wash and thinly slice the courgettes. Heat the butter with the oil in a 9-inch pan and fry the onion until lightly brown. Add the courgettes, salt, pepper and tomatoes. Cook over a moderate heat until the courgettes are tender. Lightly beat the eggs and mix them lightly into the vegetables and cook over a moderate heat until the underneath is set; continue as in previous recipe. Serve at once.

CHEESE AND TOMATO FRITTATA (*Frittata alla campagnola*)

2 servings:

6 eggs
grated cheese to taste
salt, pepper

2 oz. (4 tablespoons) butter
6 tomatoes, peeled, seeded and chopped
finely-chopped mint to taste

Lightly beat the eggs. Mix with the grated cheese, salt and pepper. Heat the butter in a 9-inch pan, add the tomatoes and fry until soft. Sprinkle with mint; add the eggs and cook until the eggs are set on the underneath. Continue as for potato *frittata* on page 66.

OMELETTE WITH CHEESE (*Frittata con formaggio*) *Campania*

4 servings:

6–8 eggs
2 tablespoons (2½) flour
salt
2 tablespoons (2½) milk
1 oz. (2 tablespoons) butter
1½ oz. Mozzarella or Bel Paese cheese,
  sliced

9 anchovy fillets
9 black olives
finely-chopped oregano to taste
6 tablespoons (7½) tomato sauce (see
  pages 160–161)

Sift the flour with the salt into a bowl. Lightly beat the eggs with the milk and stir into the flour. Heat the butter in a frying pan, one which can be brought to the table, add the egg batter and cook this until set but somewhat soft on top. Add the cheese to the top of the *frittata*. Roll each anchovy fillet into a ring and arrange these in a circle with an olive in the centre of each. Sprinkle with oregano. Put 1 tablespoon (1¼) of tomato sauce between each slice of Mozzarella. Cover the pan and cook over a moderate heat until the Mozzarella has dissolved and the *frittata* has risen. Serve in the pan.

RICOTTA OMELETTE   (*Omelette con la ricotta*)   *Campania*

2–4 servings:

8 eggs

1 cup (1¼) olive oil

½ small onion, finely chopped

salt to taste

2 leaves sweet basil, finely chopped

½ lb. tomatoes, peeled, seeded and chopped

½ lb. Ricotta cheese

4 tablespoons (5) grated Parmesan cheese

2–3 sprigs parsley, finely chopped

pepper

1½ oz. (3 tablespoons) butter

First prepare the sauce. Heat the oil, add the onion, salt, basil and tomatoes and cook over a moderate heat for 20 minutes. Beat the Ricotta in a bowl with half the Parmesan, a pinch of salt and the parsley until it is smooth. Beat the eggs with the remaining Parmesan and a pinch of pepper.

Heat half the butter in an omelette pan, pour in half the egg mixture and fry this until the underneath is a golden brown and the mixture is set and fairly dry. Place half the Ricotta filling down the middle and fold the omelette over. Slide from the pan on to a hot platter and keep it hot. Quickly make a second omelette with the remaining mixture and slide on to the platter; pour the sauce over the top of the omelettes and serve immediately.

soups  *minestre*

Under this heading come many dishes: soups thick and thin and dishes of pasta, polenta, rice etc. In fact, for many Italians the word *minestre* applies to those dishes which make up the first main course.

The origin of the word *minestre* is interesting. In the days when inns were few and far between, travellers found food and shelter in the monasteries. The monks were accustomed to receiving unexpected guests at all hours, and it was one of their daily tasks to see they were well fed on arrival. For these emergencies they had an enormous cauldron constantly simmering on the stove filled with meat, vegetables and broth to be served at a moment's notice. This became known as the *minestra*, a word derived from the Latin *ministrare*, to serve.

It is not easy to classify Italian soups. For example, *zuppa* can be translated as a soup which contains vegetables, such as *zuppa di primavera*, a spring soup made with carrots and peas. But we also have *zuppa pavese*, egg soup; *zuppa di pesce*, fish soup; or *zuppa di brodina*, broth, and mysteriously, *zuppa inglese*, which is a rum-soaked trifle or tipsy cake.

Where does minestrone come? These are also vegetable soups which the Genoese claim to have invented. However, despite Genoa's claim, the best known is Milan's minestrone. These usually, but not always, include rice or pasta and are thick and heavy.

Then there is *pasta in brodo, consommé* or clear broth garnished with tiny pasta shapes. Such soups are also labelled *zuppa di pastina*.

There are the fish soups, for which the sea coast areas are famous. Every seaside town claims to have the best, either called *zuppa di pesce* or *brodetto*, and all are a type of fish stew or chowder of assorted fish. Most include eel and dogfish and a large variety of shellfish, few of which have equivalents outside of Italy. Not many of these excellent stews or soups can be reproduced outside of their home town but it is worth trying them when travelling in Italy.

There are cold soups, a few fruit soups, and Tuscany favours a soup called *acqua cotta* (i.e. cooked water) which is vegetable broth poured over slices of bread previously soaked in beaten egg.

Apart from the easily recognized soups, there are those which are so thick they are eaten with a fork, *risi e bisi* is one such soup, although many would think it rates as a risotto; another is *zuppa di fontina*, which consists of layers of bread and slices of Fontina cheese plus a very little liquid and is baked in the oven. In the summer such thick soups with almost no liquid are served cold, especially in Rome.

CHICKEN BROTH (*Brodo di pollo*)

This broth is the basis for many Italian soups.

8 servings:

1 large boiling chicken
1 knuckle of veal or shin bone
6–8 pints (7½–10) water
1 each onion and carrot, coarsely chopped

1 leek and 1 sprig parsley, chopped
1–2 stalks celery with leaves
salt, peppercorns to taste

Put the chicken and veal bone into a large, heavy pan, add the water and bring gently to the boil. Skim, and add the onion, carrot, leek, parsley and celery to the pan. Add salt and peppercorns. Bring to a gentle boil then simmer for 3 hours. Take the chicken from the pan (it can be served separately) and continue simmering for 30 minutes. Strain the broth through a super-fine sieve or cheesecloth. Cool and keep in the refrigerator until required. Before using the broth, the fat which forms on the top must be skimmed.

If an extra clear stock is required, return the strained broth to the pan and add 2 crushed egg shells and 2 egg whites beaten until peaks form. Bring to the boil, stirring all the time, and strain again through a cheese-cloth or a sieve.

BEEF BROTH (*Brodo di manzo*)

6 servings:

2 lb. stewing beef
2–3 soup bones
1–2 carrots, coarsely chopped
1 small turnip, coarsely chopped
1–2 leeks

1–2 stalks celery, coarsely chopped
a little tomato paste
2 sprigs parsley
salt, pepper to taste

Put the meat and the bones in a large pan with 5 pints (6¼) of cold water. Bring this slowly to the boil, then skim. Cover the pan and simmer for 2 hours. Add the remaining ingredients and cook for a further 2 hours. Strain the broth through a fine sieve or cheese-cloth before using. Cool and keep in the refrigerator until required and carefully skim before using.

In Umbria broth is made with veal, mutton, goose, turkey, pigeon and duck.

PASTA IN BROTH (*Brodo con pasta*)

When using pasta such as *tripollini* or the slightly larger varieties in broth, the pasta should be cooked separately until *al dente* (see page 83), then drained and dropped into

the hot broth. If using the tiny pastas, for example *tagliarini*—which are literally flakes
—these can be dropped into boiling broth and cooked for three to four minutes. Serve
with grated Parmesan cheese.

The following list gives typical examples of pasta used in broth:

Acini di pepe peppercorn-size grains

Alfabeti alphabet shapes

Anellini little rings

Diamanti diamonds

Farfalline tiny butterflies

Fidelini spezzati broken *fidelini* or thin spaghetti

Lingue di passero sparrows' tongues

Maruzzette tiny shells, also called *conchigliette*

Nochette tiny bows

Occhi di pernice partridges' eyes

Orzo piccolo or *semi d'orzo* barley seeds

Quadrettini or *Quadrucci* squares of pasta

Raviolini mignon minute ravioli

Spaghetti spezzati broken spaghetti

Stelline or *Stellette* stars

Tortellini

Tripollini small bows

Tubetti small tubes of pasta

Vermicelli spezzati broken vermicelli (little worms)

Also used with soups are the finest kinds of noodles such as *capellini* or *capelli d'angelo*
and even the somewhat larger elbow macaroni, such as *chifferoni rigati*.

DUMPLINGS IN BROTH (*Sbrofadej in brodo*) *Lombardy*

6 servings:

3 pints (3¾) clear broth
4 eggs
6 oz. (1½ cups) flour

4 tablespoons (5) grated Parmesan cheese
salt
nutmeg

The word *sbrofadej* has been translated as dumplings for want of a better word. *Sbrofadej*
is a light, almost airy batter which falls from a slotted spoon into the pan in uneven
lengths, forming dumplings. As it cooks it turns a clear broth into an interesting soup.

Beat the eggs well. Sift the flour into a bowl, add the cheese, salt and nutmeg. Gradually stir the egg into the flour, beating it well all the time to a smooth, thick batter. Cover
with a damp cloth and leave for 2 hours.

Bring the broth to a bubbling boil. Pour the batter through the slots of a large perforated spoon—this is simpler than it sounds—directly into the boiling broth. Cook rapidly
until all the dumplings have risen to the top of the broth. This operation takes a little
over 5 minutes, so do not add the batter until almost ready to serve the soup. Serve with
grated Parmesan cheese.

VEGETABLE SOUP (*Minestrone*)

For all minestrones a good broth is required. If a beef broth is used, then parboiled pasta
will be added at the last moment, and the soup, served in bowls over slices of stale
bread, will be topped with a generous covering of grated cheese.

The vegetables used in a beef-based broth are usually carrots, turnips, beans etc. Tomatoes are added as much to give colour as flavour. In the spring when artichokes are plentiful they too are added, also endive and the various Italian beans, dried or fresh.

A minestrone made with a broth based on ham bone, hock, bacon rinds, or some of the firm Italian sausages, will usually call for the more leafy vegetables, such as cabbage, chicory, dandelion leaves, beet tops, burdock, kale etc. Pasta is not usually added to such soups, although this is by no means an invariable rule, but they too are served with grated cheese and stale bread.

6 servings:

1 small head white celery, with leaves	**endive**
2–4 onions	**tomatoes**
1–2 lb. stewing beef	**soaked and pre-cooked haricot beans**
green or French (snap) beans	**small pasta to choice** (see pages 70–71)
peas	**salt, pepper**
carrot	**grated Parmesan cheese**

No exact quantities are given for this minestrone for it is a matter of using what is available.

Wash the celery and cut it into pieces, using the leaves. Chop the onions. Put these ingredients with the meat into a large, heavy pan, fill to the top with cold water and bring gently to the boil. Skim, then simmer for 1 hour.

In the meantime prepare the remaining vegetables: the green beans should be trimmed and preferably snapped into two; the peas shucked; the carrot diced or cubed; the endive chopped; and the tomatoes peeled, seeded and chopped. Add the prepared vegetables and the haricot beans in the order given at 2–3 minute intervals. Bring the soup quickly to the boil, lower the heat and cook slowly for 30 minutes.

About 10 minutes before the soup is to be served, parboil the chosen pasta in another pan. Drain well, add it to the soup with salt and pepper; stir well and cook for 2–3 minutes until the pasta is *al dente* (see page 83).

Take the meat from the pan. If it is to be served in the soup, cut into small pieces and return to the pan to reheat; but it can be served separately. Serve the soup in deep bowls over a thick slice of stale bread and sprinkle with grated Parmesan cheese.

MILANESE VEGETABLE SOUP (*Minestrone alla milanese*) *Lombardy*

8–10 servings:

½ lb. (1½ cups) dried white beans	**¼ lb. (1 cup) green peas**
¼ lb. lean salt pork or bacon	**1 clove garlic, finely chopped (optional)**
1 large onion, diced	
3 potatoes, peeled and diced	**½ lb. (1¼ cups) Italian short grain rice**
2 carrots, sliced	**1 leaf sweet fresh basil or sage**
3 tomatoes, coarsely chopped	**2 sprigs parsley, finely chopped**
2 courgettes (zucchini) thickly sliced	**salt, pepper**
3 stalks celery, finely chopped	**grated Parmesan cheese**
½ small hard white cabbage, shredded	

Soak the beans in water overnight. Next day cook them (in fresh water) without salt until they are tender but still firm. Strain. Chop the pork or bacon, put it into a large pan and cook over a moderate heat until the fat runs freely. Add the onion and let this cook until soft but without browning. Add the remaining vegetables and garlic, stir well but gently, and cook for a few minutes. Add at least 6 pints ($7\frac{1}{2}$) of water and bring slowly to the boil. Add the beans and cook until they are quite tender. Add the rice, basil, parsley, salt and pepper and cook for 15 minutes or until the rice is *al dente* (see page 83). Sprinkle the soup with Parmesan cheese immediately before serving while still in the pan, or sprinkle each bowl of soup separately.

Instead of dried beans, fresh haricot beans or Lima beans are often used in Italy. The vegetables for this famous soup change not only according to season but also according to taste. What is important is that the vegetables are carefully cooked and are not allowed to become mushy.

VEGETABLE SOUP WITH PESTO   (*Minestrone alla genovese col pesto*)   *Liguria*

8–10 servings:

1 cup ($1\frac{1}{4}$) fresh or dried haricot beans
8 pints (10) water
salt
1 large onion, coarsely chopped
2 stalks celery, cut into thin rounds
1 large carrot, thinly sliced
6 tablespoons ($\frac{1}{2}$ cup) olive oil
2–4 courgettes (zucchini), sliced

4 medium-ripe tomatoes, peeled and
  coarsely chopped
4 large potatoes, peeled and chopped
2–3 leaves borage, finely chopped
$\frac{1}{2}$ lb. elbow macaroni (see page 71)
2 tablespoons ($2\frac{1}{2}$) pesto sauce (see
  page 164)
6 tablespoons ($7\frac{1}{2}$) Sardo Pecorino
  cheese grated

The vegetables used in this soup are changed according to availability. For example, instead of courgettes, marrow or summer squash can be used; leeks instead of onion, or both; aubergines (eggplants) are often added, so are pumpkin, peas and mushrooms, the last two both fresh and dried. In other words, this is a typical minestrone but it is distinguished from all others by the use of *pesto alla genovese*, which is a touch of culinary genius.

Elbow macaroni is shaped like an elbow (*gramigna*, small elbows, *chifferini rigati*, large elbows), and is usually available, but, when not, use any other similar type. If Sardo cheese is not available, use Parmesan cheese. If using dried beans, these should be soaked for several hours and partially cooked in unsalted water before being added to the soup.

Put the beans into a large heavy pan with the water, salt, onion, celery, carrot and 4 tablespoons (5) of oil. Bring to a gentle boil, lower the heat and simmer for about 1 hour. Add the remaining vegetables and the borage and cook until these are tender, about 30 minutes. Add the macaroni, cook until *al dente* (see page 83), stir in the *pesto*, the rest of the oil and the cheese. Serve at once.

RED BEAN SOUP (*Zuppa di fagioli*) *Lazio*

8–10 servings:

1 lb. (3 cups) red beans	2 tablespoons (2½) finely-chopped
1 stalk celery, chopped	parsley
1 large onion, chopped	1 tablespoon (1¼) tomato purée
1 large carrot, chopped	rosemary to taste
bicarbonate of soda	salt, pepper
1 tablespoon (1¼) olive oil	4 oz. (⅔ cup) short grain Italian rice
2 cloves garlic, chopped	grated Parmesan cheese

Soak the beans overnight, drain and put them into a pan with plenty of water. Add the chopped vegetables, a good pinch of soda and cook over a moderate heat for about 2½ hours.

Heat the oil, add the garlic and parsley, stir well, add the tomato purée, rosemary, salt and pepper, stir, add 1 cup (1¼) of water, stir again and continue cooking for 5 minutes. Stir this mixture into the vegetables some 30 minutes before the beans are cooked. About 5 minutes before the soup is ready, take out 1 cup (1¼) of beans, and put aside but keep warm. Rub the rest of the soup through a sieve, return it to the pan, bring to the boil and add the rice. Cook rapidly for 15 minutes or until the rice is soft. Immediately before serving, return the reserved beans to the pan, season to taste and cook for a minute or two longer. Serve the soup sprinkled with grated Parmesan cheese.

COURGETTE SOUP (*Zuppa di zucchine*) *Campania*

6 servings:

7–8 courgettes (zucchini), sliced in ½-inch rounds	3 eggs
2½ oz. (5 tablespoons) butter	4 tablespoons (5) grated Parmesan cheese
1 small onion, sliced	pepper
salt	sweet basil to taste, finely chopped
4 pints (5) vegetable stock or water	6 toasted slices bread

Heat the butter, add the onion and fry it slowly until soft but not brown. Add the courgettes and brown over a low heat. Sprinkle with salt and add the stock. Bring to the boil, lower the heat and simmer for 30 minutes.

Beat the eggs (in a soup tureen) together with the Parmesan cheese, salt, pepper and the sweet basil. Bring the soup to a quick boil and while still boiling pour it over the eggs, stirring briskly all the time. As soon as the eggs have 'cooked' serve the soup with toast and a bowl of Parmesan cheese.

RICE AND PEAS SOUP (*Risi e bisi*) *Veneto*

This celebrated and characteristic Venetian dish called a soup is so thick it is eaten with a fork. When Venice ruled itself under the Doges it was served as a regal dish on the Feast of St Mark. There are several ways in which to prepare *risi e bisi* but all with the same result. What is important is that there must not be too great a proportion of rice to peas so that it becomes all *risi* and no *bisi*, the latter the local name for peas.

6–8 servings:

1 lb. (2½) cups short grain Italian rice	**1 small onion, minced**
1 lb. peas, weight when shucked	**2–3 slices ham or bacon, diced**
butter	**4 pints (5) boiling broth**
1 tablespoon (1¼) olive oil	**salt to taste**
finely-chopped parsley to taste	**grated Parmesan cheese**

Heat 2 oz. (4 tablespoons) of butter with the oil. Add the rice and parsley, onion and ham and fry them until the onion is soft and just yellow. Add the peas and 3 cups (3¾) of broth. Cover and cook for 15–18 minutes, adding the remainder of the broth as required. When the rice is tender it should have absorbed all the liquid and be moist but not mushy. Add salt if required and serve at once sprinkled with cheese and dotted with butter.

If frozen peas are used, these should be added 7 minutes after adding the rice. However, Venetians insist that not only young and fresh peas are used in this dish but that they must come from fields near to the shores of the Venetian lagoons. *Risi e bisi* is not usually served in Venice when fresh peas are not in season.

CHESTNUT SOUP   (*Zuppa di castagne*)   *Piedmont*

6 servings:

2 lb. chestnuts	**½ teaspoon (⅔) celery salt**
3 cups (3¾) milk	**nutmeg**
2 oz. (4 tablespoons) butter	**1 cup (1¼) thin cream**
1 medium onion, minced	**finely-chopped parsley**
flour	**croûtons**
salt, pepper to taste	

Cut a small cross on each chestnut and boil them in water, to cover, for 15–20 minutes. Drain and cool. Pull off the outer and inner skins. Put the chestnuts with the milk in a pan and cook them gently for 40–60 minutes until very soft; add more milk if required. Rub them through a sieve. Heat the butter in a deep pan and lightly fry the onion until soft but not brown. Sprinkle lightly with flour, stir, add salt, pepper, celery salt and a good grating of nutmeg. Mix well, add the chestnut purée and cook gently for 10 minutes. Add the cream, bring to boiling point, then immediately remove from the heat. Garnish with parsley and serve with *croûtons*. If the soup is too thick, it can be thinned with milk, cream or a little dry white wine.

A similar soup can be prepared with unsweetened canned chestnut purée.

SPINACH SOUP   (*Zuppa di spinaci*)   *Piedmont*

6–8 servings:

2¼ lb. spinach
1½ oz. (3 tablespoons) butter
3 fillets anchovy
1 small onion, diced
salt, pepper, nutmeg

4 pints (5) clear stock or water
2–3 tablespoons (2½–3¾) milk or cream
croûtons
Parmesan cheese (optional)

Thoroughly wash the spinach or use an equivalent quantity of frozen spinach. Heat the butter, add the anchovy and onion and cook until the onion softens. Stir well, add the spinach, stir thoroughly and cook over a moderate heat until the spinach is tender. Take from the pan, drain and chop. Return the spinach to the pan, add salt, pepper and nutmeg to taste, then the stock and milk, stirring all the time. Continue cooking for 10 minutes and serve at once with *croûtons* and grated Parmesan cheese.

'COOKED' WATER   (*Acqua cotta*)   *Tuscany*

There are varying recipes for this soup, differing mainly in the quantity and variety of vegetables used.

6–8 servings:

4 pints (5) boiling water
½ lb. mushrooms
1 lb. ripe tomatoes
½ cup (⅔) olive oil
1–2 cloves garlic, finely chopped

salt, pepper
1½ oz. (½ cup) grated Parmesan cheese
2 eggs, well beaten
6–8 slices toast

Clean and thinly slice the mushrooms. Peel, seed and chop the tomatoes. Heat the oil in a heavy pan, add the mushrooms and fry them until soft. Add the garlic and tomatoes, season to taste, and cook over a brisk heat for 15 minutes. Add the boiling water, reduce the heat and cook for 1 hour, stirring for the first 5 minutes. Beat the cheese into the eggs and stir the mixture into the soup immediately before serving. Put a slice of toast in each soup bowl and pour the soup over the top.

EGG SOUP PAVESE STYLE   (*Zuppa pavese*)   *Lombardy*

6 servings:

12 eggs (2 per person)
2 oz. (4 tablespoons) butter
6 thick slices bread

grated Parmesan cheese
4 pints (5) clear broth
salt, pepper

Heat the butter and fry the bread on both sides until crisp. Put 1 slice into each soup bowl and sprinkle with Parmesan cheese. Bring the broth to a bubbling boil. Break 2 eggs on top of each slice of bread, sprinkle with salt and pepper and immediately pour over the top a cup of ABSOLUTELY boiling broth. It is important that the broth is boiling as the eggs should cook the moment the broth touches them. Try to avoid breaking the eggs for, although the flavour of the soup is not impaired, its appearance is. Repeat this procedure with the remaining eggs and broth, keeping the broth boiling all the time. When correctly prepared this is a soup with a subtle flavour.

Legend relates this soup was an on-the-spot invention of a cottage housewife in Pavia. The story goes that King Francis I of France, having lost a battle to the Spaniards, was on his way to surrender when he passed a cottage. Doubtless hungry and enticed by the aroma of soup coming from the cottage, he asked the housewife for something to eat. Afraid that her soup would not be good enough for a king, she dropped a slice of bread into a bowl, added an egg or two, poured the boiling minestrone on top and served it with grated Parmesan cheese. Her soup became famous, and it would be nice to add that the king, thus fortified, returned to fight and victory. Alas, it was not so.

EGG AND BREADCRUMB SOUP (*Brodo pieno*)   *Calabria*

6 servings:

4 eggs
3 pints (3¾) broth
6 tablespoons (7½) soft breadcrumbs
salt to taste

2 sprigs parsley, finely chopped
4 tablespoons (5) grated Parmesan
  cheese

Take out ½ cup (⅔) of the cold broth and bring the rest to the boil in a large pan. Meanwhile whisk the eggs in a bowl and add the remaining ingredients (except the Parmesan cheese). Still beating, add the reserved cold broth. When the broth in the pan is boiling, gradually add the egg and breadcrumb mixture, beating it with a whisk all the time. Cook over a low heat for 4–5 minutes, still whisking. Serve hot with Parmesan cheese. This is an Easter soup.

Lombardy has a similar soup in which the breadcrumbs are first fried in butter before being mixed with the eggs.

EGG AND CHEESE SOUP (*Stracciatelle*)   *Lazio*

6–8 servings:

3 eggs
2 tablespoons (2½) semolina
3 tablespoons (3¾) grated Parmesan
  cheese

nutmeg to taste
salt, pepper to taste
4 pints (5) chicken broth

Beat the eggs until smooth and add the semolina, cheese, nutmeg, salt and pepper. Dilute with 1 cup (1¼) of broth. Bring the remaining broth to a bubbling boil, add the egg mixture and whisk it in quickly. Reduce the heat and cook gently for 3 minutes. Serve as soon as the eggs break up into strands or 'rags'. *Stracciatelle* means 'little rags'.

EGG AND CREAM SOUP (*Zuppa alla veneziana*) *Veneto*

6 servings:

3 egg yolks
6 tablespoons (7½) cream

4 pints (5) cold clear chicken broth
6 slices toast or fried bread

Thoroughly beat the yolks with the cream. Pour the broth into a large pan, stir in the egg and cream mixture and bring slowly to the boil, stirring all the while until almost at boiling point. Put a slice of toast into each soup bowl, add the soup and serve immediately.

CLAM SOUP (*Zuppa di vongole*) *Sicily*

6 servings:

4–5 lb. small clams
2½ cups (3) dry white wine
½ cup (⅔) olive oil
1 small leek, white part only, chopped
1 small onion, chopped
2 cloves garlic, crushed

2 large cans Italian peeled tomatoes
1–2 stalks celery
salt, pepper
fresh oregano or marjoram, finely chopped and to taste
parsley, finely chopped and to taste

Scrub the clams thoroughly under running cold water. Put them into a pan with the wine and cook over a high heat until they open. Drain, reserving the liquid. The clams may be removed from their shells or left in them.

Heat the oil in a pan, add the leek and onion and fry them until brown. Add the garlic, tomatoes, celery, salt, pepper, oregano and the clam liquid. Cook over a high heat for 10 minutes. Discard the celery, return the clams to the pan and add the parsley. Cook for 1 minute only. Serve in soup bowls with garlic-flavoured bread or toast. If preferred, only 1 can of tomatoes may be used and the liquid made up with a mixture of white wine and water.

In Naples they prepare a similar soup and serve it with sliced bread fried in olive oil.

MUSSEL SOUP (*Zuppa di cozze*) *Sicily*

3–4 servings:

4 lb. mussels
½ cup (⅔) olive oil
1 clove garlic
2 large peeled and seeded tomatoes
a little chopped chilli pepper to taste

salt, pepper to taste
plenty of finely-chopped parsley and oregano
bread and garlic

Wash the mussels in several changes of water until all the grit has been removed. Scrape them well and pull off the beards. Put the oil into a pan with the garlic and cook over a moderate heat until the garlic changes colour. Discard it. Add the tomatoes, stir well, then add the mussels and chilli pepper and stir again. Cover the pan, cook for 2 minutes, shake the pan and cook another 2 minutes. Continue for 4 minutes or until all the mussels are almost but not fully opened. Take them from the pan and put aside in a bowl. Add a little salt and plenty of pepper to the pan, plus parsley and oregano. Stir well, return the mussels to the pan with the liquid which will have flowed from them into the bowl. Cover and cook for 5 minutes over a high heat until the shells are fully open. Discard any which are closed. Rub 4–6 slices of bread with garlic and put 1 slice into each soup bowl. Add the mussels and their liquid and serve at once.

FISH SOUP (1) *(Cacciucco alla livornese)* *Tuscany*

This soup, which is a speciality of Leghorn and considered by Italians as one of the glories of Mediterranean cooking, is one in which they are able to give full range to their imagination. Among the assorted fish used are cuttlefish, squid, mullet, racasse (generally unobtainable in both Britain and the United States), sea-hen, sea-bass, sea-scorpion, crab, octopus, crayfish etc. In Viareggio traditionalists like to add a stone taken from the sea for, they claim, the soup then attains its full height of perfection.

6–8 servings:

4 lb. assorted fish (see below)	**2 large onions, chopped**
salt, pepper	**3 cloves garlic**
lemon juice	**1 lb. tomatoes, peeled and chopped**
olive oil	**6 pints ($7\frac{1}{2}$) fish stock or water**
1 small head celery, cleaned and chopped	**1 cup ($1\frac{1}{4}$) dry white wine**
fresh oregano to taste	**6–8 slices crisp toast**

Generally cuttlefish is sold cleaned, even in Italy, but when this is not so, they must be carefully washed under running water, the long centre bone, the sac of ink, and the yellow deposit under the head must be removed. With squid, remove and discard the sac and rinse in cold water. If using eels, especially large ones, they should be skinned and the backbone removed. All the fish must be cleaned and trimmed, washed in plenty of cold water and patted dry. Cut off the heads and tails, leave the small fish otherwise whole, but cut the larger fish into pieces. Put the fish heads and trimmings into a pan with lightly salted water to cover. Bring to the boil, lower the heat and cook gently for 30 minutes, then strain.

Sprinkle the fish with salt, pepper and lemon juice. Heat plenty of oil in a deep pan, add the celery, oregano, onions and 1 clove of garlic and fry until brown. Add the tomatoes, stir well and cook for 5 minutes. Add 2 cups ($2\frac{1}{2}$) of the stock and the cuttlefish, squid or octopus, coarsely chopped or cut into strips. Bring to the boil, lower the heat and simmer for 15 minutes. Add the rest of the fish stock and the firmer pieces of fish. If the fish is not covered, add more water. Cook a few minutes, then add the rest of the fish, the smaller fish last of all. Add the wine and cook over a gentle heat until all the fish are tender, about 30 minutes.

Crush the remaining garlic and spread it over the toast. Arrange the toast at the bottom of a soup tureen or in soup bowls. Take out the fish with a fish slice and cover the toast with the fish or, if putting it directly into bowls, make sure each bowl has a variety of fish. Cover with the stock in which the fish was cooked and serve hot.

FISH SOUP (2) (*Brodetto di Porto Recanati*) *Marches*

Both Ancona and Porto Recanati claim the best *brodetto* along the Adriatic coast, but there is not a great deal of difference between the two versions. In Ancona they use fish from shallow waters, dip it in flour before it is fried, and add a little vinegar to the liquid, otherwise the procedure is much the same as for this recipe.

6–8 servings:

4 lb mixed fish (see below)
1 cup (1¼) olive oil
1 large onion, thinly sliced
salt, pepper

a good pinch saffron, soaked in a little water
2 cups (2½) dry white wine
6–8 slices bread
garlic

Among the fish used for this *brodetto* are: red and grey mullet, dogfish, white fish such as cod, skate or flat fish, plus any crustaceans and squid, cuttlefish, octopus etc.

Clean, trim and wash all the fish. Cut the larger ones into neat pieces leaving the small fish whole, but cut off their heads and tails. Heat the oil in a heavy pan, add the onion and cook until it is soft. Add the cuttlefish or squid and cook for 10 minutes before adding any more fish. Next add the tougher and larger pieces of fish; the smallest and most delicate last of all. Add enough water to cover, season, then stir in the saffron to give the stew a good colour. Cover and cook over a low heat for 15 minutes. Take another pan (the Italians use a large earthenware casserole) and transfer first the squid and cuttlefish to it and then the remaining fish, arranging them in layers. Strain the stock over the fish and add enough wine to completely cover. Cook over a brisk heat for 10 minutes, shaking the pan gently from time to time. While this is cooking, rub the bread generously with cut garlic and place 1 slice in each soup bowl. Serve the fish and its liquid poured over the bread.

CREAM OF FISH SOUP (*Ciuppin*) *Liguria*

6 servings:

4 lb. assorted fish
½ cup (⅔) olive oil
1 onion, thinly sliced
1 celery stalk, finely chopped
1 carrot, finely chopped
2–3 sprigs parsley, finely chopped

1 clove garlic, finely chopped
1 cup (1¼) dry white wine
1 small can Italian tomatoes
4 pints (5) boiling water
salt, pepper
triangles bread fried in oil

The fish recommended for this soup are not easy to find outside of Italy. There are some very curious fish indeed in the sea and many of these find their way to the Genoese fish markets, and into this soup. If the fish are curious, their names are even more so. We find sea-hen or the crooner and the sea-scorpion; praying-fish and sea-truffle; the sea-date, and even sea-strawberries. Among the less curious fish are the *palombo*, a relative of the mackerel, dogfish, angler-fish (*rospo*), red mullet, rock fish and brill. If none of these is available, then ask your fishmonger for the most unusual fish he has and mix them well to make an imitation *ciuppin*.

Clean and wash the fish and cut them into large pieces; bones can be removed but it is not essential at this stage. Separate the tough fish from the more tender.

Heat the oil in a large pan and gently fry the onion until soft. Add the celery, carrot, parsley and garlic and fry until brown, then add the wine. Increase the heat and cook for a few minutes until the wine has been reduced. Add the tomatoes with their liquid and the boiling water. Cook over a moderate heat for 20 minutes.

Add the fish, beginning with the tougher pieces, which will take longer to cook, adding the more tender fish later. Add salt and pepper, lower the heat and cook for 1 hour. Rub the soup through a fine sieve (or pick out all the bones and purée it in a blender). Return it to the pan and reheat. Check for seasoning and serve very hot with fried bread.

pasta, rice, gnocchi and polenta

pasta, riso, gnocchi e polenta

PASTA

That Italians are prodigious eaters of pasta is well known, even to those who have never set foot in Italy; but that there are hundreds, some say thousands, of varieties of pasta is probably not realized. To give a complete list of pasta types, plus recipes and appropriate sauces, would require not just a chapter in a book but the writing of a book on pasta dishes alone. (This has been done by Vernon Jarrett and his wife, Enrica, in their book *230 modi di cucinare la pasta*, Mondadori, 1969. But, bemoan the authors, 'we have had to leave out so much.')

There are two types of pasta dough: home-made and industrial. Home-made pasta is prepared with plain flour milled from common wheat, combined with eggs, kneaded to a firm dough and cut into simple shapes or strips to produce ravioli, lasagne, cannelloni, flat noodles etc. Industrial pasta is made with durum (hard) wheat semolina mixed with water.

Durum wheat is an Italian speciality and, although Italy's production is the highest in the world, not enough is grown to meet Italy's consumption and she has to import. Durum wheat has a yellow, translucent, double-pointed grain and from this is obtained the granular semolina used in the production of commercial pasta. It is impossible to make semolina pasta at home, since semolina, being granular, cannot be easily amalgamated with water into a dough. Only the force of machines is able to do this.

It is often thought that pasta fattens. But this, modern Italian dietitians insist, is not true, and pasta dishes are included in slimming diets. Vincenzo Agnesi claims that when the wheat germ is retained in the semolina, not only does it help towards maintaining a good digestion but it also actively helps to keep the body slim. His pasta firm, Agnesi, one of the largest and oldest in Italy, has as one of its slogans 'Eat pasta and keep slim', and produces among its products a full wheat germ supplemented pasta. Most pasta is made with semolina which has the wheat germ partially removed.

Pasta has its own long history, and its own museum, Museo Storico degli Spaghetti, which is situated in the small town of Pontedassio, near Imperia. The museum was founded in 1958 after many years of research by Vincenzo Agnesi and is housed in part of his firm's original mill. It contains an interesting collection of ancient documents, all referring to pasta: old pasta laws, copies of the statutes of the Genoese Guild of Macaroni

Makers from the year 1538, which refer to the buying of hard wheat, plus a photostatic copy of one of the most cherished documents in the Genoese Archives, the will of one Ponzio Bastone who, in 1279, left a *bariscella* or basket of dried macaroni to his heirs. This was thirteen years before Marco Polo returned from his travels to the Far East, thus demolishing the legend that it was he who introduced pasta to Italy, and proving, say the pasta makers, that macaroni, after all one of Italy's national dishes, was not only made in Italy in the early days but was considered valuable.

In the museum, apart from ancient documents, prints and engravings, there are working models of old pasta instruments used in the early production of pasta. The Agnesi family are happy to show round interested visitors to their museum, all that is required is to ask at the reception desk of the Agnesi firm in Imperia, or write to them beforehand, since, as the museum is private, it is not open to the public.

Although pasta is of Genoese origin, today it is in Naples and the South that it is more heavily consumed. Sometime during the seventeenth and eighteenth centuries the Neapolitans took over the production of pasta making, but even then there were less than fifty pasta makers in the city. Pasta was considered a luxury, to be eaten only on important days and holidays. At this time the Neapolitans were known as the 'leaf eaters'; much later they were dubbed the 'macaroni eaters'. There was a saying of the time which warned: 'There are three things likely to ruin a family—sweetmeats, hot bread and macaroni.' Macaroni was considered a dish for 'refined' palates.

Macaroni was known in England, for in 1772 it was recorded: 'the word macaroni is the name of a well-known Italian dish unknown in our country before the recent peace' (1763). It was imported by dandies ('macaronis') who had made the Grand Tour of Europe.

Most of the pasta which is eaten in Italy today is industrially produced although many housewives still prefer to prepare home-made pasta for some dishes and buy industrial pasta for others. There are small and cheap machines with a simple adjustment of cutters for producing various widths of flat noodles and shops which daily produce fresh pasta. In some of the markets one still sees the noodle woman with her little pasta machine which rolls and cuts noodles to the width and thickness required by the customer. Italians always have a stock of industrial pasta in the house and most housewives have their favourite brand, generally a local make. Pasta manufacturers all have their own mixtures, and pasta from one firm may take half or twice as long to cook as from another.

However odd it may seem, not all Italians cook pasta correctly. Vincenzo Agnesi says it is better to rely on experience than explicitly on your watch. The cooking time of pasta depends not only on the thickness of the pasta but also on the type of wheat used, the degree of hardness of the water, and the altitude above sea level etc. When cooking pasta it is essential to taste it from time to time 'in order not to miss the right point in cooking'. It must be taken from the heat the moment it has lost its raw taste, not a minute later. It is ready when it feels elastic and almost tough under your teeth, which explains the true meaning of the term *al dente*. During the boiling process, the heat slowly penetrates inside the pasta. This means that the outside of the pasta is always more cooked than the inside. Italians insist that this difference be reduced to a minimum and that the pasta be cooked in an uniform manner. The pasta surface must never be slimy, something the Italians dislike immensely. Finally, remember that pasta is greedy for water until the end, so do not over-drain it. Never, but never, pour cold water over the pasta 'to stop it boiling', this only results in a gluey mess.

The claim that there are thousands of different varieties of pasta is not quite as sensational as it might seem. Many pasta types have half a dozen different names, sometimes because the firms producing them like to try out new names, or because they are in the local patois of the area, or perhaps nothing but a whim. It is puzzling for the foreigner when in Venice to order *bigoli* only to discover it is a variety of spaghetti. The *tagliatelle* of the North is the *fettuccine* of Rome. However, it must be admitted that it is not only pasta which carries different names for the same product. For example, there are a dozen or so names for eel, and five or more for mussels.

One might ponder whether the different shapes of pasta make a difference in the flavour. The answer is 'yes', although not perhaps a great difference. Certainly a plate of *fettuccine* does taste differently to one of spaghetti or macaroni even when served with the same sauce. Also the coloured pastas, green, red and yellow, have their nuances of flavour.

Pasta can be divided into five main groups:

1. Those used for boiling: thin strings of pasta such as spaghetti, *spaghettini*, vermicelli, *bucatini* etc., including *chitarra*, guitar, pasta and the many 'hanks' of pasta, *mafaldine*, *fusilli*, *lasagnette* etc.
2. Those used for boiling and baking: tubular forms such as macaroni, *maniche*, *zita*, *occhi di lupo*, wolves' eyes, or *zitone*, *penne*, *grosso rigato*, *rigatoni*, etc.
3. Envelopes of stuffed pasta such as ravioli, *agnolotti* or *agnellotti*, *tortellini*, cannelloni etc., plus *lumache*, snails, and *manicotti*.
4. Flat pasta such as noodles, lasagne, *fettuccine* etc.
5. Fancy pastas, and this is the right term, as pasta makers have invented a myriad of patterns for their pastas: wheels, stars, butterflies, snails, little ears (the people of Brindisi are particularly proud of their *orecchiette*, also called *stacchiodde*); and shapes as tiny as peppercorns, like *lentine* or *occhiolini*, which are pastas usually served in *brodo* or clear soups.

Finally, when an Italian talks of pasta he does not only mean pasta with a sauce. He refers also to soups with pasta or *pastina*. If he wants a dish of pasta with a sauce, he asks for *pasta asciutta*; but if he wants a soup with pasta, it is *pasta* or *pastina in brodo*. Most Italians eat pasta every day, except in the North where rice is also popular. It is not considered a main dish and is followed by one or more courses. Italians are somewhat surprised when foreigners order a dish of spaghetti as a main dish. However, for those who find a plate of pasta too much if to be followed by other courses, ask for *una mezza porzione*, or half a portion.

HOME-MADE PASTA DOUGH

For ravioli, *tortellini*, cannelloni, lasagne, *tagliatelle* or *fettuccine*, and the other wide noodles.

approximately 3 servings (makes 1½ lb. of dough):

1 lb. flour   **4 eggs**
salt

Sieve the flour with a good pinch of salt in a mound on to a large pastry board. Make a hollow in the centre and break in the eggs. Work the flour from the edges of the mound into the centre and over the eggs. Work this well until a smooth dough is produced, then knead until the dough is firm and smooth to the touch. After about 10 minutes the dough should be elastic and shiny. Dip a cloth into warm water, wring it out thoroughly until almost dry and wrap the ball of dough in it. Leave for 30 minutes to rest.

To use the dough, break it into 2 pieces, roll it out, using as little pressure as possible, on a board into paper-thin sheets, and sprinkle lightly with flour to prevent sticking. At this stage the dough can be cut into the desired shapes at once and used, or it can be allowed to dry out for a further 30 minutes.

To make flat noodles such as *fettuccine* or *tagliatelle*, roll up the sheets of dough into cylindrical shapes, like making a jam or Swiss roll, and slice into narrow strips. Gently unroll, doing this with a slight tossing movement to avoid the strips sticking together. Place the strips on a lightly-floured cloth and let them dry. Use according to the chosen recipe.

Home-made noodles may be cooked immediately or, if making a large quantity, they can be kept in a refrigerator for 24 hours if they are carefully wrapped in wax paper. Home-made pasta also freezes well.

HOW TO COOK PASTA IN THE CLASSICAL MANNER

Use a very large pan. For each 1 lb. of pasta use between 10–12 pints (12½–15) of liquid and between 1½–2 tablespoons (2¼–2½) of salt.

Never add the pasta before the water is at bubbling point, then add it all at once, but slowly so that the water does not for one moment go off the boil. Stir well with a wooden spoon or fork to prevent sticking. Cover the pan for a minute or so to let the water almost boil over, then uncover and cook for the required period. Stir the pasta from time to time and take it at once from the heat when it is *al dente*, or cooked through but still firm to the bite. Strain immediately.

When cooking spaghetti or other long pasta, do not cut it into shorter lengths; its flavour is not spoilt but its appearance is. There is a saying in Bologna (and the Bolognese know about cooking), '*Conti corti e tagliatelle lunghe*', or, short bills but long noodles.

It is important that pasta is never over-cooked. Cooking times vary according to the type of pasta used. Pasta manufacturers state precisely on the package how long the different pasta should be cooked. For example, a very fine spaghetti will take 4 minutes to cook, while a slightly thicker variety will take up to 7 minutes. *Fettuccine* will take anything from 5–10 minutes. Follow this advice, plus that of Vincenzo Agnesi (see page 83) and you cannot go wrong. The following timetable gives an approximate time in minutes for cooking several types of pasta:

Abissini	12	Ditalini	7	Puntine	10
Anelli	11	Ditalini piccoli	8	Risone	12
Anellini	7	Ditalini rigati	12	Rocchetti	13
Avemaria	11	Eliche	10	Sedani	13
Bavette	7	Farfalle	12	Sedanini	10
Bucatini	9	Farfalle tonde	10	Sopra fidelini	4
Canestrini	9	Fidelini	3	Spaghetti	10

Chifferi rigati	13	Gnocchi	14	Spaghettini	6
Chifferini rigati	9	Gramigna	12	Spaghettoni	14
Chifferoni	13	Linguine	9	Stellette	10
Chifferoni rigati	16	Maccheroncelli	12	Stelline	8
Chifferotti rigati	13	Maccheroni	12	Tagliarelli	10
Chifferotti	9	Maccheroni rigati	10	Tagliatelle	12
Chinesi rigati	12	Occhi di pernice	7	Tagliatelle mezzane	10
Chinesini	13	Penne	11	Telline	8
Corallini	10	Pennette	10	Tortiglioni	14
Cravattine	11	Pennini	10	Trenette	12
Denti d'elefante	10	Pennini piccoli	11	Vermicelloni	17
Dischi volanti	12	Piselli	10	Zita	8
Ditali	12	Pisellini	9		
Ditali rigati	13	Puntette	11		

A REVOLUTIONARY METHOD OF COOKING PASTA *Liguria*
(*Un modo rivoluzionario per cuocere la pasta*)

This recipe for cooking pasta was supplied by Eva Agnesi. As she explained, when the pasta is cooked in this way and drained the water remains quite clear, proof that the pasta has retained its mineral and vitamin content.

3–4 servings:

10 pints (12) water   **salt**
1 lb. pasta

Bring the water to a rapid boil, slowly add the pasta and, as soon as the water again bubbles, let it boil for 2 minutes. Take the pan from the stove, wrap the lid in a cloth and cover the pasta. Leave for the exact prescribed time, according to the manufacturer's instructions. In other words, the pasta remains in the water precisely as long as it would be if boiling it plus the first 2 minutes. Drain, season and serve.

If cooking thick pasta, for example macaroni, let it boil for 3 minutes before taking the pan from the stove, but otherwise follow the instructions exactly.

In the following recipes either Eva Agnesi's method of cooking pasta, or the usual method, may be used.

GREEN PASTA   (*Pasta verde*)

6 servings:

¼ lb. spinach   **1 lb. (4 cups) flour**
2 eggs, lightly beaten

Wash the spinach, cut off the thick stalks and cook, without adding water, until tender. Drain thoroughly, chop and rub through a sieve. Combine the spinach and eggs, mix well and gradually add the flour; more or less may be required to make a firm, pliable dough. Continue as for normal pasta (see page 85).

RAVIOLI   (*Ravioli*)

These little envelopes of stuffed noodle pastry are almost too well known to warrant an introduction. Genoa claims not only to be the city where ravioli was created but that their ravioli is the best in the country. Naturally there is a legend concerning both origin and name. One story is that it had humble beginnings, in ships' galleys where cooks could not afford to waste food. Left-overs were finely chopped and mixed together, then placed on small squares of noodle dough, folded once and boiled. The name ravioli is similar to the Genoese *rabiole*, patois for left-overs. However, both in Chinese and Siberian cooking there are small envelopes of dough cooked with almost similar fillings, so who invented ravioli we really do not know.

Ravioli are not difficult to prepare. The dough is the same as used for other pasta; the fillings are made with meat, fish, vegetables and cheese.

RAVIOLI   (*Ravioli*)   *Liguria*

6 servings (about 60 ravioli):

pasta dough (see pages 84–85)   **grated Parmesan cheese**
filling (see above)   **tomato sauce** (see pages 160–161)

Make the pasta dough (see pages 84–85) and roll it out into 4 equal, oblong, paper-thin sheets. On 1 sheet drop tiny mounds of the chosen filling 1½ inches apart. Dip a pastry brush into cold water and sweep it in straight lines between the mounds. Place a sheet of dough evenly over the top. Work quickly so that the dough remains damp and pliable, otherwise it will crack. Firmly press down with the fingers between each mound of filling to form 2-inch squares and, with a sharp knife, a ravioli cutter, or pastry wheel, cut round the mounds to separate them. Put these aside on a floured cloth, leaving space between each, and repeat this operation with the remaining 2 sheets of dough.

Have ready a pan with 12 pints (15) of boiling, salted water and drop the ravioli into this, about 15 at a time, stirring them gently with a wooden spoon or fork. Boil until tender, 8–10 minutes. Remove carefully with a perforated (slotted) spoon and place in a layer on a hot serving plate. Sprinkle with grated cheese and a little tomato sauce. Repeat until all the ravioli are finished, placing each freshly cooked batch on top of the ravioli already on the plate, and spreading with sauce and cheese. Serve the ravioli with the rest of the sauce and grated cheese separately.

Ravioli can be made half the size and served in broth, i.e. *ravioli al brodo*.

FISH STUFFED RAVIOLI (*Ravioli di magro*) *Liguria*

These are prepared during Lent and days of abstinence.

6 servings:

pasta dough (see pages 84–85)
¾ lb. cooked fish
grated Parmesan cheese to taste

2–3 eggs, beaten
salt, nutmeg to taste

Prepare the pasta dough (see pages 84–85). Flake the fish, discarding all bones, and mix to a paste with the cheese and eggs; add salt and nutmeg. Prepare the ravioli as on page 87. Serve without a sauce.

MEAT STUFFED RAVIOLI (*Ravioli di carne*) *Lombardy*

6 servings:

pasta dough (see pages 84–85)
2 oz. (4 tablespoons) butter
1 clove garlic, finely chopped
a good sprig parsley, finely chopped
½ lb. veal, without bone
stock or water
⅓ cup (⅔) red wine

1 slice bread
a little milk
½ lb. cooked spinach
1 small onion, finely chopped
salt, pepper, nutmeg
2 eggs beaten
2 oz. (⅔ cup) grated Parmesan cheese

Prepare the pasta dough (see pages 84–85). Heat the butter and lightly fry the garlic and parsley for 2–3 minutes. Add the meat, brown it, then add just enough liquid to cover the bottom of the pan. Simmer for 20 minutes, add the wine and cook gently until the meat is tender. Soak the bread in milk and squeeze it dry. Put the meat through the fine blade of a grinder, at the same time adding the spinach, onion, bread, salt, pepper and a sprinkling of nutmeg. Mix well, bind with the eggs and beat in the cheese. Prepare the ravioli as on page 87.

RICOTTA STUFFED RAVIOLI (*Ravioli di ricotta*) *Lazio*

6 servings:

pasta dough (see pages 84–85)
1 oz. (2 tablespoons) butter
1 egg yolk
½ lb. Ricotta cheese

3 oz. (1 cup) grated Parmesan cheese
1 heaped tablespoon (1¼) finely-chopped parsley
salt, pepper to taste

Prepare the pasta dough (see pages 84–85). Pound the butter until creamy and beat in the egg yolk. When blended, add the Ricotta and Parmesan cheese and beat until the mixture is smooth. Add the parsley and seasoning. Prepare the ravioli as on page 87. Serve with a meat sauce (see pages 157–158) or a tomato sauce (see pages 160–161).

In Sardinia they make a similar Ricotta stuffing with Pecorino cheese instead of Parmesan, adding a pinch of saffron and a sprinkling of nutmeg and black pepper.

SPINACH STUFFED RAVIOLI (*Ravioli di spinaci*) *Tuscany*

6 servings:

pasta dough (see pages 84–85)	**2 oz. ($\frac{2}{3}$ cup) grated Parmesan cheese**
$\frac{1}{2}$ lb. spinach	**salt, pepper, nutmeg**
1 oz. (2 tablespoons) butter, melted	**1–2 egg yolks**

Prepare the pasta dough (see pages 84–85). Wash and cook the spinach until tender without adding any water. Drain well and chop it finely. Beat the butter into the spinach, add the grated cheese, seasoning, a generous sprinkling of nutmeg, and bind with the egg yolks. Prepare the ravioli as on page 87.

FRIED RAVIOLI (*Panzarotti alla napoletana*) *Campania*

Make small ravioli (see page 87) with any type of filling and fry them in deep boiling fat until they are amber coloured. Serve hot.

TORTELLINI *Emilia-Romagna*

A little explanation is required concerning the *tortellini*, a rather special member of the pasta family, for not only has this pasta package of stuffing a history, but it is the cause of a minor state of gastronomic cold war between two cities, Bologna and Modena, both gastronomically famous in Italy.

There is in Bologna The Learned Order of the Tortellini with an impressive list of members dedicated to the preservation of the *tortellini*, the most splendid, say the Bolognese, who claim to have created it—note they CREATED it not merely INVENTED it—of the pasta family. At their functions members wear golden red hats in the shape of a *tortellini* and a ribbon round their necks from which hangs a perfect *tortellini*, a 'navel' made in gold.

But Modena lays claim to the *tortellini* as well, and to strengthen her claim to its invention a legend or two is quoted. It is related (in Modena only, remember) that a famous pasta cook of that city dreamed one night he saw Venus arising from the sea. As he glimpsed her perfect navel, he awoke and at once rushed to his kitchen to recreate such perfection in the only way he could express himself, by rolling up a small package of pasta in the form of that perfect navel. Less exalted but no less romantic is the story of the cook who loved his employer's wife. One day, it is said, he looked through the keyhole of her bedroom door and saw her asleep in the nude—but had a view only of her perfect navel. As a token of a hopeless passion, he went sadly back to his kitchen and shaped his next batch of pasta in the form of that navel.

Had the Bolognese any answers to these stories from Modena? 'No' they replied, they just knew they had been the creators of the *tortellini* and they 'needed no fairy tales' to add to what they knew to be true.

6 servings:

pasta dough (see pages 84–85)	**2 slices Parma ham, chopped**
filling:	**2–3 slices mortadella, chopped**
2½ tablespoons (3¼) butter	**1 cup (1¼) grated Parmesan cheese**
¼ lb. lean pork, chopped	**salt, pepper, nutmeg**
¼ lb. chicken or turkey breast, chopped	**2 eggs, well beaten**

Make the pasta dough as on pages 84–85. Roll it out into a ball and leave for 20 minutes on a lightly floured pastry board covered with a cloth.

Prepare the filling. Heat the butter, add the pork and chicken (or turkey) and cook until it is a golden brown. Put twice through the coarse blade of a grinder together with the ham and mortadella. Mix in the cheese, salt, pepper and nutmeg and bind with the eggs. The mixture must be well blended.

Roll out the dough into a paper-thin sheet. Cut into circles 1½ inches in diameter. Put a little of the filling on to one half of each circle. Fold the other half of the dough over the filling to make a semicircle. Take this in the right hand and fold it round your left index finger so that the two ends curl round and slightly overlap. Press the ends firmly together and turn upwards. Spread the *tortellini* on a cloth to dry for 30 minutes.

Traditionally, *tortellini* are served with a meat sauce, *ragù* (see page 158), but recently it has become popular to serve them with hot melted butter and cream. They are also served in broth and called *tortellini in brodo*.

CANNELLONI   (*Cannelloni*)

Cannelloni are squares of pasta dough with a savoury filling, rolled like stuffed pancakes. Both home-made or industrial pasta may be used, but this is perhaps one of the times when home-made pasta is preferable. Fillings for cannelloni are a matter of imagination. Any of the ravioli fillings may be used in the following recipes, which are typical.

SPINACH AND CHEESE STUFFED CANNELLONI   (*Cannelloni di magro*) *Tuscany*

6 servings:

pasta dough (see pages 84–85)	**3 eggs, beaten**
2½ lb. spinach	**salt, pepper, nutmeg**
butter	**grated Parmesan cheese to taste**
½ lb. Ricotta cheese	**2 cups (2½) bechamel sauce** (see page 159)

Wash the spinach and cook it without water until tender. Drain and squeeze dry. Heat a little butter in the same pan, return the spinach and gently cook it for 5 minutes. Take it from the pan and chop it finely. Add the Ricotta and mix well, then add the eggs to bind the mixture. Add salt, pepper, nutmeg and Parmesan cheese to taste. Put the mixture aside but keep it warm. Make the bechamel sauce, also put it aside but keep it warm.

Roll out the pasta as thinly as possible. Cut into pieces approximately 3 × 4 inches. Have ready a wide pan with plenty of boiling, salted water and drop the pieces, one or two at a time, into the water. Cook until *al dente* (see page 83) or until the slices rise to the surface. As they cook, remove them one by one with a perforated (slotted) spoon. Lay them on a dry cloth to drain and cool.

Spread a little of the filling down the long side of each piece of pasta and roll each piece tightly as it is filled. Generously butter a shallow baking dish and arrange the cannelloni in a single layer. Cover with bechamel sauce and slivers of butter. Heat in a moderate oven (350°F., mark 4) for 15–20 minutes or until the top is a golden brown. Serve with a bowl of grated Parmesan cheese.

CANNELLONI WITH MOZZARELLA CHEESE (*Cannelloni di mozzarella*)
ILLUSTRATED PAGE 60   *Calabria*
4–6 servings:

pasta dough (see pages 84–85   **tomato sauce** (see pages 160–161)
¾ **lb. Mozzarella cheese**   **grated Parmesan cheese to taste**
butter

Prepare and cook the pasta as in the previous recipe. Thinly slice the Mozzarella. Place a slice on each square of prepared pasta and roll them up tightly. Generously butter a shallow baking dish and arrange the cannelloni on it in one layer. Cover with tomato sauce, sprinkle generously with cheese and dot with butter. Bake as in the previous recipe. Extra Parmesan may be served separately. If Mozzarella cheese is not available, use Bel Paese.

BAKED STUFFED PASTA (*Lumaconi al forno*) *Liguria*

For this the larger forms of pasta may be used, for example, *lumaconi*, big snails; cannelloni, large round tubes; *manicotti*, little sleeves; and *rigatoni*, furrowed macaroni.

4–5 servings:

1 lb. large pasta   **5 tablespoons (6¼) grated Parmesan**
3 tablespoons (3¾) olive oil   **cheese**
1 small onion, chopped   **½ lb. cooked ground meat**
1 medium-sized can peeled Italian   **pepper, nutmeg**
** tomatoes, chopped**   **2 eggs**
salt   **2–3 tablespoons (2½–3¾) milk**
1 clove garlic   **1 oz. (2 tablespoons) butter**
½ lb. Ricotta cheese

Heat the oil and fry the onion until soft. Add the tomatoes and salt and cook for 15 minutes. Add the garlic and cook quickly for 5 minutes. Put the mixture aside but keep hot.

Beat the Ricotta until smooth or rub it through a sieve. Combine with the Parmesan, meat, salt, pepper, nutmeg and eggs. Mix to a paste and add milk to moisten the mixture.

Cook the pasta until *al dente* (see page 83). Drain it and spread out on a damp cloth. Cool, then put a little of the stuffing into each pasta 'shape'. Rub a baking dish with butter, add the pasta, cover with the sauce (discarding the garlic), and cook in a hot oven (425°F., mark 7) for 15–20 minutes.

BUCATINI WITH ANCHOVY SAUCE (*Pasta ammuddicata*) *Calabria*

4 servings:

1½ lb. bucatini
8 anchovies in brine or 12 fillets in oil
1 cup (1¼) olive oil

2½ cups (3¼) breadcrumbs, coarsely
  grated
chilli or cayenne pepper

Bucatini is a long pasta, half-way in thickness between spaghetti and macaroni.

Wash the salt off the anchovies, bone them, discard the heads and tails and cut the flesh into small pieces. Heat half the oil, add the anchovies and cook, stirring all the time, until they are dissolved. Put aside but keep warm. Heat the remaining oil in another pan and fry the breadcrumbs until brown. Sprinkle with plenty of chilli or cayenne pepper, put them into a warm bowl and keep warm.

Cook the *bucatini* until *al dente* (see page 83). Drain at once, turn into a hot deep dish and stir in the anchovy sauce. Serve with the fried breadcrumbs. Cheese is NOT served with this dish.

SPAGHETTI SAILOR'S STYLE (*Spaghetti marinara*) *Campania*

4 servings:

1½ lb. fine spaghetti
6 tablespoons (7½) olive oil
1–2 onions, finely chopped
1–2 cloves garlic
2¼ lb. peeled plum-shaped tomatoes,
  fresh or canned, chopped

1 teaspoon (1¼) sugar
3 anchovies
1 tablespoon (1¼) finely-chopped basil
1 cup (1¼) grated Parmesan cheese

Heat the oil, add the onions and garlic and cook over a moderate heat until the onion changes colour. Discard the garlic. Add the tomatoes (seeds removed), sugar and anchovies and cook over a moderate heat for 15–20 minutes.

While the sauce is cooking, cook the spaghetti (see page 83) and turn it into a hot serving dish. Sprinkle with basil and 2 tablespoons (2½) of the cheese and add the sauce, stirring quickly but gently. Serve with the rest of the Parmesan cheese separately.

SPAGHETTI WITH GARLIC AND OIL (*Spaghetti aglio e olio*) *Campania*

3–4 servings:

1 lb. spaghetti
½ cup (⅔) olive oil
2–3 cloves garlic, slivered

1 sprig parsley, finely chopped
1 small pepper, seeds discarded,
  finely chopped

Cook the spaghetti until *al dente* (see page 83). Heat the oil and brown the garlic. Add the parsley and the pepper and gently fry them until the parsley and pepper are brown. Drain the spaghetti, turn it into a hot serving dish, add the sauce, toss well but lightly and serve at once, without cheese.

SPAGHETTI WITH TUNNY FISH (*Spaghetti al tonno*) *Sicily*

4 servings:

1½ lb. spaghetti
1 small can tunny (tuna) fish
2¼ lb. ripe or canned tomatoes
2 tablespoons (2½) olive oil

1–2 cloves garlic, crushed
salt, pepper
1 teaspoon (1¼) finely-chopped oregano
  or marjoram

If using fresh tomatoes, peel them, squeeze out the seeds and chop the pulp. Heat the oil, fry the garlic until brown, then discard it. Add the tomatoes, salt and pepper and cook over a good heat for 20 minutes. Flake the fish with a fork, stir it gently into the tomatoes, add the oregano, stir well, reduce the heat and cook for about 10 minutes.

Cook the spaghetti until *al dente* (see page 83). Drain and turn into a hot serving dish. Stir in the hot sauce, toss lightly and serve at once.

If preferred, canned salmon may be used in this recipe.

SPAGHETTI AMATRICIANA (*Spaghetti all'amatriciana*) *Lazio*

Rome has adopted and taken as her own this dish of spaghetti which takes its name from the small town of Amatrice in the Sabine Hills. In the original recipe *bucatini* were used, and purists claim that tomatoes do not belong to the recipe at all. However, the Roman version uses them. Bacon, crisply fried, can be used instead of the pork chaps. The cheese usually served with this dish is Pecorino, but if not available, the best substitute would be Parmesan or a mixture of Parmesan and grated hard cheese, such as Cheddar, not processed.

4 servings:

1½ lb. spaghetti or bucatini
1 lb. tomatoes
1 small sweet red pepper
½ lb. lean pork chaps or lean bacon
2 tablespoons (2½) pork fat, lard or
  olive oil

1 small onion, finely chopped
1 clove garlic
salt, pepper
1 cup (1¼) grated Pecorino cheese

Peel the tomatoes, squeeze out the seeds and chop the pulp. Dice the sweet pepper, discarding the core and seeds. Cut the pork or bacon into strips. Heat the fat and fry the pork until it is crisp and brown, take from the pan but keep it hot. Add the onion, garlic and sweet pepper to the pan and fry them gently until the onion changes colour. Discard the garlic and stir in the tomatoes. Add salt and plenty of black pepper or a good pinch of cayenne pepper—some of the Roman *trattorie* pride themselves on the pepper-hotness of this dish. Cook for 30 minutes or so.

Cook the pasta until *al dente* (see page 83). Drain and turn into a hot serving dish. Mix the bacon with the sauce and stir it well into the pasta and sprinkle with cheese— or the cheese can be stirred into the pasta and the whole dotted with slivers of butter.

SPAGHETTI CAPRI FASHION (*Spaghetti alla Capri*) *Campania*

4 servings:

1½ lb. spaghetti
1¼ lb. ripe or canned plum-shaped
 tomatoes
olive oil
salt
1 teaspoon (1¼) sugar (optional)

4 anchovies in brine or 8 fillets in oil
1 small can tunny (tuna) fish
12 black olives, pitted and chopped
5 oz. Mozzarella cheese, diced
pepper

If using fresh tomatoes, peel them, squeeze out the seeds and chop. Canned tomatoes only need chopping.

Heat 3 tablespoons (3¾) of oil, add the tomatoes and a little salt and sugar. Cook over a brisk heat for 15 minutes. Thoroughly wash the anchovies to remove the salt, wipe them dry and discard the heads and tails. Pound them together in a mortar with the tunny and olives. Rub this mixture through a fine sieve and mix with enough oil to make a thick paste. Gently heat the sauce but do not let it become hot.

Cook the spaghetti until *al dente* (see page 83). Drain, turn into a serving bowl and at once stir in the tomato sauce, the anchovy and tunny sauce, Mozzarella and pepper. Serve at once.

SPAGHETTI WITH FENNEL AND SARDINES (*Spaghetti alla siciliana*) *Sicily*

4 servings:

1½ lb. spaghetti
olive oil for frying
1 large onion, thinly sliced
1 tablespoon (1¼) tomato paste
black pepper
2¼ lb. fresh sardines

1 lb. bulb fennel
2 tablespoons (2½) raisins
1 tablespoon (1¼) pine nuts
2–3 tablespoons (2½–3¾) fried soft
 breadcrumbs

Heat 2–3 tablespoons of oil and fry the onion until soft. Add the tomato paste, pepper and 2 cups (2½) of hot water, stir well and simmer for 10–15 minutes.

Bone the sardines, discarding the heads and tails. Heat enough oil to fry the sardines until lightly browned. Take them from the pan and put aside. Thinly slice the fennel, add it to the tomato sauce, stir well, cook for 15 minutes, then add the raisins, pine nuts and a quarter of the fried sardines. Cook gently until the fennel is tender.

Cook the spaghetti until *al dente* (see page 83). Drain. Spread a layer of the sauce on the bottom of a casserole. Add about one-third of the spaghetti, spread with the sauce, add a layer of fried sardines, and another of spaghetti. Repeat until the ingredients are finished. Put the casserole into a hot oven (425°F., mark 7) and bake until almost all the sauce is absorbed. Sprinkle with fried breadcrumbs.

This dish is a speciality of Palermo. It is typical of Sicilian cooking that fried bread-crumbs are added to spaghetti or other noodles dishes when vegetables are included. If fresh sardines are not available, use fresh sprats or other small fish—but never canned sardines—as a substitute.

SPAGHETTI WITH BACON AND EGG SAUCE *Lazio*
(*Spaghetti alla carbonara*)

3 servings:

1 lb. spaghetti	**4 eggs**
2 tablespoons (2½) olive oil	**½ cup (⅔) grated Parmesan cheese**
6 thin slices bacon, diced	**½ cup (⅔) grated Pecorino cheese**
½ cup (⅔) dry white wine (or cream or milk)	**salt, black pepper**

If Pecorino cheese is not available, double the quantity of the Parmesan cheese or substitute with a strong, dry Cheddar.

Cook the spaghetti until *al dente* (see page 83). Heat the oil in a shallow casserole, add the bacon and fry it until crisp. Add the wine, lower the heat and cook until it evaporates. Beat the eggs in a bowl, add the grated cheeses and continue to beat until blended. Season. Heat the plates on which the spaghetti is to be served. When the spaghetti is ready, quickly drain it, put it once more into the pan with the bacon and stir rapidly. Add the egg and cheese mixture and stir it quickly into the spaghetti. The eggs, should, and will, cook immediately if the spaghetti is sufficiently hot. Whatever happens, the spaghetti must not be allowed to cool after the egg mixture has been added. Stir for a minute or so, no longer, and serve at once on the hot plates.

SPAGHETTI WITH A TOMATO AND BACON SAUCE *Umbria*
(*Spaghetti al guanciale*)

Guanciale is a hog's or pig's jowl, or chaps; where these are not available, use bacon.

4 servings:

1½ lb. spaghetti	**1¼ lb. ripe tomatoes, peeled and seeded**
2 tablespoons (2½) olive oil	**sprig oregano or marjoram**
¼ lb. pork or bacon, diced	**1 cup (1¼) grated Parmesan cheese**
1 onion, thinly sliced	

If ripe tomatoes are not available, use Italian canned tomatoes, drained.

Heat the oil, add the pork or bacon and fry until the fat has rendered; add the onion, stir well and cook until soft but not brown. Chop the tomatoes, add them to the pan with the oregano, bring once to the boil, reduce the heat and cook for 15–20 minutes. Remove the oregano before serving the sauce.

Cook the spaghetti until *al dente* (see page 83). Drain and turn into a hot serving dish. Add the sauce, stir it quickly into the spaghetti and serve at once with Parmesan cheese.

SAVOURY MACARONI (*Maccheroni alla calabrese*) *Calabria*

4 servings:

1½ lb. macaroni (zita)
2¼ lb. ripe tomatoes
½ cup (⅔) olive oil
1–2 cloves garlic, crushed
1 small piece chilli pepper, finely
  chopped

1 medium-sized onion, finely chopped
1½ oz. smoked ham (prosciutto),
  chopped
salt, pepper
1 cup (1¼) grated Caciocavallo cheese

Peel and chop the tomatoes, discarding the seeds. Heat the oil and lightly fry the garlic and chilli pepper. Discard the garlic, add the onion and cook until the onion is transparent. Add the ham, cook for 2–3 minutes, then add the tomatoes, salt and pepper. Bring gently to the boil, lower the heat and cook for 30 minutes, stirring occasionally.

In the meantime cook the macaroni until *al dente* (see page 83). Drain. Put a layer of macaroni into a hot serving dish, sprinkle with cheese and 2–3 tablespoons of the sauce and continue in this manner, working quickly so that the macaroni does not cool, until all the ingredients are finished. Serve immediately.

PASTA WITH RICOTTA CHEESE (*Pasta con la ricotta*) *Lazio*

The pasta used in this recipe can be any of the spaghettis, *fettuccelle*, *bavette* or *linguine*, *trenette* or *tagliatelli* etc. (see pages 85–86).

4 servings:

1½ lb. pasta
¾ lb. Ricotta cheese
3 oz. (1 cup) grated Parmesan cheese

salt, black pepper to taste
2½ oz. (5 tablespoons) butter

Cook the pasta until *al dente* (see page 83). Beat the Ricotta with a wooden spoon until light and airy and rub it through a fine sieve. Mix it with the Parmesan cheese and add salt and black pepper. Just melt the butter. When the pasta is *al dente*, drain it quickly and return it to its pan. Add the melted butter, stir rapidly and then stir in the Ricotta mixture. Mix this swiftly into the pasta and serve at once.

TRENETTE WITH PESTO (*Trenette al pesto*) *Liguria*

Trenette are matchstick-thick noodles, like a thickish spaghetti. They are used in Genoa to make this favourite dish of pasta flavoured with *pesto*. According to the Genoese, it is the finest dish of pasta in Italy.

4 servings:

1½ lb. trenette
2 medium-sized potatoes, slightly
  less than ½ lb.

4 oz. pesto (see page 164)
3 oz. (1 cup) grated Sardo or Parmesan
  cheese

Peel the potatoes and cut them into thin strips. Have ready a large pan with plenty of boiling, salted water. Add the potatoes. Cook for 2 minutes, then add the *trenette* and cook until *al dente* (see page 83). Take 2–3 tablespoons of the liquid in which the *trenette* are cooking and dilute the *pesto*. Keep this hot. Drain and turn the *trenette* into a hot serving dish. Add the *pesto* and mix it well into the pasta. Serve at once, accompanied by a bowl of grated cheese.

Italian *pesto* can usually be bought in Italian stores, although NOT always in those kept by southern Italians.

'GUITAR' NOODLES (*Maccheroni alla chitarra*) *Abruzzi-Molise*

One of the oldest methods of cutting noodles is on the so-called *chitarra*, guitar, with its wooden frame and thick steel strings, like those of the guitar. The prepared pasta dough is spread over it and rolled with a rolling pin, forcing it through the wires and producing long, sharply cut strands of pasta locally called *maccheroni alla chitarra*. Most homes in the Abruzzi area have their own *chitarra*, although there is industrially-made pasta labelled *alla chitarra*. The pasta is cooked in the usual way and served with a meat or tomato sauce and grated Provola or Scarmozza cheese.

VERMICELLI WITH CLAMS OR MUSSELS *Campania*
(*Vermicelli con le vongole o le cozze*)

4 servings:

1½ lb. vermicelli	2 cloves garlic, crushed
3½–4 lb. clams or mussels	1 clove garlic, finely chopped
salt	2–3 sprigs parsley, finely chopped
olive oil	pepper

Thoroughly scrub the clams or mussels and leave them for 1 hour in a bowl with plenty of heavily salted water. Wash them several times under running water and wipe them until they are clean and shining.

Put 4 tablespoons (5) of oil into a large pan, add the crushed garlic and cook until it browns. Discard the garlic, add the clams and cook them for 5 minutes, or until the shells open, shaking the pan from time to time. Discard those which do not open. Take the pan from the heat, carefully scoop out the clams from their shells and drop them into a bowl with their juices. Strain the juice through a fine sieve.

Heat ½ cup (⅔) of oil, fry and brown the chopped garlic, add the clams with their juice and the parsley and pepper. Cook over a low heat for 2 minutes, no longer or the clams will toughen.

Cook the vermicelli until *al dente* (see page 83). Drain and turn it into a hot serving dish and stir in the sauce. Cheese is not used with this dish.

Both home-made pasta (see pages 84–85) **or industrially-prepared pasta can be used in the following noodle recipes.**

NOODLES WITH BUTTER AND PARMESAN CHEESE *Lazio*
(*Fettuccine al burro e parmigiano*)

3 servings:

1 lb. wide noodles (fettuccine)	**2 cups (2½) grated Parmesan cheese**
8 oz. (1 cup) butter	**salt, black pepper**

Cook the *fettuccine* until *al dente* (see page 83) and drain. Turn it into a hot serving dish and mix in the butter, do not soften or melt this first, simply stir it well into the noodles; add the cheese, again stir, sprinkle with salt and pepper and serve at once.

It is important in this recipe to be generous with the butter. Spaghetti and other pasta can be prepared in the same manner.

NOODLES WITH GARLIC SAUCE (*Fettuccine aglio e olio*) *Abruzzi-Molise*

3 servings:

1 lb. wide noodles (fettucine)	**4–6 large cloves garlic, finely chopped**
½ cup (⅔) olive oil	**salt, pepper**

Cook the *fettuccine* until *al dente* (see page 83). Heat the oil, add the garlic, salt and pepper and cook over a moderate heat until the garlic browns. Drain the noodles, turn them into a hot dish, add the sauce, stir well and serve at once.

A dish for meatless days. Finely-chopped parsley or other fresh herbs can be added at the same time as the garlic. In some parts of Campania where a similar sauce is prepared, finely-chopped chilli is also added, elsewhere finely-chopped sweet pepper is used.

NOODLES BOLOGNA STYLE (*Tagliatelle alla bolognese*) *Emilia-Romagna*

The Bolognese claim not only to make the best *tagliatelle* but, like their *tortellini*, to have created it. Their story is that the cook of one of the noblemen of Bologna was inspired by the long golden tresses of his master's principal guest, no other than the notorious Lucrezia Borgia, and 'created' a pasta as 'yellow and as light as her hair'.

3 servings:

1 lb. wide noodles (tagliatelle)	**2 cups (2½) hot Bolognese sauce**
a few slivers butter	(see page 158)
2 cups (2½) grated Parmesan cheese	

Cook the noodles until *al dente* (see page 83). Drain them and turn into a hot serving dish. Sprinkle with slivers of butter, add half the cheese and half the sauce and quickly mix. Serve the rest of the cheese and sauce separately.

NOODLES WITH HARE SAUCE (*Pappardelle con la salsa di lepre*) *Tuscany*

This is one of the famous pasta dishes of Italy. Sometimes wild boar, *cinghiale*, is used instead of hare, also other game.

4 servings:

1½ lb. wide noodles	salt, pepper
legs and back of 1 hare	finely-chopped thyme to taste
2 oz. (4 tablespoons) butter	1 tablespoon (1¼) flour
2 tablespoons (2½) olive oil	1 cup (1¼) dry white or red wine
2 slices fat bacon, finely chopped	2 cups (2½) boiling meat stock
1 small onion, finely chopped	grated Parmesan cheese to taste for
1 stalk celery, finely chopped	garnish

Remove the meat from the legs and back of the hare and cut it into small pieces. Heat the butter and oil, add the bacon, onion and celery and cook gently until brown. Add salt, pepper, thyme and the hare pieces. Brown over a moderate heat. Sprinkle with flour and blend this into the sauce. Add the wine, stir well and cook over a low heat until reduced by half. Add the stock, stir, cover the pan and cook over a low heat for 2 hours.

Some 15–20 minutes before serving, cook the noodles until *al dente* (see page 83). Drain and drop them into the pan with the sauce. Toss and serve in a hot dish with grated Parmesan cheese served separately.

BAKED NOODLES BOLOGNA FASHION (*Lasagne alla bolognese*) *Emilia-Romagna*

4 servings:

1½ lb. wide noodles	
1½ oz. (1½ cups) dried Italian mushrooms	1 cup (1¼) milk
bechamel sauce (see page 159)	2–3 sprigs continental parsley, finely
Bolognese sauce (see page 158)	chopped
3 oz. (6 tablespoons) butter	pinch salt
1 clove garlic	1 cup (1¼) grated Parmesan cheese

Soak the mushrooms in tepid water, squeeze dry and chop them. Make a thin bechamel sauce, doubling the recipe on page 159, and a Bolognese sauce. Cook the noodles until *al dente* (see page 83). Drain and dry them on a cloth, carefully separating the strips.

Heat one-third of the butter, fry the garlic until brown and discard it. Add the mushrooms, milk, parsley and salt, stir and cook gently for 15 minutes.

Rub an oblong baking dish with butter. Cover the bottom with a layer of the lasagne, spread it thinly with bechamel sauce, then with the Bolognese sauce. Sprinkle with Parmesan cheese. Continue in this way until all the ingredients are used up, adding 2 layers of the mushroom mixture as well. The top layer should be of lasagne sprinkled with grated cheese and dotted with slivers of the remaining butter. Bake in a moderate oven (350°F., mark 4) until a light crust forms on the top. Serve straight from the oven.

Green lasagne is cooked in the same manner.

BAKED SAVOURY MACARONI (*Maccheroni al forno*) *Apulia*

3 servings:

1 lb. broken macaroni
2 tablespoons (2½) olive oil
4 oz. mushrooms, cleaned and sliced
4 tomatoes, peeled, seeded and chopped
2–3 sprigs parsley, finely chopped
salt, pepper

1 cup (1¼) hot water or stock
1 oz. (2 tablespoons) butter
1 cup (1¼) thin bechamel sauce (see
 page 159)
grated Parmesan cheese to taste

Heat the oil, add the mushrooms, tomatoes, parsley, salt and pepper and cook for a few minutes, stirring all the time. Add the hot water. Stir this into the sauce and continue cooking over a low heat until the tomatoes are soft.

In the meantime cook the macaroni until *al dente* (see page 83) and drain. Rub a pie dish with butter and add the macaroni. Stir in first the tomato sauce, then the bechamel sauce, add plenty of Parmesan cheese, salt and pepper to taste and bake in a moderate oven (350°F., mark 4) for 20-30 minutes. Serve hot with a bowl of grated Parmesan cheese separately.

Almost any left-over boiled pasta can be used up in this way.

BAKED NOODLES WITH PRAWNS OR SHRIMPS *Southern Italy*
(*Lasagne ai gamberetti*)
ILLUSTRATED PAGE 60

4 servings:

1½ lb. wide noodles
salt
butter
1 lb. cooked small prawns or shrimps

2 cups (2½) bechamel sauce (see page
 159)
grated Parmesan cheese to taste
6 oz. Mozzarella cheese, thinly sliced

Cook the noodles until *al dente* (see page 83), drain and pat them dry, carefully separating the strips. Rub a baking dish generously with butter and cover with a layer of noodles; add a layer of prawns, spread with sauce, add a sprinkling of Parmesan cheese and a layer of Mozzarella. Repeat this until all the ingredients are finished, the top layer being of Parmesan cheese and Mozzarella. Bake in a moderate oven (350°F., mark 4) until the top is brown, and serve at once.

If Mozzarella cheese is not available, use Bel Paese or any other mild-flavoured soft cheese.

BAKED GREEN NOODLES (*Lasagne verdi al forno*) *Emilia-Romagna*

6 servings:

1 lb. green pasta dough (see page 87)
butter
meat sauce (see pages 157–158)

1 cup (1¼) grated Parmesan cheese
bechamel sauce (see page 159)

Cut the prepared green pasta into 4-inch squares. Cook until *al dente* (see page 83), drain and place on a cloth to dry. Rub a shallow baking dish generously with butter and cover the bottom with a layer of pasta. Spread with a layer of meat sauce, Parmesan, and bechamel sauce. Continue in this manner until all the ingredients are finished, ending with a final layer of noodles. Sprinkle the top with Parmesan and 2 oz. (4 tablespoons) of melted butter. Bake in a moderately hot oven (350°F., mark 4) for 30 minutes or until the top forms a golden crust.

RICE (Riso)

RISOTTO

Italian rice is larger grained than Carolina rice or the Far Eastern rice which is used to make dry *pilaus*. An Italian risotto is far more moist than a *pilau*, but even so each grain of rice must be separate in precisely the same way as they are in a *pilau*. Moist rice does not mean that it should be sticky or gummy.

The best rice for an Italian risotto is either *arborio* or *vialone*, both Italian varieties. The former, with short, white grains, has a nutty flavour and is obtained without difficulty outside of Italy. However, if neither are available, then probably the next choice is short grain rice.

For an Italian risotto the rice must be *insaporito*, which means that it is gently fried in a *soffritto* or *battuto*: this is a finely-chopped mixture of onion, garlic, anchovies, parsley etc. lightly fried in mixed oil and butter. The rice is added, stirred, fried until transparent, then cooked by the gradual addition of stock, about 1 cup ($1\frac{1}{4}$) at a time, as the rice swells, absorbs the liquid and begins to dry out. The rice should never get completely dry and it must be kept cooking over a moderate heat.

Caution is required when cooking a risotto and it must be watched all the time it is cooking. The amount of liquid must be exactly calculated so that the rice, when cooked, will still be tender but nevertheless with that little bite, i.e., *al dente*, to each grain, so that just enough liquid is left in the pan to bubble gently.

The rice should not be strained before serving; in fact, many Italian recipes specify that the rice should be served with its tiny quantity of bubbling liquid, called *riso all' onda*, rippling rice. A risotto when cooked is usually left for a minute or so before being served to allow it to settle. This is particularly important if any flavouring has been added at the last minute since it will take a minute or so to impregnate the rice.

RISOTTO WITH TOMATO SAUCE (*Risotto al pomodoro*) *Southern Italy*

3 servings:

1 lb. ($2\frac{1}{2}$ cups) short grain Italian rice
3–4 oz. fat bacon

1 tablespoon ($1\frac{1}{4}$) Italian tomato paste
salt to taste

Dice the bacon and fry it in a large saucepan until the fat runs. Add the tomato paste, then the rice and cook for 5 minutes, stirring all the time. Add 2 pints ($2\frac{1}{2}$) of boiling water, season, cover the pan and cook for 20 minutes. Before taking the rice from the stove, stir it well.

RISOTTO MILANESE (*Risotto milanese*) *Lombardy*
ILLUSTRATED PAGE 60

3 servings:

1 lb. (2½ cups) short grain Italian rice	3½ pints (4¼) boiling broth
4 oz. (8 tablespoons) butter	½ teaspoon (⅔) saffron, soaked 20
1 small onion, chopped	minutes in a little water
2 oz. bone marrow	4 oz. (1⅓) cups grated Parmesan cheese
salt, pepper	

Heat half the butter in a large pan and gently fry the onion and bone marrow. Cook gently for 2–3 minutes so that the onion cooks until soft but does not brown. Add the rice, salt and pepper, stirring all the time with a wooden spoon. Let the rice cook until it becomes slightly transparent and then add 1 cup (1¼) of the hot broth. Continue to cook until the rice has absorbed the liquid, then add another cup. Continue cooking in this manner over a good heat, adding the remaining broth by cupfuls, stirring carefully most of the time until the rice is *al dente* and *all'onda* (see page 101). Add the saffron with its liquid about 10 minutes after the rice has been cooking and stir it well into the rice. If all the rice does not change colour, this is not important, a two-coloured risotto looks equally effective. Take the risotto from the heat and gently but thoroughly stir in the remaining butter and the cheese. Cover the pan and let the rice settle for 2 minutes. Serve the risotto at once with a large bowl of Parmesan cheese.

Dry white wine, up to a cupful, may be substituted for one of the cups of stock.

This is also called *riso alla finanziera* because the saffron makes it gleam like gold.

RISOTTO WITH FISH (*Risotto con il pesce*) *Emilia-Romagna*

4–5 servings:

1½ lb. (3¾ cups) Italian short grain rice	3 tablespoons (3¾) olive oil
3 lb. assorted small fish	3 oz. (6 tablespoons) butter
2 cloves garlic	½ lb. small cuttlefish, chopped
1 onion, coarsely chopped	½ lb. small squid, chopped
1 celery stalk, coarsely chopped	½ cup (⅔) dry white wine
2 carrots, coarsely chopped	pepper
4 pints (5) water	¼ cup (⅓) brandy (optional)
salt	

Both cuttlefish and squid are usually cleaned and prepared by the fishmongers for cooking.

First make a fish stock. Clean the small fish and put them into a large pan. Add 1 clove of garlic, the onion, celery, carrots, water and salt to taste. Bring this to a gentle boil and cook for 30 minutes. Strain through a coarse sieve, pushing through as much of the flesh as possible. Put this aside until required.

Heat the oil and half the butter. Fry the remaining garlic until it is brown, then discard it. Add the cuttlefish and squid. Fry these for 5 minutes, then add the rice and fry it until brown. Add the wine, let this evaporate and add a cupful of the fish stock. When this is absorbed into the rice, add another cupful and continue in this manner until all the stock is absorbed and the rice is *al dente* yet *all'onda* (see page 101). Add salt, plenty of pepper and finally the brandy. Cook this for 2 minutes, take the pan from the heat, add the remaining butter, turn out onto a hot platter and serve at once.

If neither cuttlefish nor squid are available, a good risotto can still be made with the remaining ingredients.

RICE COOKED WITH FISH STOCK (*Risotto col brodo di pesce*) *Emilia-Romagna*

3 servings:

1 lb. (2½ cups) Italian short grain rice
2 oz. (4 tablespoons) butter
1 small onion, finely chopped
1–2 cloves garlic, sliced
1–2 stalks celery, chopped
1 carrot, thinly sliced

2 tablespoons (2½) finely-chopped parsley
salt, pepper
3 pints (3¾) boiling fish stock
butter and Parmesan cheese to taste

Heat the measured quantity of butter, add the onion, garlic, celery and carrot and gently fry them until all the vegetables are soft but not brown. Add the parsley, rice, salt and pepper, stir and cook over a moderate heat until the rice becomes transparent, then add 1 cupful of fish stock. Cook over a moderate heat until the stock has been absorbed, then continue adding cupfuls of hot stock until the rice is *al dente* but still *all'onda* (see page 101). Stir in butter and Parmesan cheese immediately before serving.

SICILIAN RISOTTO (*Riso alla siciliana*) *Sicily*

3 servings:

1 lb. (2½ cups) short grain Italian rice
salt
olive oil
1 onion, chopped
1 tablespoon (1¼) wine vinegar
1 glass dry white wine
juice 4 lemons

½ teaspoon (⅔) mustard
2 anchovies in brine, well washed
5 large ripe tomatoes
a little oregano or marjoram, finely chopped
pepper
6–8 black olives, pitted and chopped

Bring plenty of salted water to the boil in a large pan. Add the rice, lower the heat and cook gently for 15 minutes or until the rice is *al dente* and *all'onda* (see page 101).

Meanwhile make a sauce. Heat 2–3 tablespoons (2½–3¾) of oil and fry the onion until brown. Sprinkle with vinegar and cook briskly until this evaporates. Add the wine, lemon juice, mustard and the anchovies. Mix well then rub them through a sieve. Put the sauce aside but keep hot.

Peel and chop the tomatoes and discard their seeds. Heat ½ cup (⅔) of oil, add the tomatoes and cook for 10 minutes over a good heat. Sprinkle with oregano.

Drain the rice and put into a hot serving dish. Stir in the sauce, add pepper, the tomatoes and olives and serve at once.

TIMBALE OF RICE (*Timballo di riso — Sartù*) *Campania*

Sartù is a name of unknown origin and the recipe varies from kitchen to kitchen.

3 servings:

1 lb. (2½ cups) short grain Italian rice
4 oz. (8 tablespoons) butter or other fat
3 pints (3¾) boiling stock
1–2 tablespoons (1¼–2½) olive oil
1 large mild onion, finely chopped
2 ripe tomatoes, peeled, seeded and
 chopped
a few dried mushrooms soaked in
 water for 30 minutes
8 chicken livers, coarsely chopped
salt, pepper

1 cup (1¼) chicken stock
1 cup (1¼) dry white wine
3 tablespoons (3¾) fine breadcrumbs
2 hard-boiled eggs, sliced or chopped
Parmesan cheese to taste
shelled, cooked green peas (optional)
crisply-fried diced bacon to taste
 (optional)
4 oz. sliced Mozzarella cheese
 (optional)

Heat half the butter. Dribble in the rice and cook this for 5 minutes, stirring all the time, until the rice is transparent. Slowly add the stock, stir well, cover the pan and continue cooking until the stock is absorbed and the rice is *al dente* and *all'onda* (see page 101).

While the rice is cooking, heat the rest of the butter with the oil, add the onion and fry it until soft. Add the tomato, mushrooms (drained and chopped), chicken livers, salt and pepper. Simmer for 5 minutes, add the chicken stock, stir it well into the sauce, add the wine and cook for 15 minutes, stirring from time to time.

Rub a round baking dish generously with butter and sprinkle with breadcrumbs. Mix the rice with the sauce, eggs, plenty of Parmesan cheese and the remaining ingredients, if you are using them. Bake in a warm oven (325°F., mark 3) for 1 hour. Turn off the heat and let the rice settle in the oven for 5–10 minutes before turning it out to serve. *Sartù* can be served plain or with Parmesan cheese and dotted with slivers of butter.

RICE FINANCIER'S STYLE (*Risotto alla finanziera*) *Lombardy*

4 servings:

1 lb. (2½ cups) short grain Italian rice
4 oz. (8 tablespoons) butter
1 small onion, finely chopped
8 chicken livers, chopped
½ lb. fresh mushrooms, finely chopped
1 small red pepper, finely chopped

salt, pepper
1 slice lemon peel
3 pints (3¾) boiling stock
½ cup (⅔) dry white wine
grated Parmesan cheese to taste

Heat the butter in a large pan, add the onion and cook it until soft but not brown. Add the chicken livers, mushrooms, red pepper, salt, pepper and lemon peel, and cook over a moderate heat for 5 minutes. Dribble the rice into the pan and cook until it is brown. Add the stock, a cupful at a time, stirring constantly but gently; add the wine and let the rice cook over a moderate heat with the liquid just boiling until the liquid has been absorbed and the rice is *al dente* (see page 101).

Serve with a bowl of grated Parmesan cheese.

GNOCCHI

Gnocchi is made from a basis of maize flour, cornmeal (polenta), potatoes, or semolina. It is usually served with cheese and/or a sauce. The gnocchi, which resemble dumplings, are usually poached in boiling, salted water until cooked, when they rise to the surface; they are then drained and variously treated. Gnocchi are also prepared with other mixtures, for example, spinach and Ricotta cheese.

Gnocchi has been eaten in Italy since the days of the Romans, although some people feel that they are part of the Germanic culinary influence, dating from the days when North Italy became part of the Holy Roman Empire. Certainly there is a resemblance between the Austrian or German *Knödl* and gnocchi, but why should it not have been the case of the Italians showing the Austrians something of their cooking?

However, whatever the beginning of this very essentially Italian dish, the modern Romans have adopted one version of gnocchi and rival gnocchi lovers have dubbed the Romans 'priest stranglers', *strozzapreti* or *strangolapreti*, because they say their gnocchi is so heavy 'it is enough to choke a priest'. However, the term has also been levelled at the Tuscans and Venetians for similar dishes, but in a complimentary manner; a priest, it is said, choked from euphoria while eating the local gnocchi.

POTATO GNOCCHI (*Gnocchi alla romana*) *Lazio*

6 servings:

2 lb. floury potatoes　　　　　　**butter**
salt, pepper to taste　　　　　　**meat sauce** (see pages 157–158)
½ lb. (2 cups) flour　　　　　　**grated Parmesan cheese to taste**

Peel and cook the potatoes until soft. Drain and mash. Put them into a mixing bowl with a little salt and pepper. Beat well, add the flour and mix it well into the potatoes to make a soft but firm dough; a little more flour may be needed, it depends on the flour and the type of potatoes. Knead the dough for 2–3 minutes—if the dough seems sticky, add a little more flour. Cut into 4–6 pieces and roll each piece into long cylinders ½-inch thick. Cut each cylinder into pieces 1-inch long and pinch the centre of each between the thumb and index finger. Sprinkle the cylinders with flour.

Bring a large pan filled with salted water to the boil. Drop about one-third of the gnocchi into the boiling water and let them boil rapidly; they are ready as soon as they rise to the surface. Take them out with a perforated (slotted) spoon. Drain them at once on a warm dry cloth. Repeat this operation until all the gnocchi are ready. Put them in a large shallow baking dish, sprinkle generously with slivers of butter, half the meat sauce, and the Parmesan cheese. Place in a moderate oven (350°F., mark 4) and leave between 5–10 minutes, then serve at once. The rest of the meat sauce and a bowl of Parmesan cheese is served separately.

POTATO GNOCCHI PIEDMONTESE (*Gnocchi alla piemontese*) *Piedmont*

6 servings:

gnocchi (see page 105)
salt
¼ lb. Fontina cheese

2 oz. (4 tablespoons) butter, melted and kept hot
tomato sauce (see pages 160–161)
grated Parmesan cheese to taste

Make the gnocchi as in the previous recipe but about half the size. Drop them into a pan with plenty of bubbling, boiling salted water and cook until they rise to the surface. Take them out with a perforated (slotted) spoon and place them at once on to a flat serving dish. When they are all in the dish, cover with thin slices of Fontina cheese and sprinkle with butter. Heat for 5 minutes in a hot oven. Serve the sauce and Parmesan separately.

In Piedmont, during the truffle season local cooks often add flaked white truffle to the dish immediately it comes from the oven, the combination of truffle with Parmesan cheese is delicious.

SPINACH AND CHEESE DUMPLINGS (*Gnocchi di spinaci e ricotta*) *Umbria*
ILLUSTRATED PAGE 60

6 servings:

1 lb. spinach
salt, pepper
1½ oz. (3 tablespoons) butter
10 oz. Ricotta cheese

½ lb. (2 cups) flour
1 whole egg and 1 yolk
melted butter and Parmesan cheese to garnish

Wash the spinach and cook it until tender without water, adding salt and pepper to taste. Drain, chop finely and rub through a fine sieve. Mix in the measured quantity of butter. Beat the Ricotta until smooth, add the spinach and, when well mixed, add the flour, the egg and egg yolk, salt and pepper. Get ready a large pan with boiling, salted water. Break off small pieces of the spinach mixture and, with floured hands, form these into little balls about the size of a walnut. Drop them a few at a time into the boiling water. When they rise to the surface, take them from the pan with a perforated (slotted) spoon and put them on to a hot plate. Pour over them hot melted butter to taste and grated Parmesan cheese.

The gnocchi may also be placed in a hot dish and put into a hot oven for 10 minutes and are then known as *malfatti di spinaci*.

POLENTA (*Polenta*)

This is called variously a porridge, mush, or pudding and is usually made with maize flour. It is a descendant of the ancient Roman's *pulmentum*, which was served both as a soft porridge and a hard cake, and made with primitive flours. Later, in Renaissance times, polenta was made from ground barley and chestnut flour (it still is in Corsica).

Maize was not brought to Italy until sometime in the seventeenth century when a sack of it was unloaded from the cargo of a trading ship in Venice. As most good things in those days came from Turkey, the maize, although from recently-discovered America, was called *granoturco*, or Turkish corn, as it is to this day. In Venice polenta is made from white maize and here it thrives as in no other part of the country.

Polenta is prepared and served in a variety of ways, hot or cold, sweet and savoury. The following recipes give the traditional way of cooking polenta, that is, long, slow cooking with plenty of stirring. However, an instant polenta is now on the Italian market and is being used with enthusiasm. It takes precisely five minutes to cook.

Although polenta can be cooked in any type of large, heavy pan, Italians like best of all to use a *paiuolo*, a copper pan which oddly enough is not tin lined.

In the United States, where polenta is probably as popular as in Italy, it is called cornmeal.

POLENTA—A General Recipe
ILLUSTRATED PAGE 60

It is difficult to say definitely how much water is required with polenta, it depends on the quality and age of the polenta flour. A fair direction is 1 lb. of polenta flour to $2\frac{1}{2}$ pints ($3\frac{1}{4}$) of water for a firm polenta, and about 3 pints ($3\frac{3}{4}$) for one of a soft consistency. However, most packaged cornmeal has fairly precise instructions on the package.

6–8 servings:

1 lb. ($3\frac{3}{4}$ cups) polenta flour　　　　　**salt**
water

Bring the water to a furious boil, add salt and gradually the polenta, and stir to prevent lumps forming. Cook over a moderate heat for 30–40 minutes with the water boiling all the time, or until the polenta is the consistency of mashed potatoes. Stir again and again. If a thicker polenta is required, let it cook another 20–25 minutes or until it is impossible to stir any longer.

Soft polenta can be served sprinkled with salt and pepper, and with a tomato, mushroom or meat sauce poured over the top, then sprinkled with grated Parmesan cheese.

Hard polenta is shaped on to a board and allowed to cool, and then sliced with a string or with a wooden polenta knife.

Sliced polenta is served cold with a very hot sauce—any of the vegetable, meat or fish sauces used for pasta may be used, and grated cheese is added, except with the fish sauces.

POLENTA WITH ITALIAN SAUSAGES (*Polenta pasticciata con salsicce*) *Umbria*

6–8 servings:

soft polenta (see page 107)
3 oz. (6 tablespoons) butter
1½ lb. Italian pork sausages

tomato sauce (see pages 160–161)
salt, pepper
grated Parmesan cheese to taste

While the polenta is cooking, heat the butter and gently fry the sausages until they are brown all over. Add the sauce, salt and pepper and simmer gently for 30–40 minutes. Taste for seasoning. Turn the polenta out on to a flat, hot serving dish, make indentations on the top, fit in the sausages and pour tomato sauce over all. Sprinkle generously with Parmesan cheese.

Some Italians prefer to skin the sausages and coarsely chop them before they are fried.

POLENTA FRITTERS (*Frittelle di polenta alla lodigiana*) *Lombardy*

3–4 servings:

thick polenta (see page 107)
2 eggs, well beaten
breadcrumbs

fat for deep frying
tomato sauce (see pages 160–161)

Make a thick polenta, using half the quantity of flour. Take it from the pan and turn into a mixing bowl. Beat until smooth then spread it on a polenta or pastry board or marble slab to the thickness of half an inch. Let it cool. Cut out small rounds with a floured cutter or small glass. Dip each round into beaten egg and roll in breadcrumbs. Heat the fat, add the polenta rounds, a few at a time, and fry until a golden brown. Take from the pan with a perforated (slotted) spoon and drain quickly on absorbent paper. Serve on a hot dish with tomato sauce served separately.

fish  *pesci*

The variety of fish in Italy's fish markets is fascinating. The shapes are bizarre, the colours fantastic, and the fish vary from whitebait to the gigantic tunny (tuna) with its beef-red flesh, and the swordfish, equally monstrous, salmon-pink in colour and fearsome looking with its pointed sword, often on display. There is also the pale pink *vitello del mare*, 'veal of the sea' or shark.

Italians eat everything which comes out of the sea. Since much of their sea fish is Mediterranean it is not easy to find a counterpart in Britain or the United States. In the rivers and lakes the fish are more familiar, such as trout, salmon, salmon-trout, perch, pike, carp etc.

After pasta, fish is probably the most important source of Italy's food. Some seven hundred million fish are taken annually from Italian waters. To name more than a selection is impossible. Apart from those already noted, we find anchovies, sardines, shad, eel, cod—eaten both fresh and dried—bream of several kinds, angler-fish—a large ugly member of the grouper family—whiting, snapper, grayling, and varying kinds of flat fish: sole, flounders etc. There are all the many crustaceans (Apulia is celebrated for its shell-fish), the usual plus the unusual, such as the sea-date, a shellfish the shape of a date and the sea-urchin, with a flavour between the oyster, mussel and lobster. Sea-urchins live in clusters, clinging to the rocks and can only be collected with pincers or gloved hands for they are covered with sharp spines. There are also cuttlefish, squid, octopus and other mollusks, including oysters, scallops, mussels, conch, clams, sea truffles etc.

One of the best known of the Italian crustaceans is scampi, a name under which many crustaceans are disguised. It was originally the Venetian name for the giant Adriatic prawn which grows up to six inches in length. Its body is pale amber, almost colourless, with a thin shell and no claws. The flesh is tender with a shrimp-like flavour, and it is cooked in a variety of ways. Very good are the *langouste*, crawfish or rock lobster, which is commonly found in Mediterranean waters. Among the best are the Sardinian *langouste* or to use the Italian name, *aragosta* or *arigusta*.

Eels are popular in most parts of Italy. Grosseto has its *capitone*, which in December is exported to Rome and Naples for the Christmas Eve feast. Pisa, better known for its leaning tower, favours the blind baby eel called *lecee*, dialect for *cieche*, caught in large numbers at the mouth of the Arno river. Flavoured with sage, they are cooked in oil. Comacchio, in Emilia-Romagna, which lies below the level of the sea amidst miles of lagoons, produces some of the fattest eels in Italy. These are made into rich stews; roasted on a spit over charcoal; or marinated in wine vinegar, flavoured with orange and lemon juice, raisins, pine nuts and chopped candied peel. Also highly rated in this area is the *passera di valle*, a relative of our lemon sole, and the *canocchie*, which are like shrimps or small prawns.

Lombardy has its lake fish, salmon-trout etc., and a small golden carp. It is said the golden carp are descendents of goldfish thrown into Lake Garda which had mated with the local carp. Whatever their ancestry, these golden fish are as good to look at as to eat. Lake Como, also in Lombardy, enjoys a reputation for eel, trout, carp, salmon-trout and *missoltitt*, a speciality of Lecco, which are small shad, dried and packaged in boxes between layers of bay leaves. Milan, capital of Lombardy, offers pike, perch and carp cooked in white wine, as well as numerous salt fish dishes.

Venice has a huge repertoire of fish dishes, often named in the local dialect which confuses even Italians. For example, *sfogi in saor* is *sogliole in sapore*, or fried sole. Quieter than Venice is nearby Chioggia from where most of the fish sold in Venetian fish markets comes. It is a pleasant fishing town at the western extremity of the lagoon, where small fishing boats, locally called *bragozzi*, bring ashore some of the finest fish of the Adriatic.

Apart from fish taken from the seas along the coast and lagoons, the Venetians have ventured further afield and brought back with them *baccalà* or *stoccafisso* to produce one of the best-known dishes of Venice, *baccalà alla vicentina*.

The sea also provides Genoa and the Ligurian coast with much raw material for good eating, especially for their classic soups or stews. Incidentally, if a menu lists fried toad tail, remember it is only the *rospo* tail, which makes good eating, and called *lotte* or *baudroie* in France, and in some parts of Italy *boldro* and *pescatrice*. Its Adriatic name, *rospo*, does mean toad and is a reference to its sadly hideous head which is always cut off before reaching the market.

Umbria has no coastline but plenty of lake fish with a slightly marshy flavour from Lake Trasimeno. Neighbouring Marches, with its long coastline, boasts some of the principal fishing ports of Italy, such as Ancona and San Benedetto del Tronto. From the latter port fishermen sail far and wide in search of fish.

Southern Italy has some splendid fish and equally good fish dishes. Swordfish and tunny take pride of place, but there is red mullet, sea-bass, *spigola*, and *dentice*, dentex, a pink-shaded fish with a white flesh. Fresh sardines and anchovies are plentiful.

Fish plays an important part in the cooking of the South. Indeed, there are many fish dishes which should tempt visitors in this area: octopus as cooked in Posillipo, with garlic, olives, capers and parsley; or as cooked in the small harbour of Santa Lucia, in earthenware pans with tomatoes and peppers, *polpi alla luciana*. Noodles and other pasta with fish are extremely well prepared in Naples, not surprising of course, since both fish and pasta are important to the Neapolitans.

Apulia has an abundance of fish, much of which is caught by trawler fleets operating offshore. The Taranto oysters have been famous for centuries and the ancient Romans preferred them above all others; the modern Romans no less so today. Bari has several local fish dishes, one of curled octopus, *pulpe rizze* or *polpi arricciati*; a number of mussel dishes, they are called *cozze* here, such as fried mussels, or mussels stuffed with bread-crumbs, garlic, parsley, cheese and olive oil and cooked in a tomato sauce. The Bari fish soup is called *caimbotte*.

Along the heel and toe of Italy there are many fine fish markets but Taranto's market makes all others seem, as H. V. Morton puts it in his book *A Traveller in Southern Italy*, 'merely a sideshow', adding, 'the fish market of Taranto is a museum of the southern sea: I was told that there are nearly a hundred different varieties of fish and shellfish to be seen here, and I think I have seen them all.'

Sicily, where the tunny (tuna) provides food and a living for the people, has a strange, brutal fish battle, *tonnare*, which takes place every year in the mating season when the tunny emerge to the surface seeking a mate. They are 'channelled' through enclosed areas leading to what is graphically described as 'the chamber of death' formed by fishing boats parked close together to make the channel walls, while below they drag an extra strong net. As the fish rise to the surface the nets are slowly pulled on board the boats, the fish clubbed to death in the diminishing water, and yanked aboard. As the men work they chant, while the *rais*, or leader, yells encouragement. The whole scene, the chanting, the yelling, the fish thrashing in the nets, plus the clubbing, is not a pleasant sight, dramatic though it undoubtedly is.

Sardinia, like Sicily, has a plentiful supply of fish and many of their best dishes are prepared with fish. Two popular fish soups or stews are *la cassola*, a highly-spiced fish stew, and a variety of *buridda* in which dogfish and skate are the main ingredients. There are also spit-roasted eels; grilled, stuffed baby squid; baked and stuffed mussels, both cooked in the local Vernaccia wine; stuffed anchovies; magnificent lobsters which are exported abroad; and fresh sardines with fennel. Sardines are fished in large quantities in Sardinian waters, hence their name.

CARP IN WHITE WINE (*Carpione in vino bianco*)   *Lombardy*

6–8 servings:

3 lb. carp	3 sprigs parsley, finely chopped
3 tablespoons (3¾) olive oil	1 cup (1¼) dry white wine
1 medium-sized onion, minced	salt, pepper
1½ oz. (3 tablespoons) butter	1 tablespoon (1¼) white wine vinegar
1 tablespoon (1¼) flour	1–2 large lemons

Carp is a good table fish but it needs considerable washing in running water to free it from its muddy flavour. It must be scaled, and if the scales are difficult to remove, dip the fish for a minute in hot water. Cut off the head and make sure the gall stone, which lies at the back of the head, is removed otherwise the fish will have a bitter flavour. Clean it well, wipe dry and cut into thick steaks.

Heat the oil in a thick, shallow pan and fry the onion until soft. Knead the butter with the flour. Stir it into the oil, add the parsley and wine and cook over a moderate heat, stirring all the time, until the sauce is thick. Add the fish, salt, pepper, vinegar and warm water to cover. Stir gently, cover the pan and simmer for 30 minutes, stirring occasionally, turning the fish one or twice. Serve the carp in its sauce, garnished with wedges of lemon.

FRIED ANCHOVIES (*Acciughe o alici in padella*) *Liguria*

4 servings:

2 lb. fresh anchovies	2–3 sprigs parsley, finely chopped
flour	½ cup (⅔) dry white wine
1 cup (1¼) olive oil	1 tablespoon (1¼) wine vinegar
1 clove garlic, finely chopped	salt, pepper

The anchovy is a small herring-like saltwater fish with a white flesh of delicate flavour which, in the Mediterranean, is eaten fresh, salted in brine, or preserved in oil. The best and the largest—they grow up to 8 inches although the usual size is 2½–3 inches—come from the Mediterranean, but some are caught in the Channel in French or British waters.

The flavour of cured anchovies develops only after the anchovy has been pickled in brine for some months, as a result of fermentative changes. Therefore, it is not possible to use anchovy fillets in oil as a substitute for fresh anchovies, although quite often they can be used instead of anchovies in brine. Anchovy fillets in brine or oil sharpens the appetite for meat and drink, and in certain dishes it heightens the flavour of the ingredients used.

Clean the anchovies, wash and dry them. Split and bone them, and roll in flour; or they can also be fried whole. Heat the oil and gently fry the garlic and parsley, add wine, vinegar and finally the anchovies. Add salt and pepper. When the anchovies are tender, take them from the pan and serve hot.

Sprats and other small fish can be prepared in the same manner.

DOGFISH WITH PEAS (*Palombo con piselli*) *Lazio*

6 servings:

6 slices dogfish	1 tablespoon (1¼) tomato purée
2 lb. peas, shucked	2–3 sprigs parsley, finely chopped
¼ cup (⅓) olive oil	salt, pepper
½ small onion, thinly sliced	

The dogfish of the Mediterranean is the black-mouthed dogfish. Many fish of different species and even of different families find themselves on the British fishmonger's slab under the name dogfish, while dogfish is often sold as rock salmon. The customer who asks for dogfish will never be quite sure what he is getting. Much depends on locality, as well as local names. A variety of mackerel also comes under this definition. However, most fish sold as dogfish is cleaned, skinned and disguised, and its preparation involves little work.

Wash the fish in salted water and leave it to drain. Heat the oil in a wide, shallow pan over a low heat. Fry the onion until soft and dilute the tomato purée in 1 cup (1¼) of water. Stir this into the oil, then add the peas and parsley and cook gently for 15 minutes. Add the fish, season and cook for 8 minutes on each side or until tender. Serve hot in the sauce.

EEL WITH PEAS (*Anguilla con piselli*) *Tuscany*

4–6 servings:

2–2½ lb. freshwater eel	salt, pepper
3 lb. peas, shucked	1 cup (1¼) dry white wine
3 tablespoons (3¾) olive oil	1 tablespoon (1¼) tomato paste
1 small onion, thinly sliced	4 tablespoons (5) warm water
1 clove garlic, pounded	finely-chopped parsley

When buying eel make sure it is absolutely fresh; the best are freshwater eels.

Cut off the head, clean and skin the eel and cut it into pieces some 2½ inches long. Wash and dry carefully. Heat the oil in a deep frying pan, add the onion and garlic, cook until they change colour, add the eel and season. Fry gently until brown, add the wine, the tomato paste diluted in the water, stir, then add the peas. Cook gently for 30 minutes; add more water if required. Just before serving, sprinkle with parsley.

FISH FILLETS IN WHITE WINE (*Filetti di pesce al vino bianco*) *Umbria*

4–5 servings:

2 lb. fillets sole, plaice or other flat fish	a few white grapes or sultanas
butter for frying	salt
1 tablespoon (1¼) strained lemon juice	½ cup (⅔) white wine

Heat the butter but do not let it brown. Add the fillets, lemon juice and grapes. Cover and cook for 10 minutes. Uncover, turn the fillets, sprinkle with salt, add the wine and bring to a quick boil. Lower the heat and simmer for 10 minutes.

FILLETS OF FLOUNDER IN CREAM SAUCE *Marches*
(*Filetti di pesce passero in salsa*)

6 servings:

2½ lb. flounder fillets, plaice or other flat fish	3 tablespoons (3¾) grated Parmesan cheese
2 pints (2½) fish stock	1 cup (1¼) cream
2 oz. (4 tablespoons) butter	½ lb. white grapes, seeded and halved
½ lb. mushrooms, sliced	salt, white pepper to taste
1 oz. (¼ cup) flour	

Heat the stock, add the fillets, 2 or 3 at a time, and cook them until just tender. Take from the pan, put aside but keep hot and moist. Continue to simmer the stock.

Heat half the butter and fry the mushrooms until tender. Knead the remaining butter with the flour and stir it into the stock. Cook, stirring all the time until it thickens. Take the pan from the heat, add the cheese, beat well, then stir in the cream. Rub a casserole with butter, arrange a layer of fish at the bottom, and sprinkle with grapes and mushrooms. Repeat until all the ingredients are finished. Sprinkle lightly with salt and pepper, cover with the sauce and bake in a moderate oven (350°F., mark 4) for 15 minutes or until the top is a golden brown.

MARINATED MACKEREL (*Maccarelli marinati*) *Calabria*

3–6 servings:

6 small mackerel	**3 peppercorns**
salt	**3 cloves**
1 large onion, sliced	**$\frac{3}{4}$ pint (2$\frac{1}{4}$ cups) dry white wine**
2 carrots, sliced	**$\frac{3}{4}$ pint (2$\frac{1}{4}$ cups) wine vinegar**
1 bay leaf, crumbled	**1–2 lemons, sliced**
3 sprigs parsley, finely chopped	

Clean the mackerel, chop off the heads and tails and scale. Wash the fish in plenty of cold, salted water, wipe them dry and leave for 1 hour on a plate, sprinkled lightly with salt.

Cover the bottom of a large casserole with the onion, carrots, bay leaf and parsley. Add the peppercorns and cloves. Wipe the salt from the mackerel and lay them on top of the vegetables. Add the wine and vinegar. Bring to a slow boil, cover the pan, lower the heat, then cook for 10 minutes. Take from the stove and leave the fish still covered in the liquid until cold. Take them out with a fish slice and arrange on a serving dish. Sprinkle with a little of the liquid (strained) and garnish with lemon. (The marinade can be strained and used again with fish.)

MACKEREL IN A TOMATO SAUCE (*Sgombro in salsa di pomodori*) *Sicily*

3–6 servings:

6 mackerel fillets	**2–3 sprigs parsley, finely chopped**
salt, black pepper	**tomato sauce** (see pages 160–161) **or 1**
4 tablespoons (5) olive oil	**large can Italian tomatoes, mashed**
1 large onion, thinly sliced	**a little fresh oregano or marjoram**
1–2 cloves garlic, minced	**$\frac{1}{2}$ cup ($\frac{2}{3}$) water**

Wash and dry the fish and lightly sprinkle them with salt and pepper. Heat the oil, add the onion and garlic; when they change colour add the parsley, stir, and cook for 1–2 minutes. Add the tomato sauce or mashed canned tomatoes and the oregano. Cook for 5 minutes if using tomato sauce; 15 minutes if using canned tomatoes. Add the fillets and the water, cover and cook for 10 minutes. Carefully turn the fillets, then cook another 10 minutes. Serve with fried bread.

RED MULLET (*Triglie*)

Red mullet are usually sold already scaled but, if not, scaling must be done with care as the skin is delicate. Cleaning is a matter of taste. Some mullet connoisseurs insist that the intestines should be left in (like the trail of small game birds) as this increases their flavour.

RED MULLET SIMMERED IN WINE (*Triglie saporite*)
ILLUSTRATED PAGE 117

6 servings:

12 small mullet	plain flour
salt, pepper	1 oz. (2 tablespoons) butter
lemon juice and oil	1 cup (1¼) white wine

Leave the fish whole and clean them through the gills. The scales are usually already removed.

Rub the fish lightly with salt and pepper, then with lemon juice and oil. Sprinkle with flour.

Heat the butter in a large frying pan (all the fish should cook at the same time), and add the fish. Gently cook first on one side for 1 minute, then on the other. Add the wine and cook until this gently boils. Lower the heat, cover the pan and cook for 5–7 minutes over a moderate heat until the fish are tender.

Serve with a green salad (see page 44) or, if preferred, a tomato sauce (see pages 160–161).

RED MULLET COOKED IN TOMATO SAUCE (*Triglie alla livornese*)   *Tuscany*

4 servings:

1 lb. small red mullet	salt, pepper
flour	2 lb. tomatoes, peeled, seeded and
1 cup (1¼) olive oil	chopped
1 small onion, finely chopped	2 sprigs parsley, finely chopped
1–2 stalks celery, chopped	

Prepare the mullet as in the previous recipe and roll them in flour. Heat half the oil, add the onion, celery, salt and pepper and fry until the onion is brown. Add the tomatoes and cook them over a moderate heat until the sauce is thick. In another pan heat the rest of the oil and fry the mullet until brown; transfer them to the tomato sauce and cook slowly for 5 minutes. Serve, preferably in the pan, with the sauce and sprinkled with parsley.

BAKED RED MULLET (*Triglie al forno*)   *Apulia*

3–6 servings:

6 medium-sized red mullet	½ cup (⅔) white wine
salt	½ lb. green olives, pitted
½ cup (⅔) olive oil	

Sprinkle the mullet with salt and arrange them in a shallow casserole. Trickle the oil over them, sprinkle with wine and bake in a moderate oven (350°F., mark 4) for about 20 minutes, turning them once with extreme care as they break up easily. Add the olives about 5 minutes before the fish are ready.

MUSSELS AU GRATIN (*Cozze gratinate*) *Sicily*

3–4 servings:

2–3 lb. mussels
generous ½ cup (⅔) dry white wine
salt, pepper
1 tablespoon (1¼) white vinegar
1 small onion, coarsely chopped

parsley, finely chopped
1 clove garlic, finely chopped
breadcrumbs
1 tablespoon (1¼) strained lemon juice
3 tablespoons (3¾) olive oil

Wash and scrub the mussels and remove the beards—or these can be removed when the shells open. Put them into a pan with the wine, pepper, vinegar and onion. Cover and cook over a good heat until the shells open, shaking the pan from time to time; this helps the shells to open. Take them from the pan and pull off the upper part of the shells; discard any that have not opened. Arrange the mussels in their half shells on an oven-proof dish and sprinkle with parsley, garlic, breadcrumbs, lemon juice, salt, pepper and oil. Put them in a hot oven for a few minutes and serve at once with wedges of lemon.

The liquid from the mussels should not be thrown away, it is extremely good and can be used to flavour a fish sauce, stew or soup.

OCTOPUS COOKED IN TOMATOES (*Polipo affogato ai pomodori*) *Campania*

4–5 servings:

1 octopus, weighing about 2½ lb.
½ cup (⅔) olive oil
2–3 cloves garlic, finely chopped
1 small red pepper, whole

1 lb. ripe tomatoes, peeled and chopped
finely-chopped parsley to taste
salt, pepper
1–2 lemons

Clean the octopus, turn out its inside bag, and remove the eyes and the beak, which is at the bottom of the bag, if this has not been done by the fishmonger. Wash the octopus well and pound it firmly with a wooden mallet to tenderize it. Put it into a casserole with the oil, garlic, red pepper, tomatoes, parsley, salt and pepper, cover and cook gently for 1½–2 hours or until the octopus is tender. Discard the red pepper. Take out the octopus with a perforated (slotted) spoon and cut it into small pieces. Return these to the pan and cook until reheated. Turn the octopus and its sauce into a deep serving dish and serve hot with wedges of lemon. It can also be served cold.

In Liguria there is a particularly small and tender octopus called *moscardini* much liked locally, which is also cooked in the same manner.

Trout with a green sauce (page 123); red mullet simmered in wine (page 115); ingredients for mixed fried fish (page 126)

STUFFED SARDINES (*Sarde ripiene*) *Liguria*

6 servings:

2 lb. fresh sardines	**6 leaves sweet basil or marjoram, finely**
salt	**chopped**
2 slices white bread	**2 eggs, beaten**
1 lb. spinach	**½ cup (⅔) olive oil**
2 tablespoons (2½) grated Parmesan	**1 tablespoon (1¼) pine nuts**
cheese	**1½ oz. (1 cup) soft breadcrumbs**
2 cloves garlic, finely chopped	**butter**
2–3 sprigs parsley, finely chopped	**1 lemon**

The true sardine is the young of the pilchard and it is found only in European waters. In the Pacific and Atlantic, small fish called sardines are the young of herrings, belonging to the same family as pilchards and anchovies. Fresh sardines have an entirely different flavour from those that are canned.

Wash the sardines, cut off the heads and slit the bodies open lengthwise down the belly to remove the backbone. Sprinkle with salt and leave them to drain on a sloping board.

Soak the bread in water and squeeze it dry. Wash the spinach thoroughly and cook it without water until tender. Drain, press dry and finely chop it. Mix together the spinach, bread, cheese, garlic, parsley, basil, eggs, salt and 2 tablespoons (2½) of the oil to make a filling. Stuff each sardine with a little of the filling, close and re-shape. Pour the remainder of the oil into a round baking dish. Arrange the sardines in the dish, like the spokes of a wheel, and sprinkle with pine nuts, breadcrumbs and slivers of butter. Bake in a moderate oven (350°F., mark 4) for 15–20 minutes. Serve the sardines in the dish in which they were baked with wedges of lemon.

Failing fresh sardines, small herrings make a good substitute.

SCAMPI COOKED ON A SPIT (*Spiedini di scampi*) *Veneto*

6 servings:

3 lb. scampi, about 24	**olive oil**
salt, pepper, flour	**2 large lemons as a garnish**

This recipe assumes that large fresh scampi are being used, not frozen ones. If using frozen scampi, ignore the first instructions.

Cut off the scampi tails and discard the bodies. Using a sharp knife, cut out the underside part of the tail shells and take off the meat. Impale the meat on 4 skewers, about 6 on each. Sprinkle them lightly with salt, pepper and flour. Grill the scampi for 7–8 minutes, brushing them often with oil and turning the skewers frequently to prevent burning or over-cooking. Serve the scampi immediately they are cooked, sprinkled lightly with oil and garnished with wedges of lemon.

Chicken Tuscany style (page 147); green salad (page 44); stuffed meat loaf (page 143)

FRIED SCAMPI (*Scampi fritti*)   *Veneto*

6 servings:

24 large scampi	**1–2 eggs, well beaten**
olive oil	**fine breadcrumbs**
salt, pepper	**lemon**

Prepare the scampi as in the previous recipe. Heat plenty of oil in a deep frying pan. Season the scampi, dip them into egg and then into breadcrumbs. Fry them for 5–6 minutes or until golden on all sides. Serve hot garnished with thick slices of lemon.

SALT FISH VENICE STYLE (1) (*Baccalà alla vicentina*)   *Veneto*

There are many versions of salt fish cooked *alla vincentina*, some simple, others so elaborate that they become 'a noble dish for ruddy unassuming people'. It is usually served with polenta.

4–6 servings:

2 lb. salt fish, pre-soaked	**milk**
½ cup (⅔) olive oil	

Salt fish, in Italy *baccalà* and *stoccofisso*, is usually cod but can also be haddock and ling, dried and preserved in salt. It used to require days of soaking before it could be cooked but nowadays it is mostly sold pre-soaked. However it is still marketed unsoaked or partially soaked; the unsoaked variety is naturally the cheapest.

Soak the fish overnight. Drain, skin and bone it. Cut into serving pieces. Heat the oil and fry the fish until it browns. Take it from the pan, put into another pan, cover with milk and cook over a low heat until the milk has been absorbed. Serve with sliced polenta (see page 107).

SALT FISH VENICE STYLE (2) (*Baccalà alla vicentina*)   *Veneto*

4–6 servings:

2 lb. salt cod	**8–10 fillets anchovy, chopped**
1 cup (1¼) olive oil	**½ cup (⅔) dry white wine**
1 small onion, finely sliced	**2 pints (2½) milk**
2–3 cloves garlic, crushed	**½ teaspoon (⅔) ground cinnamon**
2–3 sprigs parsley, chopped	**black pepper**

Soak the fish overnight; next day skin, bone and cut it into serving pieces. Heat the oil, add the onion and garlic and fry until brown. Add the parsley, anchovies and wine and cook until this has evaporated. Add the fish, cover with milk and sprinkle with cinnamon and pepper. Bring to the boil over a moderate heat. Cover and put into a slow oven (325°F., mark 3) and cook for 4–5 hours or until the fish is tender and all the liquid has evaporated. Stir from time to time. Serve with sliced polenta (see page 107).

MARINATED FRIED SOLE (*Sfogi in saor*) *Veneto*

4 servings:

1½ lb. sole fillets	1 tablespoon (1¼) wine vinegar
flour	salt, pepper
olive oil	¼ cup (⅓) pine nuts
1 lb. onions, sliced	pinch ground cinnamon
1 teaspoon (1¼) sugar	¼ cup (⅓) sultanas (white raisins)

This dish is traditionally served on the evening of the Feast of the Holy Redeemer, the third Sunday in July, a day of great celebration.

Roll the fillets in flour and shake off the excess. Heat plenty of oil and fry the fillets until golden on both sides. Take them from the pan and drain. In the same oil, fry the onions until soft and add the sugar, vinegar, salt, pepper and 1 tablespoon (1¼) of water. Bring this to the boil and cook for a few minutes. Add the nuts, cinnamon and sultanas and mix well. Put a layer of fish into a casserole and add a layer of the onion mixture. Repeat until all ingredients are finished. Cool and leave for several hours or overnight in a cool place. Serve cold.

SOLE WITH MARSALA (*Sogliola al marsala*) *Lazio*

2 servings:

1 sole, filleted	butter
1 egg, well beaten	salt, pepper
fine semolina	dry Marsala

Wash the fillets and pat them dry. Dip each one into the egg, then coat with semolina, pressing it firmly down into the fish. In a large, shallow pan heat enough butter to fry the fillets until cooked but not browned. Sprinkle them with salt and pepper and pour 1 tablespoon (1¼) of Marsala over each fillet. Serve the fish in their sauce.

Plaice or American flounder can be cooked in the same manner.

SWORDFISH (*Pesce spada*)

What good eating this fish provides, its pale rose-pink flesh with a delicate flavour is a worthy rival to the salmon. However it is now disowned by the Americans and Japanese because of its high mercury content. It is a large, meaty fish weighing anything from sixty to three hundred pounds, yet of the mackerel family.

Messina in Sicily is famous for its swordfish; it is here one sees the swordfish boats lined up ready to sail or just returned from a successful encounter. They are curious craft, long and narrow, not unlike the shape of the fish they hunt, with a high steel mast on top of which is the look-out where sits the *guardino*. From his vantage point he can spot the fish as they swim in the clear water and steer the boat towards them, providing the spearmen perched at the end of a horizontal steel mast with a good aim. Modern boats are a great improvement on the old-fashioned ones which simply offered the look-out man a pole on which to perch, and the unfortunate harpoonist a precarious-looking walk-out resembling the pirate's walking plank.

Swordfish fishermen are superstitious. Women are not allowed on the look-out as they believe it brings bad luck. It is debatable whether many women would like to be perched some sixty feet above water. The fishermen always sing as they pass between the famous rock of Scylla and the whirlpool (Charybdis), perhaps to delude the monster of the seas, for the entrance to the Straits of Messina is narrow and fishermen remember the legend of the monster who snatched up those surviving sailors who had been fortunate to escape the whirlpool.

Sicilians are masters of the art of cooking swordfish and not only is the veal-textured flesh eaten, the liver and heart are cooked, and the roe, like caviar, is also considered a delicacy.

BAKED SWORDFISH (*Pesce spada al forno*) *Sicily*

4 servings:

1½ lb. swordfish	salt, pepper
¼ cup (⅓) olive oil	1 tablespoon (1¼) each chopped oregano
1 small onion, chopped	and capers
2 lb. tomatoes, peeled and chopped	12 green or black olives, pitted
½ glass dry white wine	lemon

Wash and skin the fish and cut it into steaks. Heat the oil and lightly brown the onion; add the tomatoes, wine, salt and pepper. Cover the pan and cook gently for 15 minutes. Add the oregano, capers and olives. Lightly rub a baking dish with oil, add the fish steaks, pour the sauce over the top and bake in a moderate oven (350°F., mark 4) for about 30 minutes. Serve garnished with thick wedges of lemon.

A similar dish is served in Imperia (Liguria) where immigrant Sicilians catch swordfish in great quantities.

GRILLED SWORDFISH (*Pesce spada alla griglia*) *Sicily*

4 servings:

4 swordfish steaks	1 tablespoon (1¼) finely-chopped
3 tablespoons (¼ cup) olive oil	oregano
juice 1 large lemon	salt, black pepper
	wedges lemon

Skin the fish steaks. Mix the oil, lemon juice, oregano, salt and pepper in a shallow bowl, add the steaks and leave for 1 hour, turning them occasionally.

Grill the steaks 4 minutes on each side, brushing well with the dressing as they cook. Serve at once with lemon.

Other firm fish steaks may be cooked in the same way.

TROUT (*Trota*)

The lakes and rivers of Italy are well stocked with trout. In Calabria they prize the trout caught in the rivers of the Sila region. They are often grilled on the spot over an open fire, or if taken home, steamed and served with an oil and lemon dressing. In Piedmont, trout are cooked on top of a mixture of chopped vegetables to which raisins, garlic and herbs are added. In Basilicata, they grill their trout, first smearing it with garlic-flavoured butter, and serve it with an oil and lemon dressing.

TROUT WITH A GREEN SAUCE (*Trota in salsa verde*) *Umbria*
ILLUSTRATED PAGE 117

4 servings:

2 lb. trout
1 stalk celery and 1 small onion,
  coarsely chopped
1 sprig parsley
salt
2 eggs

1 tablespoon ($1\frac{1}{4}$) capers
2 pickled gherkins, finely chopped
2 sprigs parsley, finely chopped
1–2 anchovy fillets, chopped
juice 1 lemon
approx. 1 cup ($1\frac{1}{4}$) olive oil

Thoroughly wash and clean the trout under running cold water. Put it into a pan with the celery, onion, and 1 sprig of parsley, sprinkle lightly with salt and cover with water. Cover the pan and cook gently until the flesh is tender, 10–15 minutes.

While it is cooking, prepare the sauce. Beat the eggs in a mortar or in a blender, add the capers, gherkins, 2 sprigs of parsley, anchovies and lemon juice and pound or blend them to a thick paste. Gradually add the oil until the paste is the consistency of mayonnaise and pour this into a sauceboat.

Take the fish from the pan, let it cool, then carefully remove the bones without breaking the flesh too much. Arrange it on a serving plate and sprinkle with parsley and lemon juice. Serve the sauce separately.

GRILLED FRESH TUNNY FISH (*Tonno fresco in gratella*) *Sardinia*

As well as swordfish, tunny (tuna) is also in disgrace with the Americans and Japanese because of its mercury content. It is a saltwater fish and the largest as well as the most useful member of the mackerel family. It can grow to an enormous size, but usually smaller fish are caught and marketed; the smaller tunny are the best. The flesh is meaty but very dry and firm, and lends itself particularly well to being canned in oil.

6 servings:

2 lb. fresh tunny (tuna), thinly sliced
$\frac{1}{2}$ cup ($\frac{2}{3}$) wine vinegar
olive oil

salt, pepper
juice 1 lemon

The best part of the tunny for grilling is cut from the belly. Spread out the slices on a large platter, sprinkle them with vinegar and leave for 30 minutes in a cool place. Wipe the fish dry. Clean the platter, return the fish and pour over it about $\frac{1}{2}$ cup ($\frac{2}{3}$) of olive oil, then sprinkle with salt and pepper. Leave it for 2 hours in a cool place, turning occasionally. Drain.

Grill the fish slices for 5 minutes on both sides. Serve at once, sprinkled with lemon juice and a little olive oil.

TUNNY FISH IN MARSALA   (*Tonno al marsala*)   *Sicily*

4–6 servings:

2–3 pieces tunny (tuna)
2 cloves garlic, slivered
a little mint, chopped
salt, pepper
½ cup (⅔) olive oil

1 small onion, thinly sliced
butter
1 lb. ripe tomatoes, chopped and sieved
¾ cup (1) dry Marsala

Skin the pieces of fish and with the point of a knife, make tiny slits all over them. Into these push slivers of garlic and mint. Sprinkle with salt and pepper and put aside.

Heat the oil and fry the onion until golden. Add the fish pieces, brown them all over, take them from the pan and drain. Rub a casserole with butter, add the fish, sprinkle with salt and pepper and cover with the onion and tomatoes. Add the Marsala. Cover the pan and bake in a moderate oven (350°F., mark 4) for 45–60 minutes. Serve the fish on a hot platter, the sauce poured over the top.

The pieces of fish used for this recipe should be cut from the tail or, as the Sicilians say, the *tarantelle*.

FRIED WHITEBAIT   (*Bianchetti fritti*)   *Liguria*

4 servings:

1 lb. whitebait
oil for deep frying
flour

3 sprigs parsley
1–2 lemons, cut into wedges

Whitebait is a small silvery-white fish, of which there are some seventy species.

In a deep frying pan with a frying basket, heat plenty of oil. Prepare the whitebait. If it is necessary to wash them, do so carefully and pat them dry on a cloth. Dust them with flour, shaking off any excess. Fry the parsley in the hot oil until crisp, remove and drain it. Put the first batch of whitebait into the hot oil and fry them until crisp; they will take 1–2 minutes. Shake the basket gently to make sure the whitebait do not stick together. Drain. Repeat this operation with the rest of the fish (some cooks return them to the hot oil again for an extra crisping). Serve garnished with the parsley and lemon.

WHITING IN VINEGAR SAUCE   (*Merlano* or *Nasello in salsa d'aceto*)   *Sardinia*

6 servings:

6 small whiting, about 1 lb. each
salt
1 oz. (2 tablespoons) butter
½ cup (⅔) wine vinegar

sprig rosemary
1 clove garlic, finely chopped
pepper

The *merlano* which is really a variety of small cod, is the Italian equivalent of the whiting, to which it is related. As they are small, fragile fish they do not travel well and should only be eaten when fresh.

Scale and clean the fish, slit their bellies open from head to tail and remove the head and backbone. Wash them in salted water, dry and arrange them flat, bellies down, in a buttered, shallow baking dish. Sprinkle lightly with salt and dot with butter. Bake in a moderate oven (350°F., mark 4) for 25 minutes or until the fish is tender and lightly browned.

Pour the vinegar with $\frac{1}{2}$ cup ($\frac{2}{3}$) of water into a small pan; add the rosemary, garlic and pepper. Bring this to the boil slowly, simmer for 5 minutes, strain and pour the sauce over the fish just before serving.

FRIED FROGS' LEGS (*Cosce di rane fritte*) *Lombardy*

Although frogs are not fish they are aquatic creatures and custom has placed them among the fish dishes. It is only the tender and delicate white meat from the legs which is eaten. Thomas Coryat, a somewhat neglected British traveller of the seventeenth century, wrote: 'I did eat fried Frogges in this citie (Cremona), which is a dish much used in many cities of Italy; they were so curiously dressed, that they did exceedingly delight my palat, the head and the forepart being cut off.'

Usually frogs' legs are sold prepared for cooking and in pairs.

6 servings:

36 pairs frogs' legs	**flour**
olive oil	**salt**
lemon juice	**wedges of lemon**
parsley, chopped	

Wash the frogs' legs in cold water, wipe them dry and then marinate them for 1 hour in a little oil, lemon juice and parsley. Heat plenty of oil in a deep pan. Drain and dry the frogs' legs, roll them lightly in flour and brown them quickly all over. Sprinkle with salt and serve garnished with wedges of lemon.

FRIED FROGS' LEGS IN BATTER (*Rane fritte*) *Piedmont*

6 servings:

2 lb. frogs' legs, skinned and cleaned	**$\frac{1}{4}$ lb. (1 cup) flour**
white wine	**salt**
3 whole eggs	**olive oil for deep frying**
milk or cream	**1 lemon cut into wedges**

Wash the legs in cold water and wipe them with a damp cloth. Leave them in a bowl with wine to cover for several hours. Prepare a batter. Whisk the eggs with very little milk or cream. Beat the mixture into the flour, add salt and beat until the mixture is like a thick smooth cream. Leave for 1 hour in a cool place.

Have ready a deep frying pan with plenty of boiling oil. Take the legs from the marinade, dry carefully, dip them in the batter, and drop gently into the hot oil. Fry until golden brown, 10–12 minutes. As soon as they are done, take them from the pan and drain quickly. Serve at once with wedges of lemon.

STEAMED FLATFISH (*Sogliola al piatto*) *Apulia*

2 servings:

1 sole	**chopped garlic to taste**
olive oil	**plenty finely-chopped parsley**
salt	**1 lemon**

Clean and trim the fish but keep it whole. Place it on an oval fireproof plate and rub it with oil. Sprinkle with salt and garlic and cover it with the parsley. Put the plate into a shallow pan with bubbling water; the water should not cover the fish. Cover the pan and cook until the fish is tender, about 10–15 minutes. Serve with lemon.

MIXED FRIED FISH (*Fritto misto di pesce*)
ILLUSTRATED PAGE 117

This is a mixture of fish chosen according to season, taste and availability. It can be a mixture of fried sole fillets (dipped usually in egg and breadcrumbs first), scampi, cuttlefish, squid, octopus etc.; a mixture of any of the small fish; or cubes of firm white fish. Providing the fish is fresh, varied, and fried until a golden brown, any combination can be used. Serve with thick wedges of lemon.

FISH STEW (*La cassola*) *Sardinia*

8 servings:

4 lb. assorted fish (see below)	**3 sprigs parsley, finely chopped**
salt	**1 lb. ripe tomatoes, peeled and chopped**
½ cup (⅔) olive oil	**2 cups (2½) dry white wine**
2 cloves garlic, finely chopped	**dried chilli pepper to taste**
1 large onion, finely chopped	**6 slices fried bread**

Assorted fish in Sardinia means dogfish, eel, mullet, skate, sea-bass, gurnard, sea-scorpion and bream or any of the mollusks, i.e. octopus, squid, cuttlefish, plus crab and crayfish.

Clean the fish, cutting off heads, tails, fins etc. Cut the larger fish into neat pieces and wash them in salted water. If using crayfish, cut the tail into small pieces and split the body into two. Put the fish ends, etc., into a large pan and cover with cold, salted water. Bring gently to the boil and cook slowly for 30 minutes. Strain but keep hot.

In another pan heat the oil until very hot. Add the garlic, onion and parsley. Stir and cook until the onion changes colour; add the tomatoes and wine, stir well and cook for 15 minutes. Take ½ cup (⅔) of the hot fish stock from the pan, add it to the tomato mixture, then add the cuttlefish, squid or octopus, all coarsely chopped, salt to taste and the chilli pepper. Cook over a moderate heat for 20 minutes. Add the pieces of firm fish, cook these for 5 minutes, then add the crayfish. Cook gently for 15 minutes; finally add all the remaining fish, plus another cup or two of the fish stock, and cook over a moderate heat until all the fish are tender. Test for seasoning. Put a slice of fried bread into each bowl, cover with the fish and its liquid and top up each bowl with the strained fish stock. Serve at once.

Traditionally a type of ship's biscuit, not bread, should be eaten with this stew.

meat  *carni*

The quality of meat in Italy is variable and the methods of butchering differ from those of most countries. In general Italian butchers cut across the natural muscle separations, and meat is nearly always de-boned. This makes cuts of meat unrecognizable to foreigners. To add to the confusion, butchers throughout the country either have different cuts of meat or they give similar cuts other names. Only one cut of meat seems to remain the same, the fillet, *filetto*. For those foreigners living in Italy it is best to remember that 'when in Rome do as the Romans', and learn the local names.

Most Italians prefer their meat underdone. The Florence *bistecca* can be positively raw, *blu* or *quasi cruda*, unless one asks for *al sangue*, rare, *cotta a puntino*, medium-rare, or *ben cotta*, well done.

Padua, with the largest meat market in Italy, claims the finest meat, in particular beef. Tuscany also has a strong claim to the best beef which comes from one of the oldest, tallest and heaviest breeds of cattle in the world, the *chianina*, whose other important characteristic is its rapid growth. They are large enough for slaughter between fifteen and seventeen months, thus producing a red meat which is not 'baby beef' owing to its size, but neither true beef nor true veal. It is called *vitellone* or large veal, and is roughly the same age as veal in the United States and Britain. It is virtually without fat.

Florence has two meat dishes made from the *vitellone* which are its pride: *bistecca alla fiorentina* and *costata alla fiorentina*, both of which are rib steaks on the bone cut from a young steer, at least an inch thick (priced by their weight in restaurants). They are grilled over charcoal, seasoned with salt and pepper, brushed with olive oil and served with wedges of lemon. Perugia, Umbria's capital, has a cut of veal steak called *mongana* which it considers rivals Florence's *bistecca*.

Italians are veal eaters. It has even been suggested that the word Italy was derived from the word *vitella*; certainly the people of the peninsular were veal eaters before they were known as Italians. On the subject of veal the Tuscans are divided, a not unusual state. South of Florence the Tuscan word for veal is *vitella*, which really means heifer; north of the city it is *vitello*, meat from a calf, an animal which has lived for two or even three months and, say its detractors, often from an even older beast that has simply grown fat in idleness.

There is no such thing as force feeding or quick fattening of pigs in Italy, with the result that pork is of fine quality, firm and lean. Justifiably pork is the pride of Umbria. It would be interesting to know just how many pigs are consumed in Umbria in a year. In Perugia's market one butcher slices and sells a whole spit-roasted pig on each of four mornings a week. Such roasted pigs are sold all over Umbria. Some people take the pork home, others bring a split roll and buy slices of pork to make a sandwich which is consumed on the spot. The butcher supplies the salt.

It does not take much searching to discover the pig, which is raised in the green hills of Umbria and fed on a diet of bran and acorns. It provides a great deal of the alimentation, together with its by-products, to the people of this region. Roast pig is the traditional dish of Umbria. One writer comments that during the festivals, 'these are truly sad days for the pigs, destined to live not more than a year for the satisfaction of man's palate, and find themselves in the oven when they are barely adolescent', but Umbrians see to it that their pigs 'are surrounded by an affection and care during their short stay on earth' —for obvious reasons.

The most unlucky pigs of all, though, are those born in Sardinia which are slaughtered at the age of two or three months. They are cooked *alla bandita*, in a hole dug in the ground between layers of hot embers and wood and liberally seasoned with herbs.

In Umbria the *porchetta*, or young pig, is thoroughly cleaned, filled with its chitterlings, herbs (especially rosemary), spices, fennel, salt, pepper and garlic, and roasted in an oven or on a spit until the meat is tender and the skin crisp and brown.

The most famous of the Umbrian pigs are from Norcia. When a Roman talks of a *norcina* he means not a citizen of Norcia but a pork butcher; and a *norcinaria* is a pork butcher's shop. Among all the usual products of the pig are hams; sausages of every conceivable kind including salami, blood sausages and frying sausages; lard; chitterlings; and, in Norcia, a liver sausage called *mazzafegati dolci*, which is flavoured with garlic, fennel and pine nuts.

The unfortunate, docile looking lamb must surely wish the Italians had fewer holidays during which it is traditional to eat lamb. Lamb meat is usually of good quality, especially in Rome where lamb is sold young. It is not rare to find that a leg of lamb weighing two pounds is the largest in the shop; loin and rib chops are little more than bite-size.

There are hundreds of different ways of cooking lamb in Italy: roasted either on a spit or in the oven, hunter's style, country style etc. In Rome it is the very young lamb which is most favoured, in particular *abbacchio*, unweaned or milk-fed lamb which has never eaten grass. One Roman speciality is the *braciolette a scottadito* (burn-your-fingers cutlets) or small cutlets grilled and thus named because they are traditionally turned over with the fingers, an operation which must be swiftly performed or the fingers are burnt. Another Roman dish is *brodettato*, a stew made with small pieces of lamb, flavoured with an egg and lemon sauce.

Offal, sold only in specialist shops, plays an important role in Italian cooking: liver, brains, sweetbreads, tongue, heart, tripe, kidneys are always available, both from veal and lamb. Offal is not cheap for it is much in demand as Italians, with their usual culinary sense, have made dishes from them of which they are justly proud. Venice boasts of its *fegato alla veneziana*, a dish of paper-thin slices of liver sautéed with sliced onions. Umbria has its *testina di agnello fritta*, fried lamb's head served with slices of lemon. Romans appreciate *testarelle di abbacchio*, lamb's head seasoned with salt, pepper and rosemary and baked in the oven, basted with olive oil. Rome also serves *coda di bue alla vaccinara*, or oxtail simmered in a tomato and celery sauce; also *coratella d'agnello*, considered a workman's dish of lung, heart, liver and spleen fried in olive oil, heavily salted and flavoured with onions. It is supposed to promote drinking.

A more elegant dish of offal is Milan's *finanziera di pollo*, or chicken livers cooked in Madeira; or Calabria's *quagghiariddi*, tripe stuffed with a mixture of salami, cheese and parsley and bound with egg. A speciality from Catanzaro, also in Calabria, is *morseddu*, a dialect word which means 'big bite', basically liver, lungs and heart from the pig or calf cooked in a tomato sauce, flavoured with red peppers and garlic and spread on squares of toasted bread. It is eaten without a knife or fork, hence the name.

Italian cold meats are a joy to eat and imposing to look at, and it is quite impossible to give a complete list of them; there is virtually every kind of meat anyone would wish to buy. The newcomer to Italy is tempted to buy too much for the choice is so wide, so it is comforting to know that one may buy as little as one *etto*, roughly three and a half ounces of each type of meat and thus, in time, probably run the gamut. Probably Bologna with its vast pig population, all of which are finally turned into sausages or pressed preserved meats of some kind, has the finest variety, but Umbria is surely a close second.

POT ROASTED BEEF (*Manzo al grasso d'arrosto*) *Lombardy*

4–6 servings:

2 lb. beef, rolled and tied
3 oz. (6 tablespoons) butter
1 tablespoon (1¼) flour

boiling stock or water
salt, black pepper

Heat the butter, add the flour and stir to a brown roux. Gradually stir in 1 cup (1¼) of stock and add the meat, salt and pepper. Cover and simmer for 4 hours, basting frequently with more hot stock.

To serve, cut the meat into medium-thick slices and arrange them on a hot platter with the gravy poured over the top.

BEEF COOKED IN RED WINE (*Carbonata*) *Valle d'Aosta*

6 servings:

6 slices lean beef (rump or chuck)
3 oz. (6 tablespoons) butter
4–6 onions, sliced
4 tablespoons (5) flour

1 bottle red wine
salt, pepper
nutmeg

Heat the butter, add the steaks and brown them all over. Transfer the meat to a casserole. In the same fat fry the onions until soft, sprinkle them with flour, stir well and cook until they are a golden brown. Spread them over the meat, cover with red wine, season with salt and pepper, add a good sprinkling of nutmeg, and cook over a moderate heat for about 40 minutes.

BEEF STEAK IN A TOMATO AND OREGANO SAUCE *Campania*
(*Bistecca alla pizzaiola*)

Also called *costa di manzo pizzaiola* and *fettine di manzo alla pizzaiola*, this dish is often prepared with veal (*vitellone*) cutlets. *Bistecca* are large rib steaks from a young animal (see page 127).

6 servings:

6 beef steaks	**1 lb. tomatoes, peeled, seeded and**
½ cup (⅔) olive oil	**coarsely chopped**
salt, pepper	**1 tablespoon (1¼) finely-chopped**
2–3 cloves garlic, crushed	**oregano**

Heat the oil in a large heavy frying pan. Add the steaks 2 or 3 at a time, the pan should not be crowded, and fry them on both sides. Sprinkle them with salt, take from the pan but keep hot. Brown the garlic, add the tomatoes and oregano, salt and pepper, and cook for 8 minutes. The tomatoes must be soft but not cooked to a pulp. Return the steaks and simmer until they are tender.

A similar recipe from Naples adds 1 lb. of chopped onions to the sauce and 2 tablespoons (2½) of cream.

VENETIAN STEWED BEEF (*Pastizzada alla veneta*) *Veneto*

6–8 servings:

3–4 lb. beef	**2 cloves**
3 oz. (6 tablespoons) butter	**pinch powdered cinnamon**
1 small onion, finely chopped	**1 pint (2½ cups) red wine vinegar**
salt, pepper	**2 stalks celery, coarsely chopped**
½ cup (⅔) Marsala	**1 sprig rosemary**
½ cup (⅔) white wine	**salt**
marinade:	**5–6 peppercorns**
2 cloves garlic	

Mix the marinade ingredients in a bowl, add the meat and leave for 12 hours. Take out the meat and wipe it dry.

Heat the butter in a heavy pan and gently fry the onion; add the meat, brown it all over, add salt, pepper, Marsala and white wine. Cover the pan and simmer for 3 hours or until the meat is tender.

To serve, slice the meat and spread with its gravy.

STEWED BEEF (*Stracotto*) *Tuscany*

6 servings:

2½–3 lb. lean beef in one flat piece	**1 clove garlic**
strip of larding or bacon fat, diced	**salt, pepper**
2 leaves sage	**½ oz. (1 tablespoon) butter**
1 sprig rosemary	**1 tablespoon (1¼) flour**

Stud the meat with the fat. Pound the herbs, garlic, salt and pepper to a paste and spread it over the beef. Roll and tie it up neatly and put into a heavy pan. Add water to half-way up the side of the meat, cover and cook over a moderate heat until almost all the liquid has been absorbed and the meat is tender. Turn occasionally.

Take the beef from the pan, put aside but keep hot. Knead the butter and flour together, stir into the remaining liquid and cook until it is thick, stirring all the time. To serve, slice the meat and strain the sauce over the top.

BRAISED BEEF IN BAROLO WINE (*Manzo brasato al barolo*) *Lombardy*

6–8 servings:

3 lb. beef, round or topside	**1 bottle Barolo (dry red wine)**
green herbs to taste, chopped	**1 oz. (1 cup) dried mushrooms**
2 carrots, chopped	**flour**
1 stalk celery, chopped	**½ lb. bacon fat, chopped**
1 onion, chopped	**2 tablespoons (2½) olive oil**
2 cloves garlic	**1 onion, minced**
6 peppercorns	**salt**
1 bay leaf	

Put the meat into a large bowl and add the chopped herbs and vegetables, garlic, pepper-corns, bay leaf and wine. Leave for 12–24 hours in the refrigerator, turning occasionally. Soak the mushrooms in tepid water for 30 minutes.

Take the meat from the marinade, dry it and roll in flour, shaking off any excess. Strain the marinade. Heat the bacon fat and oil together, add the minced onion and, when it changes colour, add the meat and brown it all over. Add salt, the mushrooms with their liquid, and the marinade. Bring to a slow boil then simmer for at least 3 hours —but up to 6 hours is allowed; or cook the meat for 3 hours one day and again the next day for an hour or two, this improves its flavour. Do not stint on the wine in this recipe.

To serve, slice the meat thickly and strain the sauce directly over it.

BABY LAMB (*Abbacchio alla romana*) *Lazio*

The best cuts of baby lamb are the leg and loin as the shoulders are too lean.

4 servings:

2 lb. lamb, leg or loin	**½ cup (⅔) red wine vinegar**
1½ oz. (3 tablespoons) lard	**1–2 sprigs rosemary**
salt, pepper	**½ clove garlic**
½ cup (⅔) white wine	**4 anchovy fillets, chopped**

Wipe the meat with a damp cloth and cut it into cubes. Heat the lard and quickly brown the meat. Add plenty of salt and pepper, stir, add the wine and vinegar and cook for 5 minutes. Add the rosemary, garlic and anchovies, cover the pan and cook slowly for 20–30 minutes until the meat is tender and the sauce like a dark thick glaze which covers the meat. Discard the rosemary and garlic before serving.

LAMB WITH SWEET PEPPERS (*Agnello con peperoni*) *Abruzzi-Molise*

6 servings:

3 lb. lamb	**2 cups (2½) dry white wine**
salt, pepper	**8 sweet peppers, yellow and red**
flour	**4 tomatoes, peeled and chopped**
4 tablespoons (5) olive oil	**1 bay leaf**
2 cloves garlic, crushed	

Wipe the meat with a damp cloth and chop it into small pieces. Sprinkle with salt and pepper and roll it lightly in flour. Heat the oil, add the garlic, and when it is brown, add the meat and brown it well. Add the wine. Cut the peppers into wide strips, discarding the core and seeds. Add these with the tomatoes and bay leaf to the pan and cook over a moderate heat for 30–40 minutes or until the meat is tender.

ROAST LAMB WITH POTATOES AND ONIONS *Campania*
(*Agnello al forno con patate e cipolle*)

6 servings:

3 lb. leg lamb	**½ cup (⅔) olive oil**
1 clove garlic, finely chopped	**1½ oz. (3 tablespoons) lard**
a sprig rosemary	**12 small onions**
salt, pepper	**2 lb. new potatoes**

Wipe the meat with a damp cloth. Make small incisions with the point of a sharp knife in the flesh and insert into these the garlic and rosemary. Rub the meat with salt and pepper, put it into a roasting pan, brush with oil and spread with lard. Roast in a hot oven (450°F., mark 8) until tender, 1–1½ hours.

Trim the onions, scrub the potatoes and add them to the roasting pan after 15 minutes cooking. Turn the meat occasionally and baste.

Lamb is cooked in this way throughout Italy.

LAMB STEW (*Spezzatino di agnello*) *Lazio*

6 servings:

3 lb. lamb, leg or shoulder	**juice 1 lemon**
flour	**salt, pepper**
4 oz. (½ cup) butter	**1 cup (1¼) white wine**
4 slices fat bacon, diced	**1 tablespoon (1¼) tomato paste**
1 small onion, chopped	**1 cup (1¼) stock**
1 stalk celery, chopped	

Wipe the meat with a damp cloth and cut it into cubes. Dredge them with flour. Heat the butter and bacon, add the meat and brown it well. Add the onion, celery, lemon juice, seasoning and wine. Dilute the tomato paste with the stock, add it to the pan and cook for 1–1½ hours or until tender.

STEWED MUTTON   (*Stracotto di castrato*)   *Tuscany*

6 servings:

3–4 lb. boned mutton	1 clove garlic, finely chopped
2 oz. pork fat or ham for larding	a few sage leaves, finely chopped
½ cup (⅔) olive oil	1 sprig parsley, finely chopped
1 onion, sliced	1 cup (1¼) dry white Chianti
2 carrots, finely chopped	salt, pepper
2 stalks celery, finely chopped	1 cup (1¼) stock

Mutton is the nearest translation of *castrato*, the meat of a castrated ram which, although more tender than the flesh of a regular ram or ewe, is still not a tender meat; but it has a very distinctive and strong flavour which is much appreciated by many Italians.

Lard the meat with strips of fat pork and tie it securely into a good shape. Heat the oil, add the vegetables and herbs, then the meat and brown it all over. Add the wine, let this cook for a few minutes and add salt, pepper and the stock. Cook over a low heat, tightly covered, until the meat is very tender, about 3 hours depending on the quality of the meat. If necessary, add a little more hot stock.

Take the meat from the pan, cut it into medium-thick slices, strain the sauce over the top and serve hot.

POT ROAST LEG OF MUTTON   (*Cosciotto di castrato*)   *Abruzzi-Molise*

6 servings:

3–4 lb. leg mutton	1 stalk celery, finely chopped
salt, pepper	1 cup (1¼) dry white wine
¼ lb. sliced fat bacon	1 lb. tomatoes, peeled, seeded
fresh rosemary	and chopped
½ cup (⅔) olive oil	2–3 sprigs parsley, chopped
2 cloves garlic, crushed	fresh oregano or marjoram to taste,
1 onion, finely chopped	chopped
2 carrots, finely chopped	

Wipe the meat with a damp cloth and rub it lightly with salt and pepper and leave for 1 hour. Wrap it in slices of bacon and tie them on securely. Push rosemary under the bacon.

Heat the oil in a heavy pan, add the garlic, chopped vegetables and the meat. Brown the meat evenly all over. Add the wine, raise the heat and cook quickly for a few minutes. Add the tomatoes and herbs and enough water to come one-third up the side of the meat. Cover, lower the heat and simmer for 1½ hours or until the meat is tender, basting occasionally. Take out the meat and discard the bacon. Strain the sauce. Serve the meat and sauce separately.

ROAST FILLET OF PORK IN MILK (*Arrosto di maiale al latte*) *Veneto*

5–6 servings:

2½ lb. pork fillet
1 sprig rosemary
2 oz. (4 tablespoons) butter

2–3 sage leaves
salt, pepper
2 pints (2½) milk

Trim the pork and tie it up neatly with string to preserve its shape while cooking. Push the rosemary in the middle. Heat the butter in a casserole, add the sage, fry it a little, add the meat and brown it all over. Add salt and pepper. In another pan bring the milk just to the boil, pour it over the pork and cook slowly until the meat is tender. The sauce will be creamy and a golden brown. Take the pork from the pan and slice it.

A variation is to take the meat from the pan, slice and keep it hot and cook sliced mushrooms in the sauce, or these can be cooked separately and poured over the top of the meat when serving. Yet another variation is to add a sprinkling of grated truffle, with or without the mushrooms.

1 *Salame tipo milano*
2 *Coppa*
3 *Salame tipo varzi*
4 *Mortadellina*
5 *Salame milano bindone*
6 *Salame milano bindonetto*
7 *Capocolo*
8 *Culattello*
9 *Negronetto*
10 *Salame casalingo*
11 *Zampone belle pronto*
12 *Salsiccia italiana*
13 *Salame ligure*
14 *Salsiccia tipo napoletano*
15 *Zampone*
16 *Provolone*
17 *Coppa di zibello*
18 *Mortadella con il pistacchio*
19 *Provoloncino*
20 *Cacietta*
21 *Cotechino*
22 *Negronetto*
23 *Parma ham*
24 *Mortadella*
25 *Reggianetto*
26 *Salame mugnano*
27 *Bel Paese*
28 *Campagnolo*
29 *Pecorino*
30 *Provolone picante*
31 *Dolcelatte*
32 *Parmesan*
33 *Gorgonzola*
34 *Fontina*

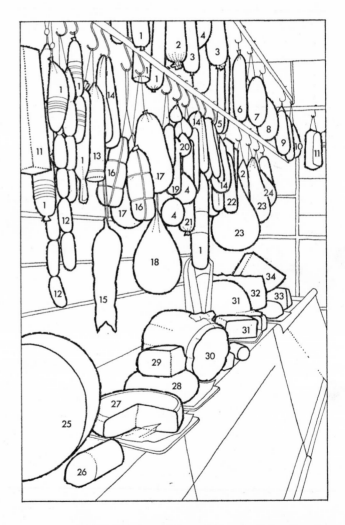

The interior of Parmiaggani, Soho, London, showing the wide variety of Italian cheeses and sausages.

PORK CHOPS FLAVOURED WITH FENNEL   *Tuscany*
(*Costolette di maiale al finocchio*)

6 servings:

6 medium-thick pork chops	**salt, pepper**
2 tablespoons (2½) olive oil	**¼ teaspoon (⅓) fennel seeds**
1 clove garlic	**red Chianti**

Heat the oil in a heavy frying pan, brown the garlic and discard it. Rub the chops with salt, pepper and fennel seeds and fry them on both sides until brown. Add a little Chianti and continue cooking until the chops are tender.

PORK CHOPS WITH ONIONS   (*Braciole con cipolle*)   *Umbria*

6 servings:

6 loin pork chops	**salt, pepper**
olive oil	**¼ cup (⅓) dry white wine**
3 large mild onions	

Peel the onions and cut them into halves horizontally. Heat ¼ cup (6 tablespoons) of oil, add the onions and cook gently until soft; sprinkle lightly with salt and pepper. Rub the chops all over with a little oil and grill them slowly on both sides until brown and tender. Place them in a shallow baking dish, sprinkle with the wine, salt and pepper and top each with half an onion. Bake in a moderate oven (350°F., mark 4) for 10 minutes.

DRUNKEN PORK CHOPS   (*Maiale ubriaco*)   *Tuscany*

3–6 servings:

6 medium-sized pork chops	**salt, black pepper**
butter for frying	**red wine, preferably Chianti**
juice 1 lemon	

Rub a large heavy frying pan with butter. Rub the chops with lemon juice and sprinkle them with salt and black pepper. Heat the pan, add the chops and, over a moderate heat, brown them on both sides. Add wine to cover and simmer the chops until tender, turning them once or twice. Most of the wine will evaporate but what is left should be poured over the chops immediately before serving.

Sliced oranges in Marsala (page 168); Ricotta cream cake (page 166); coffee, lemon and strawberry water ices (pages 169–170)

BRAISED VEAL SHIN BONES (*Ossobuco* or *ossibuchi*) *Lombardy*

This is one of the great dishes of Milan and it is always served with rice, usually *risotto alla milanese* (see page 102). There are two highlights with an *ossobuco*: its flavouring, the *gremolata*, and the marrow from the bones. A small marrow fork is supplied to help dig out this delicacy which is usually spread on chunks of bread.

6 servings:

6 veal shin bones between 2½–3 inches long, or veal shank with plenty of marrow and some meat attached	**½ cup (⅔) dry white wine**
salt, pepper	**6 large ripe tomatoes, peeled, seeded and chopped**
flour	**1 clove garlic, minced**
4 oz. (½ cup) butter	**1 teaspoon (1¼) grated lemon rind**
	2 tablespoons (2½) minced parsley

The bones should be cooked in a shallow pan which holds them comfortably standing upright so that the marrow does not fall out.

Sprinkle the bones with salt and pepper and dredge them lightly with flour. Heat the butter, add the bones and brown them all round. Turn the bones so that they are standing upright, add the wine, cook for 10 minutes, then add the tomatoes. Cover the pan tightly and simmer until the meat on the bones is so tender it almost falls off, about 1–1½ hours.

Mix the remaining ingredients and sprinkle over the top 3 minutes before serving.

VEAL 'BIRDS' (*Uccelletti di vitello* or *Braciolette ripiene*) *Tuscany*

Many are the different names and stuffings for this favourite way of cooking both veal and beef prepared throughout Italy. These stuffed meat rolls are called 'birds' because they are cooked in the manner of small birds.

6 servings:

12 thin slices veal or beef	**2 tablespoons (2½) sultanas (white raisins)**
2 slices bread	**12 strips fat bacon**
2 cups (2½) pine nuts	**olive oil**
2 tablespoons (2½) finely-chopped parsley	**½ cup (⅔) white wine**
2 tablespoons (2½) grated Parmesan cheese	

Soak the bread in water and squeeze it dry. Pound the meat until thin but unbroken. Combine the bread with the nuts, parsley, cheese and sultanas to make a stuffing. Cover each slice of meat with a strip of bacon, add a little stuffing, roll it up and fasten each roll with a toothpick. Heat enough oil to cover the bottom of a large heavy frying pan, brown the veal rolls all over, then add the wine and simmer until tender, about 20 minutes.

BREADED VEAL CUTLETS (*Costolette alla milanese*) *Lombardy*

This is a recipe of Spanish origin said to have been brought by the Spanish troops of Charles V to Italy. It flourished in Milan and was praised as an Italian dish in an official report to the Austrian Emperor Franz Josef. It became the rage in Vienna and was named *Wiener Schnitzel*. Only young, tender veal can be used for this recipe.

6 servings:

6 veal cutlets with bone	**fine dry breadcrumbs**
salt	**4 oz. ($\frac{1}{2}$ cup) butter**
2 eggs, well beaten	**lemon**

Trim the cutlets, pound them gently until flat, and nick them lightly round the edges to prevent curling during cooking. Sprinkle with salt and coat with egg and breadcrumbs, pressing the breadcrumbs well down.

   Heat the butter in a heavy pan and fry the cutlets rapidly until brown on both sides. Watch the heat for if it is too high the butter will burn. Reduce the heat and simmer for 5 minutes or until tender. Serve with lemon.

VEAL CUTLETS COOKED IN WHITE WINE *Lombardy*
(*Arrostini annegati al vino bianco*)

3 servings:

6 small veal cutlets	**1 sprig sage**
flour	**1 sprig rosemary**
2 oz. (4 tablespoons) butter	**1 cup ($1\frac{1}{4}$) dry white wine**
1 oz. (2 tablespoons) fat bacon, diced	**salt**

Wipe the cutlets with a damp cloth, pat them dry and nick round the edge of each to prevent curling while cooking. Dredge them with flour. Heat the butter and bacon in a heavy frying pan. Fry the sage and rosemary for 1 minute. Add the cutlets and brown on both sides. Pour off the fat and discard the herbs. Add the wine and a pinch of salt and cook over a low heat for 20–30 minutes. Turn the cutlets once or twice and baste frequently. When serving, spoon a little of the sauce over each cutlet.

VEAL WITH TUNNY FISH (*Vitello tonnato*) *Lombardy*

6 servings:

2 lb. leg veal	**salt, pepper**
1 cup ($1\frac{1}{4}$) dry white wine (optional)	**7–8 oz. can tunny (tuna) fish**
1 carrot, 1 stalk celery, 1 onion, all chopped	**3 anchovy fillets**
	2 egg yolks
juice 1 lemon	**$\frac{1}{4}$ cup ($\frac{1}{3}$) olive oil**
2 bay leaves	**1 tablespoon ($1\frac{1}{4}$) capers**
2 cloves	

Soak the veal for 30 minutes in cold water. Dry it thoroughly and put it into a pan with the wine, vegetables, 2 teaspoons (2½) of lemon juice, bay leaves, cloves, salt and pepper. Bring slowly to the boil, lower the heat and cook until the veal is tender. If using *vitella da latte*, milk calf, it will take about 1½ hours; older veal somewhat longer. When the meat is tender, take it from the pan, pat it dry and leave uncovered until cold.

Pound the tunny in a mortar (or purée it in a blender) with the anchovies, then rub it through a fine sieve. Beat the egg yolks separately with the remaining lemon juice, then add enough oil, drop by drop, to make a fluid dressing. Add the tunny paste and whisk until the dressing is creamy. Lastly add the capers.

Cut the veal into thin slices and spread each slice lightly with dressing. Arrange them in a serving dish and spread with the remaining dressing. Cover and leave in a cool place for several hours before serving. Garnish with slices of lemon and fresh parsley. Use either as an antipasto or as a main dish.

The veal can be left up to 3 days in the sauce. There are 2–3 recipes for this dish, varying only slightly.

VEAL CUTLETS WITH MARSALA (*Scaloppine di vitello al marsala*) *Lazio*

3–4 servings:

1½ lb. veal cutlets, without bone	4 oz. (8 tablespoons) butter
salt, pepper	½ cup (⅔) dry Marsala
flour	2 tablespoons (2½) stock or water

Pound the cutlets until thin. Sprinkle with salt and pepper and lightly coat them with flour. Heat the butter in a frying pan, add all the veal and brown quickly on both sides over a high heat. Pour the Marsala over the top and cook 1 minute longer. Put the cutlets in a serving dish, quickly stir the stock into the gravy, scrape the pan, pour the sauce over the cutlets and serve.

Piccata al marsala are thin slices of veal cooked in the same manner. Only young, tender veal can be cooked in the above fashion.

VEAL CUTLETS WITH HAM (*I 'saltimbocca'* or *Saltimbocca alla romana*) *Lazio*

The literal translation of *saltimbocca* is 'jump in the mouth', and when tender, thin slices of veal are cooked, it almost does that. This is a recipe which originated in Brescia but was 'naturalized' by the Romans.

6 servings:

12 3-inch-long thin slices veal	12 leaves fresh sage
4 thin slices prosciutto (smoked ham)	3 oz. (6 tablespoons) butter
salt, pepper	

Gently pound the veal pieces until they are very thin. Cut each slice of *prosciutto* into 3 pieces. Sprinkle the veal lightly with salt and pepper, put 1 leaf of sage on to each piece, cover with a slice of *prosciutto* and secure with a toothpick. Heat the butter in a pan large enough to take all the *saltimbocca* at the same time (however, if you cannot fry them simultaneously, start frying with only half the butter, adding the rest with the next batch). Fry the *saltimbocca* over a brisk heat; if the meat is tender, as it should be, they will take about 5 minutes to cook. Serve immediately.

A little white wine is often quickly stirred into the butter and strained over the *saltimbocca* immediately before serving.

MIXED BOILED MEATS (*Bolliti misti o bollito misto*) Piedmont

Although of Piedmont origin, this great dish is served throughout the northern and the central provinces of Italy, but it is not easily imitated outside the country. It consists of a fine selection of boiled meats which may include chicken, beef, spiced sausages, *zampone* (which is stuffed pig's foot), tongue, pig's knuckle, trotter and head. On special occasions turkey and capon are added. At its best, which is in Piedmont, it is superb; and it is at its most dramatic (in my experience) at the La Rosetta Hotel in Perugia, where an enormous dish of unsliced boiled meats (including a pig's head in season) is brought on a trolley to the table for the client to make his choice and have sliced in front of him.

It is not a dish easily prepared at home for a small family, for the character of the dish lies in both the quantity and the variety of the meats.

This is a dish of meat with which vegetables are served, usually white haricot beans, cabbage and potatoes, and essentially a bowl of *salsa verde* (see page 163). The meats are all served hot on a large platter, surrounded by the vegetables.

MIXED FRY (*Fritto misto*)

This is one of the well-known Italian specialities which, basically, is a mixture of fried meat, vegetables, etc., all fried separately and served on a large platter. Naturally the *misto* differs from region to region and several towns lay claim to the best, Milan in particular. Emilia, for example, calls its selection *grande fritto misto all'emiliana*. However, since all the mixtures must be seasonal, those wanting to prepare a *fritto misto*, typical of the country rather than of one region, can choose any of the following vegetables (some of which, like cauliflower flowerets, must be parboiled before frying), plus any meat which is piquant, small and takes to the frying pan: lamb, pork or veal cutlets; sliced veal and beef; chicken and turkey breasts; liver, kidneys, brains, sweetbreads; smoked ham or even bacon can be used.

VEGETABLES: The most suitable are courgettes (zucchini) with their flowers (the latter dipped in batter); aubergines (eggplants) cut into cubes; baby artichokes in batter; and celery.

CROQUETTES: These can be made from any ground meats or rice; potatoes, mixed and mashed and other vegetables.

FRITTERS: Oddly, apple fritters are popular (at least in Emilia); cheese fritters; leftover noodles mixed with grated cheese and bound with an egg, make good fritters (another speciality from Emilia and, naturally, they use *tagliatelle*); in fact, any kind of light savoury fritter may be added to this splendid dish of 'how to use up the little bits in the refrigerator'.

It is customary to use two or three of any of the above mentioned ingredients, up to perhaps six. It is important with any *fritto misto* that everything is of the best quality and, as far as possible, all of equal size. It is equally important that the *fritto misto* must be served immediately it is cooked, for fried foods are not worth eating lukewarm. Serve with thick slices of lemon.

SWEETBREADS WITH MUSHROOMS (*Animelle di vitello coi funghi*) *Tuscany*

6 servings:

1½ lb. calves' sweetbreads	½ cup (⅔) white wine
flour	½ cup (⅔) olive oil
3 oz. (6 tablespoons) butter	1 clove garlic, finely chopped
1 small onion, sliced	1 lb. mushrooms, sliced
salt, pepper	2–3 sprigs parsley, finely chopped

Blanch the sweetbreads, i.e. put them into cold water and bring to a slow boil. Boil gently for 10 minutes. Drain and plunge them into cold water. Cut away all the membrane. Put the sweetbreads between 2 plates with a weight on top and leave them for 2 hours. Dredge with flour.

Heat half the butter, fry the onion until soft, add the sweetbreads, brown them, season with salt and pepper, and add the wine. In another pan heat the oil with the remaining butter, fry the garlic until brown, discard it, add the mushrooms, a pinch of salt, and the parsley. Cook over a low heat for a few minutes. Add the sweetbreads and liquid, stir gently and simmer for 2 minutes.

KIDNEYS WITH LEMON (*Rognoni di vitello trifolati*)

2–4 servings:

2 veal kidneys	finely-chopped parsley to taste
2 tablespoons (2½) olive oil	juice 1 lemon
salt, pepper	

Remove the fat and skin from the kidneys and slice them thinly. Heat the oil, then add the sliced kidneys and cook them quickly, stirring all the time—they should cook over an almost dry pan. Add the salt, pepper and parsley and finally the lemon juice, stirring all the time. Cook for a minute or so longer and serve at once.

TONGUE IN A SWEET-SOUR SAUCE *Tuscany*
(*Lingua di bue o di vitello in salsa agrodolce*)

4–6 servings:

2 lb. cooked tongue	1 tablespoon (1¼) each pine nuts and raisins
2 oz. (4 tablespoons) butter	
2 tablespoons (2½) flour	1 heaped tablespoon (1½) grated orange peel
red wine and stock mixed	
2 tablespoons (2½) brown sugar	¼ cup (⅓) red Chianti

Heat the butter, add the flour, stir until the mixture is smooth and then add enough wine and stock to make a medium-thick sauce. Add the sugar, pine nuts, raisins and orange peel and cook for 15 minutes, stirring occasionally. Add the tongue, cook until hot, add the Chianti, stir, and cook gently for another 10 minutes.

This sauce also goes well with cooked ham.

LIVER AND ONIONS (*Fegato alla veneziana*) *Veneto*

3 servings:

¾ lb. calves' liver, sliced paper-thin	½ cup (⅔) dry white wine (optional)
1½ oz. (3 tablespoons) butter	1 tablespoon (1¼) minced parsley
2 tablespoons (2½) olive oil	salt, pepper
2 large onions, thinly sliced	

Heat the butter and oil together, add the onions and fry them until soft. Add the liver and lightly brown it on both sides. If adding wine, do so at this point and simmer for 5 minutes. Sprinkle with parsley, salt and pepper. Serve at once.

PORK LIVER FRIED ON A SPIT (*Fegatelli di maiale alla toscana*) *Tuscany*

3–6 servings:

1½ lb. pig's liver	a little rosemary
½ lb. pig's caul, cut into 6 squares	4 tablespoons (5) olive oil
8 small squares fat bacon	salt, pepper
4 bay leaves	

Buy the liver in 1 piece and cut it into 6 pieces. Wrap each piece in a square of caul and thread the pieces on to 2 skewers. At both ends and between each piece of liver, thread a square of bacon fat and half a bay leaf. Sprinkle with rosemary. Heat the oil in a shallow pan, add half as much water, and the salt and pepper. Stir the mixture well until it is hot, add the skewers of meat and cook until the liver is tender, turning frequently.

STUFFED MEAT LOAF (*Polpettone alla siciliana*) *Sicily*
ILLUSTRATED PAGE 118

6 servings:

1 lb. beef in 1 slice (topside)	hard-boiled eggs, sliced, to taste
2 slices bread, crustless	a few strips salami, to taste
milk	diced Caciocavallo cheese, to taste
1¼ lb. ground beef	2 tablespoons (2½) olive oil
2 eggs, beaten	1 onion, thinly sliced
3 tablespoons (3¾) grated Pecorino or Parmesan cheese	1 cup (1¼) red wine
salt, pepper	1 tablespoon (1¼) tomato paste
finely-chopped parsley to taste	¼ cup (⅓) water

Soak the bread in a little milk until soft, then squeeze it dry. Mix it with the ground beef, eggs, cheese, salt, pepper and parsley in a bowl and work the mixture until blended. Put aside.

Spread out the beef on a board and pound it firmly until thin. Sprinkle with salt and pepper and spread with the filling, then with the hard-boiled eggs, salami and Cacio-cavallo. Roll up neatly to a thick sausage shape and secure with string.

Heat the oil in a heavy pan and fry the onion until soft. Add the meat roll and brown it all over. Sprinkle with salt and pepper, add the wine and tomato paste diluted with water. Cover and simmer until tender.

Serve hot or cold cut into thick slices. If served hot, spread with the sauce.

LAMB BRAINS   (*Cervelli di agnello alla napoletana*)   *Campania*

3–4 servings:

4 lamb brains	**12 black olives, pitted and chopped**
olive oil	**breadcrumbs**
2 tablespoons (2½) dry white wine	**2 oz. (4 tablespoons) butter, melted**
1 teaspoon (1¼) capers	

Soak the brains for 20 minutes in cold water. Drain them. Put them into a pan, cover with fresh cold water and bring to the boil. Drain, rinse in cold water and pat dry. Rub the bottom of a casserole with oil, add the brains, wine, capers and olives. Sprinkle with breadcrumbs and the melted butter. Bake in a hot oven (450°F., mark 8) for 10–15 minutes or until the top is brown.

TRIPE FLORENTINE STYLE   (*Trippa alla fiorentina*)   *Tuscany*

6 servings:

2½ lb. parboiled tripe, cut into strips	**salt, pepper**
2–3 tablespoons (2½–3¾) olive oil	**1 teaspoon (1¼) lemon juice**
1 small onion, sliced	**2 cloves garlic**
3 oz. (scant ¼ cup) ground beef	**good grating nutmeg**
2 teaspoons (2½) tomato paste	**stock or water**
½ cup (⅔) dry white wine	**Parmesan cheese, grated**
1 sage leaf, chopped	**finely-chopped parsley or mint to taste**

Heat the oil in a heavy pan, add the onion and fry it until soft. Add the ground meat, stir well into the onion with a fork to prevent it forming a lump, and add the tomato paste diluted with the wine, sage, salt, pepper, lemon juice, garlic and nutmeg. Cook slowly to a thick sauce. Remove the garlic. Add the tripe and just enough stock to cover it. Stir until the sauce coats the tripe. Add 1 tablespoon (1¼) of Parmesan, cover the pan and cook gently for about 1 hour or until the tripe is very tender. Serve hot, sprinkled with Parmesan cheese and parsley.

This is a recipe from Nonna Pia who, at 81 years of age, runs the family restaurant, Tripoli, in Lucca and still does the cooking.

SAUSAGES   (*Salsicce*)

Italian sausages are usually available in Italian stores in Britain and the United States.

PORK SAUSAGES COOKED WITH WHITE GRAPES   *Umbria*
(*Salsicce con l'uva fresca*)

3–4 servings:

1½ lb. pork sausages	**2 tablespoons (2½) olive oil**
1 lb. white grapes	**2 tablespoons (2½) white wine or water**

If using large firm grapes, peel and seed them; seedless grapes can be left as they are.

Prick the sausages with a fork. Heat the oil, add the wine, then the sausages and cook until they brown, 10–15 minutes. Add the grapes, cover the pan and cook gently for 15 minutes. Serve the sausages in their sauce.

WHITE CABBAGE WITH PORK SAUSAGES (*Verzada*) *Lombardy*

4 servings:

8 Italian sausages	**3–4 thin slices streaky bacon**
1 large firm white cabbage, about 2 lb.	**1 medium-sized onion, minced**
salt	**2–3 tablespoons (2½–3¾) wine vinegar**
2 oz. (4 tablespoons) butter	

Wash the cabbage in plenty of cold, salted water, discard any coarse or badly bruised leaves. Cut it into 4. Shred finely and discard the hard core. Heat the butter in a heavy pan, add the bacon, fry until its fat is rendered, then fry the onion until soft. Add the cabbage, stir until it is well coated with fat, cover the pan and cook over a moderate heat until the cabbage begins to soften. Add the vinegar and salt to taste and stir well. Prick the sausages with a fork and arrange them on top of the cabbage. Cover the pan and cook over a low heat for about 1 hour. Serve the cabbage on a platter garnished with the sausages.

SAUSAGE AND POTATO PIE (*Pasticcio di patate con le salsicce*)

Abruzzi-Molise

4–6 servings:

½ lb. pork sausages	**pepper**
2 lb. floury potatoes	**1½ oz. (⅓ cup) grated Parmesan cheese**
salt	**lukewarm milk**
butter	**2 egg yolks, beaten**
nutmeg	

Wash the potatoes and cook them, in their skins, in boiling, salted water until tender. While they are cooking, prepare the sausages. Pull off the skins, crumble the meat with a fork and fry them in their own fat over a low heat for about 15 minutes or until they are brown. Sausages vary, so exact cooking time is difficult to give.

Drain the potatoes, cool and peel them. Rub them through a potato masher and mix with 2 oz. (4 tablespoons) of butter, a good sprinkling of nutmeg, pepper, Parmesan, and enough milk to make them creamy. Add the egg yolks, beat them well into the potatoes, then add the sausage meat and mix well. Pour this mixture into a well-buttered deep baking dish and bake in a moderate oven (350°F., mark 4) for about 20 minutes or until a light brown crust has formed on the top.

Minced fresh pork can be used instead of sausages.

poultry and game  *pollame e cacciagione*

The Italians consider that some of their finest dishes are based on poultry. They rarely cook chickens weighing less than one pound. Also they distinguish hens from seven months old calling them *pollastra*, pullets, prizing them for their tenderness and general flavour. Until as recently as the 1950's no self-respecting Italian cook would consider buying other than live poultry. Most country women still buy them this way and so do many others in the towns. One often sees a couple of Italian housewives gossiping in the street carrying a patient live fowl. However, supermarkets with their dressed and frozen chickens have also brought in their wake the poulterer who handles dressed chickens, although still free-range.

Every bit of the chicken is used in Italy, including the feet, glands and innards for making a soup stock. Such 'bits' can also be bought in the markets, cleaned and ready for cooking. In the South chitterlings are made with the innards of the chicken, not with pork as they are elsewhere.

Spit-roasted chicken flavoured with rosemary has become almost a national Italian dish. It is sold in the supermarkets, the delicatessen stores and, of course, served in all the rotisseries, garnished with lemon.

Apart from chickens, Italians have a great fondness for turkey, capon, duck, goose and guinea fowl, and especially rabbit, the latter is generally available throughout the year and in some areas it is one of the cheapest Italian meats, in others the dearest.

A game bird is almost any bird which flies and sometimes it seems that no birds fly in Italy. There are of course game laws, but many small birds, protected in Britain and the United States are shot in this country. Thrush cooked on a spit is considered a delicacy; their flesh is well-flavoured with olives, on which they feed. In Veneto and Lombardy small spit-roasted birds, larks, thrushes and fieldfare are served in a rich sauce with polenta.

There is a good supply of furred game. Wild rabbit and hare among the smaller creatures, deer and wild boar among the larger. Sardinia has plenty of the last named. Once the Sardinians hunted the moufflon, a species of wild sheep, but almost to extinction, so this is now protected by law.

Italy does have a game season, but it appears that the season is not always closely observed. However, during the season the choice of game in the poultry and game shops in Italy is positively bewildering.

CHICKEN HUNTER'S STYLE (*Pollo alla cacciatora* or *Pollo alla fiorentina*) *Tuscany*

4 servings:

4 lb. chicken, cut into 4
½ cup (⅔) olive oil
2–3 slices streaky bacon (pancetta)
1 clove garlic, crushed
1 small onion, thinly sliced
salt, pepper to taste
1 cup (1¼) boiling chicken stock

1 cup (1¼) dry white wine
½ lb. mushrooms, sliced
1 lb. ripe tomatoes, peeled, seeded and chopped
2–3 sprigs parsley, finely chopped
fresh herbs to taste

Heat the oil in a wide, shallow pan and add the bacon, garlic, onion and chicken. Fry these over a good heat until the chicken is brown. Add the remaining ingredients. Stir gently to coat the chicken, cover and cook over a moderate heat for 1¼–1½ hours or until tender. Discard the garlic and serve the chicken in the sauce.

Many recipes are labelled hunter's style and the Italians argue among themselves whether this or that ingredient should be included, in particular tomatoes. Many *cacciatori* recipes are more elaborate than the above, others more simple.

Guinea hen, *faraona*, is cooked in the same way.

CHICKEN WITH GREEN OLIVES (*Pollo con olive verdi*) *Apulia*

4 servings:

3½–4 lb. chicken, cut into 4
2 tablespoons (2½) olive oil
3 oz. (6 tablespoons) butter
1 large onion, finely chopped
1–2 cloves garlic, finely chopped
2 sweet peppers, cored, seeded and quartered

½ lb. mushrooms, sliced
2 large tomatoes, peeled and halved
salt, pepper
½ cup (⅔) dry white wine
½ lb. green olives, pitted
½ cup (⅔) cream

Heat the oil and the butter together. Fry the chicken until it is brown. Take it from the pan and put aside. Add the onion, garlic, sweet peppers, mushrooms and tomatoes to the pan, mix them well and put the chicken on top. Add salt, pepper and the wine. Cover and simmer for 1¼–1½ hours or until the chicken is tender. Add the olives and cream, stir gently and taste for seasoning.

CHICKEN TUSCANY STYLE (*Pollo al mattone*) *Tuscany*
ILLUSTRATED PAGE 118

A *mattone* is a round, thick cooking platter made from red brick terracotta and glazed on the top. With it goes an exceptionally heavy 'lid' of the same material.

I doubt whether a *mattone* is available in England; failing one, follow the directions using instead a thick, heavy frying pan and a lid on which a heavy weight can be placed. The result in flavour will be much the same, but not quite since earthenware does impart a certain something of its own.

Have ready either 2 halves of a small, tender chicken or some chicken pieces. Rub these lightly with oil and sprinkle with pepper. Rub the platter with oil, just enough to prevent sticking, add the chicken pieces, cover with the lid and cook over a low heat until tender and a golden brown, about 30 minutes if the heat is low.

Cooked in this manner, the chicken retains all its moisture and flavour. It may be served with a green salad (see page 44) or garnished with grilled onion, parsley or other green herbs.

The platter will take either 2 chicken halves or several chicken pieces.

CHICKEN PARMESAN (*Pollo al parmigiano*) *Emilia-Romagna*

4–6 servings:

4–6 chicken breasts	½ cup (⅔) dry Marsala
1 cup (1¼) grated Parmesan	¼ lb. mushrooms, thinly sliced
olive oil	salt, pepper
1 clove garlic	2 tablespoons (2½) finely-chopped
2 tablespoons (2½) flour	parsley
1 cup (1¼) chicken stock	

Coat the chicken breasts in Parmesan, pressing the cheese well in. Heat plenty of oil in a heavy frying pan. Add the chicken breasts and brown them on both sides. Take them from the pan and transfer to a casserole. Take out all but 2 tablespoons (2½) of the oil from the pan. Add the garlic and cook until it is brown and discard it. Add the flour and stir to a roux. Gradually stir in the stock until the mixture is thick. Add the remaining ingredients and cook for 10 minutes. Pour the sauce over the chicken and bake in a moderate oven (350°F., mark 4) for 30 minutes.

Thinly-sliced young veal is cooked in the same manner.

ROAST DUCK GENOA STYLE (*Anitra arrosto alla genovese*) *Liguria*

3–4 servings:

4–5 lb. duck	salt, pepper
½ cup (⅔) olive oil	3–4 tablespoons (3¾–5) hot stock
1 good sprig parsley, chopped	juice 1 lemon
1 sprig rosemary	

Put the duck into a deep dish. Combine the oil, parsley and rosemary and rub this over the duck. Sprinkle with salt and pepper; leave for several hours, turning the duck from time to time and rubbing back the oil which drips off it. Put the duck on the rack of a roasting pan. Heat the oven to very hot (450°F., mark 8) for 5 minutes, reduce the heat to moderate (350°F., mark 4), then add the duck and roast it approximately 1½ hours, allowing 20 minutes per pound. Prick the skin from time to time to let the fat run freely. After 1 hour, take the duck from the oven and pour off the fat. Pour the stock and lemon juice over the duck, return it to the oven and continue cooking until tender, basting it from time to time with its drippings.

DUCK WITH OLIVES (*Anitra alle olive*) *Liguria*

4–5 servings:

5–6 lb. duck	1 small onion, diced
salt, pepper	1 small carrot, diced
sage to taste	1 teaspoon ($1\frac{1}{4}$) minced parsley
1 bay leaf	1 cup ($1\frac{1}{4}$) red wine
2 tablespoons ($2\frac{1}{2}$) olive oil	$\frac{1}{2}$ lb. green or black olives, pitted

Rub the inside of the duck with salt and pepper; add the sage and bay leaf. Heat the oil in a deep casserole and quickly brown the duck all over. Take it from the pan and prick the skin over the breast and thighs. In the same oil, brown the onion, carrot and parsley. Return the duck, add the wine, bring it to the boil and cover tightly. Lower the heat to simmering and cook for $1\frac{1}{4}$ hours or until the duck is tender. Take out the duck. Strain the sauce, return it to the pan, add the olives and simmer for 3–4 minutes. Cut the duck into serving pieces and cover with its sauce.

STUFFED ROAST TURKEY (*Tacchino ripieno arrosto*) *Lombardy*

8–10 servings:

8–10 lb. turkey	1 clove garlic, minced
$\frac{1}{4}$ lb. prunes	1 onion
2 lb. chestnuts	$\frac{1}{4}$ lb. ($1\frac{1}{3}$ cups) grated Parmesan cheese
salt, pepper	2 eggs, well beaten
$\frac{1}{4}$ lb. beef	2 cups ($2\frac{1}{2}$) white wine
$\frac{1}{4}$ lb. pork or veal	mace, rosemary and sage, finely
$\frac{1}{4}$ lb. pork sausage	chopped
olive oil	4 slices bacon

Soak the prunes overnight; stone and chop and put them into a mixing bowl. Nick a cross in the chestnuts and cook in lightly-salted water for 20–25 minutes. Peel and finely chop and add them to the prunes. Grind the meats, skin and crumble the sausages, and chop the turkey liver, heart and gizzard. Heat a little oil and lightly fry the garlic, onion and the ground meats. Mix with the prunes and chestnuts, add the cheese and eggs and mix thoroughly, then add half the wine. Stuff this mixture into the turkey cavity and close the openings.

Rub the turkey with oil, sprinkle with salt, pepper and the herbs and cover with the bacon slices. Put on the rack of a large roasting pan and roast in a moderate oven ($350°$F., mark 4) for $3\frac{1}{2}$ hours or until tender. Baste frequently with the drippings from the pan and the remainder of the wine.

TURKEY BREASTS FRIED IN BUTTER   (*Petti di tacchino fritti*)   *Lazio*

2–3 servings:

¾ lb. turkey breast, boned and skinned   **4 oz. (½ cup) butter**
salt   **wedges of lemon**

Remove any nerves in the meat and gently hammer the breast with a mallet. Lightly sprinkle with salt. Heat the butter in a heavy frying pan and add the turkey breast. Cook on one side until golden; turn and cook on the other. Serve with wedges of lemon.

Alternatively, the turkey breast can be dipped in beaten egg, lightly coated in breadcrumbs and fried in butter.

Chicken breasts are cooked in the same manner.

RABBIT WITH GREEN OLIVES   (*Coniglio con olive verdi*)   *Sicily*

4 servings:

1 large rabbit   **1 oz. (2 tablespoons) butter**
2 large onions, thickly sliced   **1 tablespoon (1¼) flour**
2 stalks celery, thickly sliced   **2 cups (2½) boiling water**
2 large carrots, thickly sliced   **salt, pepper**
1 bay leaf   **12 large green olives, pitted**
1 oz. (2 tablespoons) lard   **1 tablespoon (1¼) capers**

Joint the rabbit and put it into a pan with 2 cups (2½) of cold water; add the onions, celery, carrots, bay leaf and lard. Simmer for 30 minutes. Remove the rabbit pieces and bring the rest to the boil. Knead the butter and flour together, stir it into the stock and cook slowly until the mixture is thick. Gradually add the boiling water, stirring until the sauce is smooth. Return the rabbit, add the remaining ingredients and cook until the rabbit is tender.

RABBIT COOKED WITH MUSHROOMS AND BACON   *Liguria*
(*Coniglio con funghi e pancetta*)

4–8 servings:

1–2 rabbits, jointed   **meat or game stock**
olive oil   **mixed rosemary, thyme and bay leaf**
1–2 onions, coarsely chopped   **   to taste**
flour   **3 slices streaky bacon, diced**
1 teaspoon (1¼) tomato purée   **1 lb. mushrooms, thickly sliced**
salt, pepper

Heat enough oil in a pan to fry the rabbit pieces and the onions to a golden brown. Pour off the oil, sprinkle the rabbit lightly with flour, add the tomato purée, salt, pepper and enough stock to cover; bring this to the boil, add the herbs, cover the pan and cook very gently for 30 minutes. Transfer the rabbit to a casserole. Strain the sauce. Spread the bacon and mushrooms over the rabbit and cover with the sauce. Cover and bake in a hot oven (450°F., mark 8) until the rabbit is tender.

WILD RABBIT HUNTER'S STYLE (*Coniglio selvatico alla cacciatora*) *Basilicata*

4 servings:

1 large rabbit, jointed
red wine
1 oz. (2 tablespoons) butter
2 tablespoons (2½) olive oil
1 onion, chopped

2 cloves garlic, thinly sliced
salt, pepper to taste
1 cup (1¼) warm stock
1 sprig rosemary

Wash the rabbit and leave it to marinate overnight in red wine to cover. Take the rabbit pieces from the marinade, drain and dry them well. Heat the butter and oil together, add the onion and garlic and lightly fry until soft. Add the rabbit and lightly fry until brown. Season, add the stock and simmer for 30 minutes. Add the rosemary, the wine in which the rabbit was marinated, cover and cook slowly until the rabbit is tender.

FRIED RABBIT (*Coniglio fritto*) *Liguria*

2–3 servings:

1 young rabbit, jointed
juice 1 lemon
salt, pepper

4–5 thin slices fat bacon
2 tablespoons (2½) olive oil

Soak the rabbit pieces in cold water for several hours. Dry each piece carefully then rub with lemon juice, salt and pepper. Chop the bacon. Heat the oil, add the bacon and fry it until crisp. Add the rabbit pieces and fry them gently until tender. Serve hot.

SALMI OF WILD DUCK (*Anitra selvatica in salmi*) *Lazio*

3–4 servings:

1 wild duck
salt, pepper
6 oz. (¾ cup) butter
olive oil
2–3 sprigs parsley, finely chopped

1 very small onion, minced
1 clove garlic, minced
juice 1 orange
1 cup (1¼) dry Marsala

The flavour and treatment of wild duck depends much on the time of the year and the duck's feeding habits. If the flavour is mild, it needs only to be wiped with a damp cloth (after it has been plucked and drawn); if strong, it needs washing and stuffing with an apple or celery. Remove the stuffing before serving the duck.

Sprinkle the duck inside with salt and rub it with half the butter. Put the giblets aside. Heat the remaining butter with a little oil in a casserole on top of the stove. Add the duck and brown it all over. Chop the giblets and mix them with the parsley, onion and garlic. Heat a little oil in a small pan, add the giblet mixture and cook over a moderate heat. Add salt, pepper, orange juice and Marsala. Bring quickly to the boil to blend the mixture and baste the duck frequently with this.

Take the duck from the pan, strain the liquid (a little cream and extra Marsala may be added) and serve it separately.

ROAST HARE (*Lepre arrosto*) *Piedmont*

6 servings:

1 hare, about 2 lb.
6–8 strips fat bacon
salt, pepper
4 oz. (½ cup) butter
1 small onion, finely sliced

hot stock
1 cup (1¼) cream
1 tablespoon (1¼) flour
a sprinkling nutmeg
juice 2 lemons

Wipe the hare with paper towels, wrap it well with the bacon, and sprinkle with salt. Heat the butter in a casserole, add the onion and when it changes colour add the hare. Put it into a hot oven (425°F., mark 7) and roast for 30 minutes, basting frequently with hot stock. Lower the heat to moderate (350°F., mark 4) and continue cooking for 1–1¼ hours. When the hare is quite tender, take it from the casserole, place on a hot serving dish and keep hot. Put the casserole on top of the stove, add the cream, sprinkle in the flour and stir it until smooth. Add the nutmeg, salt, pepper and lemon juice. Stirring all the while, bring the sauce to a quick boil. Strain it over the hare and serve garnished with wedges of lemon.

SALMI OF HARE (*Lepre in salmi*) *Umbria*

6 servings:

1 hare
1 stalk celery, chopped
1 onion, chopped
1 carrot, chopped
1 clove garlic, minced

2 bay leaves
1 teaspoon (1¼) juniper berries
salt, pepper
4 cups (5) red wine
4 oz. (½ cup) butter

Wipe the hare, cut it into pieces and put into a bowl with the remaining ingredients except the butter. Leave for 24 hours. Take out the pieces of hare, dry them thoroughly and strain the marinade. Heat the butter in a large pan and fry the hare until brown. Add the strained marinade, cover and cook slowly until the hare is tender. Remove to a hot serving dish. Strain half the sauce over the hare. Serve with polenta and spread with the remaining sauce.

Rabbit is also cooked in the same manner but requires half the time for marinating.

PARTRIDGES IN CREAM (*Pernici alla panna*) *Veneto*

4 servings:

4 partridges
juice 2 large lemons
salt, pepper
4 thin strips fat streaky bacon

1½ oz. (3 tablespoons) butter
sage, rosemary
1 cup (1¼) cream

Rub inside the partridges with lemon juice and sprinkle them with salt and pepper. Tie a strip of bacon over each bird. Heat the butter in a large casserole, add the partridges and brown them all over. Add the herbs and the rest of the lemon juice, and just enough hot water to avoid burning. Cover the casserole and cook for 20–30 minutes or until the birds are tender. Add the cream and let this heat. Take the partridges from the pan, place on a hot dish and strain the sauce quickly over them. Serve at once.

PARTRIDGE IN SOUR SAUCE (*Pernici in salsa d'aceto*) *Sardinia*

3 servings:

3 partridges	**2 tablespoons (2½) wine vinegar**
1 onion, chopped	**salt**
2 celery stalks, chopped	**1 tablespoon (1¼) parsley, finely**
2 carrots, chopped	**chopped**
salt	**1 tablespoon (1¼) capers, finely chopped**
sauce:	
½ cup (⅔) olive oil	

Put the partridges into a pan with the onion, celery, carrots, a little salt and water to cover. Cover the pan and simmer for 30 minutes or until the birds are tender. Take the partridges from the pan and cut each into two. Arrange them on a serving dish but keep hot. Combine the oil, vinegar, salt to taste, parsley and capers. Pour this dressing over the partridges immediately before serving.

PHEASANT COOKED WITH MUSHROOMS AND RED WINE *Piedmont*
(*Fagiano con funghi e vino rosso*)

3 servings:

1 pheasant 2½–3 lb.	**2 stalks celery, chopped**
1 oz. (1 cup) dried mushrooms	**1 small onion, chopped**
salt, pepper	**1½ oz. (3 tablespoons) butter**
2 tablespoons (2½) tomato paste	**4 tablespoons (5) olive oil**
2 cups (2½) stock	**dry red wine**
2 carrots, chopped	

Soak the mushrooms in tepid water for 30 minutes. Drain and chop them. Wipe the pheasant with a damp cloth and sprinkle both the inside and outside lightly with salt and pepper. Dilute the tomato paste with 3 tablespoonfuls (3¾) of stock and mix with the vegetables. Heat the butter and oil in a casserole, add the pheasant, brown it over a quick heat, and add 1 cup (1¼) of wine. Cook uncovered over a high heat until the wine is reduced by half. Lower the heat and add the mushrooms and the tomatoes and vegetable mixture. Add the stock and cover and cook over a moderate heat until the pheasant is tender, 40–60 minutes. Check from time to time to see whether additional liquid is required; if so, stock, mushroom liquid, red wine or water can be added.

PHEASANT IN RED WINE (*Fagiano al vino rosso*)

3 servings:

1 pheasant	**2 bay leaves**
1 onion, chopped	**salt, pepper**
3–4 carrots, chopped	**2 cups (2½) dry red wine**
1 stalk celery, chopped	**1 tablespoon (1¼) olive oil**
2 cloves garlic, chopped	**4 slices bacon, chopped**
1 sprig rosemary	**1½ tablespoons (2½) flour**

Cut the pheasant into 4 pieces and put it together with its liver into a deep bowl. Add the onion, carrots, celery, garlic, rosemary, bay leaves, salt, pepper and wine. Cover and leave in a cool place for 2 days.

Take the pheasant and liver from the marinade and thoroughly dry. Heat the oil, fry the bacon, add the pheasant and liver, brown all over and sprinkle with flour. Strain the marinade and pour it over the top. Cover and simmer for about 1 hour or until the bird is tender. Take the pheasant pieces from the pan, put aside but keep hot. Skim off the fat, bring the gravy to the boil and strain it over the pheasant.

QUAIL WITH OLIVES AND WINE (*Quaglie con olive verdi e vino bianco*) *Lazio*

3–6 servings:

6 quail	**2 sage leaves**
salt, pepper	**12 green olives, pitted and chopped**
2½ tablespoons (3¼) olive oil	**1 oz. (2 tablespoons) butter**
3 slices lean bacon, diced	**½ cup (⅔) stock**
1 onion, minced	**2 tablespoons (2½) brandy**
1 carrot, diced	**6–8 cups (7½–10) hot boiled rice**
½ cup (⅔) white wine	

Rub the quail with salt and pepper inside and out. Heat the oil and quickly brown the quail. Add the bacon, onion and carrot and cook over a high heat for 5 minutes. Add the wine, sage, salt and pepper and cook 5 minutes more. Add the olives, butter and stock. Lower the heat and simmer for about 20 minutes until the quail are tender and the liquid is reduced to half. Warm the brandy, pour this over the quail and ignite it; this is for flavour not glamour. Arrange a ring of rice on a hot serving dish and place the quail in the centre. Scrape off every bit of sauce and dripping from the pan, stir, and pour it over the top.

QUAIL COOKED IN WHITE WINE (*Quaglie al vino bianco*) *Piedmont*

3–6 servings:

6 quail	6 peppercorns
4 oz. ($\frac{2}{3}$ cup) raisins	1 bay leaf
pine nuts	2 cloves
6 thin slices fat bacon	salt, pepper
1 oz. (2 tablespoons) butter or oil	2 cups ($2\frac{1}{2}$) dry white wine
2 small onions, finely chopped	1 cup ($1\frac{1}{4}$) cream
1–2 cloves garlic, finely chopped	croûtons

Soak the raisins in white wine or water until plump. Put a few of these together with a few pine nuts into each quail. Wrap them securely in a slice of bacon. Heat the butter in a casserole large enough to hold the birds comfortably. Add the onions and garlic and, as they change colour, the peppercorns, bay leaf, cloves and finally the quail. Season, add the wine, cover and cook gently for about 30 minutes. Discard the bacon. Place the quail on a hot serving dish, strain the sauce and return it to the pan. Stir in the cream and bring gently almost to the boil. Pour a little of the sauce over the quail and serve the rest in a sauceboat. Garnish with *croûtons* and serve at once.

LEG OF WILD BOAR IN A SWEET-SOUR SAUCE *Sardinia* (*Cosciotto di cinghiale in agrodolce*)

12–14 servings:

1 boned leg wild boar, 10–12 lb.	salt to taste
5 oz. (10 tablespoons) butter	$\frac{1}{2}$ cup ($\frac{2}{3}$) wine vinegar
$\frac{1}{2}$ lb. fairly salt fat bacon, diced	2 oz. (2 squares) bitter cooking
1 stalk celery, coarsely chopped	(baker's) chocolate, grated
3 carrots, coarsely chopped	$\frac{1}{2}$ cup ($\frac{2}{3}$) cream
2 onions, coarsely chopped	1 tablespoon ($1\frac{1}{4}$) pine nuts
3 cloves garlic, coarsely chopped	$1\frac{1}{2}$ oz. ($\frac{1}{4}$ cup) sultanas (white raisins)
2 cloves	$1\frac{1}{2}$ oz. (3 tablespoons) sugar
2 bay leaves	1 tablespoon ($1\frac{1}{4}$) chopped candied
10 peppercorns	orange peel
1 bottle red wine	

Heat the butter and bacon in a large pan and, when the bacon fat begins to run, add the boar meat. Brown it all over, add the celery, carrots, onions, garlic, cloves, bay leaves and peppercorns. Let these ingredients brown and cook for 15 minutes. Add the wine, bring the whole to a quick boil and let the wine evaporate by half. Add salt and cook over a moderate heat for 3 hours or until the meat is tender. Take it from the pan, put aside but keep hot. Rub the gravy through a sieve and return it to the pan. Add the vinegar and the remaining ingredients, stir well and cook for 10 minutes or until the sauce has thickened. Pour some of the sauce over the meat and the rest in a sauceboat. Serve at once.

A saddle of boar is cooked in the same manner as the leg. Many cooks prefer to marinate the meat before cooking it, a precaution aimed at tenderizing the meat which can be tough.

marinade:

1 cup (1¼) olive oil
a little chopped onion, carrot and
  celery
1 each clove garlic and bay leaf

a little thyme and oregano
6 peppercorns
1 teaspoon (1¼) salt
½ pint (2¼ cups) red wine

If using a marinade, take the wine from the quantity suggested in the list of ingredients.

Heat the oil, add the vegetables and cook them for 5 minutes. Add the remaining ingredients and simmer for 15 minutes, stirring from time to time. Cool and pour the marinade over the meat. Leave from 24–36 hours.

Take the meat from the marinade and wipe it dry. Strain the marinade and add it at the same time as the rest of the wine to the pan.

VENISON COOKED IN RED WINE *(Capriolo al vino rosso)* *Sardinia*

4 servings:

3 lb. venison
2–3 tablespoons (2½–3¾) olive oil
1 carrot, coarsely chopped
1 small onion, coarsely chopped
1 stalk celery, coarsely chopped
1 good sprig parsley, coarsely chopped
a little thyme, coarsely chopped

1 bay leaf
1 clove garlic, chopped
salt, pepper
1 cup (1¼) red wine
3 oz. (6 tablespoons) butter
6 strips fat bacon, diced

Heat the oil, add the vegetables, herbs, garlic, salt and pepper, stir, then add the wine. Cover the pan and cook gently for 30 minutes. Rub the mixture through a sieve adding, if necessary, either more wine, water or stock to ease it through.

Heat the butter and the bacon and fry until the bacon is rendered; add the venison, let this brown, sprinkle with salt and pepper and add the vegetable stock. Cover the pan and cook until the meat is tender.

If preferred, the venison can be marinated in the red wine marinade of the previous recipe. However, if marinating the meat, omit the red wine listed among the ingredients and use instead half the marinade or 1 cup (1¼) of it.

sauces  *salse*

Sauces are as important in Italian cooking as they are in French cooking; the number of sauces served with pasta alone is impressive. Usually Italian sauces are less subtle than the French, but still extremely good. The following recipes represent a selection of the most interesting; many others have been incorporated in the chapter on pasta.

It is not always possible to say exactly how many servings a sauce recipe will produce since it depends on how it is used and on individual appetites.

MEAT SAUCE (1) (*Sugo di carne*) *Liguria*

For 1 lb. pasta—3 servings:

1 oz. (1 cup) dried mushrooms	**1 cup (1¼) red wine**
3 oz. (6 tablespoons) butter	**salt, pepper to taste**
1 cup (1¼) olive oil	**flour**
½ lb. finely-ground beef or other meat	**½ lb. ripe tomatoes, peeled and chopped**
3 slices fat bacon, chopped	**1 bay leaf**
1 medium-sized carrot, chopped	**1 sprig thyme**
1 stalk celery, chopped	**2 cloves**
1 onion, chopped	

Soak the mushrooms in tepid water for 30 minutes and chop them. Heat half the butter with all the oil in a large pan, fry the meat and bacon until brown, then add the carrot, celery and onion. Fry until brown, add the wine, salt and pepper and cook until the wine has evaporated. Knead the remaining butter with an equal quantity of flour. Take the pan from the stove and add the kneaded butter, stirring it well into the sauce. Return the pan to the stove and cook for a few minutes before adding the tomatoes, mushrooms, bay leaf, thyme and cloves. Cook for 10 minutes, add hot water to cover, cover the pan and cook for 1 hour. Before s erving, remove the herbs and cloves.

MEAT SAUCE (2) (*Salsa di carne*) *Calabria*

For 1 lb. pasta—3 servings:

1 lb. (2 cups) ground meat
flour
3–4 tablespoons (3¾–5) olive oil
1 large onion, finely chopped
1 small carrot, grated
1 tablespoon (1¼) finely-chopped parsley

½ cup (⅔) red wine
1 large can Italian tomatoes
1 cup (1¼) meat stock
½ lb. fresh mushrooms, finely chopped
salt, pepper

Sprinkle the meat lightly with flour. Heat the oil, fry the onion until soft and add the carrot and parsley. Cook over a moderate heat for 10 minutes. Add the meat, stirring constantly to prevent lumps forming, and cook it until brown. Pour in the wine, stir and cook over a high heat for 3 minutes. Chop the tomatoes (or rub them through a sieve), stir them into the sauce, add the stock, mushrooms, salt and pepper, and cook gently for 1 hour or until the sauce is fairly thick.

BOLOGNESE MEAT SAUCE (*Ragù*) *Emilia-Romagna*

There is no true Bolognese sauce. The French have their classic version of it but not the Italians. A Bolognese, Corrado Contoli, wrote in his book *Cucina Romagnola*: '*La composizione del ragù si presta a molte versioni ed ogni tavola lo presenta con un gusto più o meno diverso.*' The following recipe from Bologna is as genuine a *ragù* as any can be.

For 1–1½ lb. spaghetti—4 servings:

2 oz. (4 tablespoons) butter
3 tablespoons (3¾) olive oil
1 each onion, carrot, celery stalk, finely chopped
1 clove garlic, minced (optional)
2–3 slices fat bacon (pancetta)
½ lb. each pork and beef, ground

3–4 chicken livers, chopped (optional)
2–3 Italian-style sausages, skinned, the meat crumbled
½ cup (⅔) dry white wine
½ lb. ripe tomatoes, peeled, seeded and chopped

Heat the butter and oil in a wide, shallow pan. Add the vegetables (except the tomatoes), garlic and bacon and cook over a low heat until they begin to change colour. Add the pork and beef, the chicken livers (if using them) and the sausage meat. Cook gently until they begin to brown. Add the wine and cook until the wine is more or less evaporated. Rub the tomatoes through a sieve or mouli grater (or use a diluted tomato paste), add this purée to the pan, stir well, then cook gently for 1½ hours. Stir from time to time and, if necessary, add a little water or stock.

Here are some variations: add dried and soaked or chopped fresh mushrooms to the above ingredients; use all beef and no pork; add 2–3 tablespoons (2½–3¾) of milk and cream towards the end of the cooking—some cooks in Bologna do this—or a sprinkling of freshly-grated nutmeg, or marjoram and parsley, or sugar.

In essence, a *ragù bolognese* is a people's sauce, not a sauce of *haute cuisine* and, although basically all recipes agree, there are differences not only between every restaurant cook or chef but between family cooks as well.

BECHAMEL SAUCE (*La besciamella*) *Emilia-Romagna*

2 oz. (4 tablespoons) butter
2 oz. (½ cup) flour
1 pint (2½ cups) milk

white pepper, to taste
salt to taste
nutmeg to taste

Heat the butter in a thick pan, add the flour and stir for a few minutes with a wooden spoon to make a roux. Heat the milk to boiling point and gradually add it to the roux, stirring all the time until the sauce is thick and smooth. Add the pepper, salt and nutmeg, and still stirring, continue cooking for another 5 minutes; the sauce should have the consistency of thick cream. If it is not to be used immediately, cover the pan and stand it in a large pan of hot water. This prevents a thin skin forming on the top of the sauce.

This sauce, with slight variations, is prepared throughout Italy. For example, a walnut-sized knob of butter is often beaten into the sauce after it has been taken from the heat.

SAUCE FOR GAME (*Salsa ghiotta*) *Umbria*

6 servings:

1 cup (1¼) each red and white wine
1 cup (1¼) wine vinegar
½ cup (⅔) olive oil
2–3 thin slices smoked ham, chopped
½ lemon, peeled and sliced

1 clove garlic, bruised
a little sage and rosemary
4–6 juniper berries
salt, pepper
6 chicken livers

Put all the ingredients (except the chicken livers) into a pan (preferably of terracotta, say the Umbrians) and cook over a moderate heat for about 30 minutes. Chop the chicken livers, add these to the pan, discard the garlic, sage and rosemary and cook until the liquid is reduced by half.

Serve the sauce hot with any kind of game meat.

SAVOURY SAUCE   (*Salsa peverada*) *Veneto*

6 servings:

¼ lb. chicken livers, finely chopped
3–4 anchovy fillets, finely chopped
¼ lb. sausage (sopressa veneta—see
  below)
2–3 sprigs parsley, finely chopped
½ cup (⅔) olive oil

1–2 cloves garlic
salt, pepper to taste
¼ cup (⅓) dry white wine or wine vinegar
1 teaspoon (1¼) lemon juice
grated rind ½ lemon

Combine the livers, anchovies, sausage meat (crumbled), and parsley. Heat the oil, brown the garlic, add the savoury mixture, sprinkle lightly with salt and pepper and stir gently. Add the wine, lemon juice and rind, and simmer until the sauce is thick and the sausage meat well cooked, 20–30 minutes. Serve hot with poultry or game, or with cold, sliced polenta (see page 107).

Sopressa veneta is made with mixed ground pork and beef and greatly prized locally.

ITALIAN SAUCE (*Salsa all'italiana*)

1 oz. (1 cup) dried mushrooms	salt, pepper
2 oz. (4 tablespoons) butter	½ cup (⅔) sweet white wine
1 tablespoon (1¼) parsley, finely chopped	1 teaspoon (1¼) tomato paste
	½ cup (⅔) hot meat stock
1 small onion, finely chopped	juice ½ lemon

Soak the mushrooms in tepid water for 30 minutes, dry and chop them finely. Heat the butter, add the mushrooms and parsley and cook for 5 minutes, stirring all the time. Add the onion, salt and pepper, stir well and, when the onion changes colour, add the wine. Cook gently until the wine is reduced. Dilute the tomato paste with the stock, add it to the pan and cook gently for 5–10 minutes. Just before serving, add the lemon juice.

Serve with roast or boiled meat, including chicken.

DRIED MUSHROOM SAUCE (*Salsa di funghi*) *Emilia-Romagna*

For 1 lb. pasta—3 servings:

1 oz. (1 cup) dried mushrooms	1 small carrot, diced
1 oz. (2 tablespoons) butter	1 stalk celery, finely chopped
1 tablespoon (1¼) olive oil	1 tablespoon (1¼) tomato paste
2–3 strips fat bacon	4 tablespoons (5) meat stock
1 small onion, minced	

Soak the mushrooms for 30 minutes in tepid water. Dry and chop them. While the mushrooms are soaking, heat the butter and oil together, add the bacon and fry until the fat runs. Add the onion, carrot and celery, brown lightly and add the mushrooms. Dilute the tomato paste with the stock, add it to the pan and cook until the sauce reaches the desired thickness.

Use this sauce with pasta and rice dishes, especially spaghetti. The sauce should be stirred into the spaghetti as soon as it is drained.

TOMATO SAUCE (1) (*Sugo finto*) *Lazio*

For 1½ lb. pasta—4 servings:

2 oz. (4 tablespoons) butter	½ clove garlic, finely chopped
2 tablespoons (2½) olive oil	2 sprigs parsley, finely chopped
2 oz. piece fat bacon, finely chopped	hot meat stock
1 small onion, finely chopped	2 lb. ripe tomatoes, peeled, seeded and chopped
1 celery stalk, finely chopped	
1 carrot, finely chopped	salt, pepper

Heat the butter and oil. Add the bacon, fry this for 2 minutes, then add the onion, celery, carrot, garlic and parsley and fry for 5 minutes. Moisten with a few tablespoonfuls of hot stock to give the mixture, *soffritto*, time to brown without burning.

Add the tomatoes, season with salt and pepper and cook half covered for about 30 minutes, stirring from time to time. The Romans call this 'mock' sauce.

TOMATO SAUCE (2) (*Salsa di pomodoro*) *Campania*

For 1½ lb. spaghetti—4 servings:

2 lb. ripe tomatoes, peeled, seeded and chopped
½ cup (⅔) olive oil
1 small onion, finely chopped
1–2 stalks celery, finely chopped

1 medium-sized carrot, finely chopped
1 teaspoon (1¼) sugar
salt, pepper
basil, parsley to taste, finely chopped
1 cup (1¼) stock

Heat the oil and fry the onion, celery and carrot until they change colour. Add the tomatoes and the remaining ingredients and cook over a good heat for 30 minutes. If preferred, the sauce can be rubbed through a sieve or puréed in a blender, in which case it is only necessary to chop the tomatoes.

SAUCE PIQUANTE (*Salsa piccante*) *Campania*

3 tablespoons (3¾) olive oil
2 tablespoons (2½) wine vinegar
1 small can Italian tomato paste
salt, pepper

1 teaspoon (1¼) sugar
1 teaspoon (1¼) continental mustard
4 hard-boiled egg yolks, mashed

Put the oil into a small pan, add the vinegar and stir well. Add the tomato paste, stir until blended and add the salt, pepper and sugar. Bring gently to the boil, reduce the heat and simmer for 10 minutes. Take from the heat and stir well. Add the mustard, stirring it well into the sauce, then the yolks. Cool, then chill and serve with fish.

ANCHOVY SAUCE (*Salsa acciughata*) *Southern Italy*

8 salted anchovies
6 tablespoons (7½) olive oil

1 large clove garlic

Wash the salt off the anchovies and split them down the middle. Pull out the centre bone and mash the flesh to a fine paste. Heat the oil, add the garlic and fry until it browns. Discard the garlic, add the anchovy and mix well. Serve with boiled meats and spaghetti.

  This sauce, when served with spaghetti, is poured straight from the pan on to the pasta and well mixed.

GARLIC AND ANCHOVY SAUCE (*Bagna cauda*) *Piedmont*

½ cup (⅔) olive oil
4 oz. (½ cup) butter
2–3 cloves garlic, finely chopped
6 anchovy fillets, chopped

pinch salt
1 small white truffle, thinly sliced
a few leaves basil, finely chopped
  (optional)

Heat the oil and butter in an earthenware pot over hot water. In another pan cook the garlic until it is soft, then add the anchovy fillets. Cook until the anchovies have dissolved to a paste and add salt, the truffle and basil (if used, the basil must first be browned in butter).

It is usual to serve the *bagna cauda* (hot bath) in the pot in which it has been cooked and to keep the sauce hot at table on a spirit stove. It is used as a 'dip' for a variety of raw vegetables: celery, artichokes, endive and, in particular, cardoon.

CAPER SAUCE (*Salsa di capperi*) *Southern Italy*

2 tablespoons (2½) capers
1–2 sprigs parsley
3 salted anchovies or 6 anchovy fillets

½ cup (⅔) wine vinegar
½ cup (⅔) olive oil

Chop the capers, parsley and the anchovies—thoroughly wash off the salt from the anchovies if not using fillets. Put them into a small pan with the vinegar and cook over a good heat for 8–10 minutes. Rub this through a sieve or, better still, purée in a blender and return to the heat for a few minutes. Add the oil, stirring all the time.

Serve hot with boiled meats, vegetables, and grilled or fried fish.

LEMON AND OIL SAUCE (*Salmoriglio*) *Sicily*

juice 2 large lemons
1 cup (1¼) olive oil
1 tablespoon (1¼) parsley, finely
   chopped

2 teaspoons (2½) oregano or marjoram,
   finely chopped
salt to taste

Pour the oil into a warm bowl and add 3 tablespoons (3¾) of hot water, beating all the time, then, still beating, add the remaining ingredients. Put the bowl in another pan with hot water and cook the sauce, still beating, until it is hot. Serve immediately with fish, meat or chicken.

LEMON SAUCE (*Salsa al limone*) *Southern Italy*

juice 1 lemon
1 oz. (2 tablespoons) butter
1 oz. (¼ cup) flour
1 pint (2 cups) warm milk or chicken
   stock

salt
2 egg yolks, well beaten
1 tablespoon (1¼) finely-chopped
   parsley
1 teaspoon (1¼) capers

Heat the butter, add the flour and stir to a roux. Cook for a few minutes, stirring all the while. Gradually add enough warm liquid to make a smooth sauce. Add salt and cook for 10 minutes, still stirring. Take from the heat and cool. Whisk in the egg yolks. Return the pan to the heat and gently reheat the sauce, stirring constantly. Add the parsley, capers and lemon juice. Stir over a low heat until well blended.

Serve with hot or cold assorted meats, with chicken or with fish.

GARLIC SAUCE (*Aglio o aioli*) *Abruzzi-Molise*

4 cloves garlic
salt
1 egg yolk

olive oil
juice 1 lemon

Chop the garlic and pound it in a mortar with a little salt to a paste. Beat the yolk until smooth and gradually add it to the garlic. Mix well, then, drop by drop, add oil until the mixture is the consistency and texture of a very thick cream. Gradually dilute with the lemon juice, using the whole of the lemon. This sauce can also be made in a blender.

Aglio e olio con peperone has pimiento added, and, in Campania, finely-chopped hot chilli as well.

Use with fish and pasta.

GREEN SAUCE (*Salsa verde*) *Piedmont*

1 large bunch parsley, minced	milk
2 salted anchovies, washed free from salt	1 clove garlic, finely chopped
1 hard-boiled egg yolk	olive oil
1 tablespoon (1¼) soft, fresh bread-crumbs	salt, pepper

Fillet the anchovies and chop them finely together with the egg yolk. Soak the bread-crumbs in a little milk and squeeze them dry. Put these ingredients, with the parsley and the garlic in a mortar (or purée them in a blender) and pound to a paste. Add, drop by drop (as for mayonnaise) enough oil to make a fairly liquid sauce, beating well between each addition. Test for seasoning before adding salt and pepper.

Serve particularly with cold meats, *bollito*, with fish and with pasta.

PINE NUT SAUCE (*Salsa di pinoli*) *Liguria*

4 servings:

4 oz. roasted pine nuts	2–3 sprigs parsley, chopped
inside of bread roll	salt to taste
1 tablespoon (1¼) wine vinegar	½ cup (⅔) olive oil

Soak the bread in the vinegar then squeeze it dry. Put the bread, pine nuts, parsley and salt into a mortar (or purée them in a blender) and pound to a smooth paste. Gradually add the oil and stir until the oil is completely blended into the paste.

Serve with boiled meat, fish and hard-boiled eggs.

WALNUT SAUCE (*Salsa di noci*) *Liguria*

½ lb. walnuts, ground	5–6 tablespoons (approx. ½ cup) olive oil
1 clove garlic, chopped	
finely-chopped marjoram to taste	½ cup (⅔) thick cream
1 tablespoon (1¼) pine nuts (optional)	

Pound the first 4 ingredients to a paste. Add the oil, mix well, then add the cream; the sauce should be fairly fluid and creamy.

Serve with pasta. In Liguria they serve it with *pansoti*, pot-bellied, a member of the ravioli family, or boiled celery and turnips. When serving this sauce with pasta, butter and grated Parmesan or Pecorino cheese are served as well.

GREEN HERB SAUCE (*Pesto alla genovese*) *Liguria*

The Genoese naturally claim to have invented this sauce—but they say the same in Provence with their *pistou*. It is made from freshly-picked basil leaves—housewives collect them from fields and gardens—pounded in a mortar with garlic until a paste. Traditionalists say that this can be achieved only with a marble mortar, but the modern housewife often uses a blender which saves time, and the flavour seems the same. According to the Ligurians, he who eats *pesto* in Genoa never leaves. If fresh basil is not available, the next best thing is a jar of Ligurian-made *pesto*, not quite the same but better than no *pesto*.

For 1 lb. *trenette*—3 servings:

2 large bunches basil leaves, finely chopped

6 cloves garlic

2 teaspoons (2½) pine nuts

a few leaves marjoram, finely chopped

3 oz. (1 cup) grated Pecorino (Sardo) cheese

approx. 1 cup (1¼) olive oil

2–3 tablespoons (2½–3¾) boiling water

Pound in a mortar (or purée in a blender) the first 4 ingredients. Gradually add the cheese and continue pounding until the paste is smooth. Slowly stir in enough oil to make a liquid sauce and finally add the hot water.

HORSERADISH SAUCE (*Salsa di rafano*)

To serve hot with boiled meats.

1 tablespoon (1¼) grated fresh horse-radish

¾ oz. (1½ tablespoons) butter

¾ oz. (3 tablespoons) flour

½ cup (⅔) stock

1 teaspoon (1¼) sugar

Heat the butter, add the flour and stir to a roux. Gradually add the stock, stirring all the time until the mixture is creamy—if the sauce seems too thick, add a little more stock. Add the sugar and horseradish, mix well and cook gently for 10 minutes, stirring frequently.

sweet dishes  *dolci*

Most Italians prefer to finish their meal with a bowl of mixed fruit, or fruit with cheese, in particular pears with Gorgonzola. There are special occasions, usually family ones, when the housewife makes a special effort and bakes a cake or a pie herself, but generally she sends her husband off to the *pasticceria* where he can choose his favourite *torta* from an incredibly vast assortment of extremely sweet creations.

Sicilians are sweet-toothed and many Italian sweet recipes originate from Sicily. They are also the promoters of ice-cream, *gelato*, and sorbet, *granita*, an art said to have been taken from the Arabs who occupied their island centuries ago. Sicilians still make superb ice-cream of all flavours.

Difficult cakes and *torte* have not been included in this chapter as it seems a useless exercise to ask British and American housewives to bake cakes etc. which the average Italian housewife does not often do herself.

'GREEN' PIE (*Torta verde*) *Tuscany*

A speciality of Lucca, *torta verde* is not usually baked at home but by a local specialist. It is a flan with a delicious though curious filling of finely-chopped stale bread soaked in wine or water, cooked Swiss chard which gives it colour but oddly no flavour, dried grapes, pine nuts, mixed candied peel, baking powder, vanilla flavouring, grated lemon rind, sugar, grated Parmesan cheese, egg yolks, maraschino and a dry local vermouth. The result is sweet and rich.

Torta verde is served on festive occasions with a glass of wine.

RICE CAKE (*Torta di riso*) *Tuscany*

Another Lucca speciality and similar to *torta verde* (see above). This flan has a filling of rice which is cooked until soft in milk flavoured with raisins, grated lemon rind, vanilla, candied peel, sugar, maraschino and dry vermouth.

165

MASCHERPONE CREAM   (*Crema di mascherpone*)   *Lombardy*

4 servings:

2 eggs, separated
2 tablespoons (2½) fine sugar

½ lb. Mascherpone cheese
1–2 tablespoons (1¼–2½) rum

Beat the egg yolks with the sugar until thick. Whisk the whites until stiff. Beat the yolks into the cheese until blended. Add the rum, beat again and fold in the whites. Spoon the mixture into glasses and chill. Serve with wine biscuits.

RICOTTA CREAM CAKE   (*Cassata alla siciliana*)   *Sicily*
ILLUSTRATED PAGE 136

6 servings:

1 lb. (2 cups) Ricotta cheese
½ lb. (1 cup) fine sugar
4 oz. (4 squares) bitter (bakers')
  chocolate
1 teaspoon (1¼) vanilla extract

pinch salt
4 tablespoons (5) rum
chopped mixed candied fruits to taste
1 lb. round sponge cake
icing (confectioners') sugar

Rub the Ricotta through a sieve, add the sugar and beat well. Grate the chocolate and beat three-quarters of it into the cheese. Add the vanilla, salt and rum and beat until the mixture is fluffy. Add the candied fruits.

Cut the sponge cake into 3 slices. Place 1 in the bottom of a mould into which it just fits. Spread with one-half of the cheese mixture, cover with sponge, spread with the remaining Ricotta and cover with sponge. Press this down lightly, put a weight on top and leave in the refrigerator overnight. To serve, sprinkle with icing sugar and the remaining chocolate.

'TIPSY' CAKE OR TRIFLE   (*Zuppa inglese*)   *Sicily*

No one seems quite sure why this sweet is thus named; certainly it has nothing to do with soup. But this type of sweet dish has been popular in Italy since the nineteenth century, about the time when the British began visiting Italy in fairly large numbers. There are countless recipes for it, some extremely complicated, others moderately simple.

6 servings:

1 lb. sponge cake
1–1½ cups (1¼–2¼) rum or sweet Marsala
zabaione (see page 170)

1 cup (1¼) whipping cream
chopped glacé or candied fruits—
  cherries, pineapple, lemon etc.

The sponge should be 8–9 inches in diameter and thick enough to cut into 3 equal layers. Place the bottom layer in the dish on which the *zuppa inglese* is to be served. Pour over it one-third of the rum or enough to just soak it. Spread it with half the *zabaione*. Add the second layer of sponge, another third of the rum and the remaining *zabaione*, then the last slice of sponge. Pour the remaining rum over the top. Although the sponge should not be completely soggy, it must be evenly soaked, with no dry patches. Put it into a refrigerator until ready to be served. Before serving, spread whipped cream over the top and sides and garnish with the *glacé* fruits.

CHEESE PIE (*Torta di ricotta*) *Sicily*

6 servings:

½ lb. flaky pastry	4 eggs
4 oz. (¾ cup) almonds	4 oz. (½ cup) fine sugar
2 lb. Ricotta cheese	a little vanilla or almond flavouring

Roll out the pastry and line a 9-inch pie dish with this. Put aside.

Blanch, toast and coarsely chop the almonds. Beat the Ricotta until smooth. Beat the eggs with the sugar and flavouring until thick. Add this to the Ricotta, beating all the time until the mixture is smooth. Add the almonds, then turn into the prepared pie dish. Bake in a moderate oven (350°F., mark 4) for 35–40 minutes or until a thin skin has formed over the top. Turn off the heat, open the oven door slightly and let the *torta* cool in the oven.

FRESH FIGS IN RUM SYRUP (*Fichi in sciroppo*)

6 servings:

2 lb. firm green or purple figs	½ cup (⅔) rum
½ lb. (1 cup) sugar	

Wash the figs and drain them well. Dissolve the sugar with 1 cup (1¼) of water over a low heat, bring to the boil and cook for 5 minutes. Add the figs, reduce the heat and simmer until quite tender. Turn into a bowl and leave until cool. Arrange the figs in a preserving jar and add the syrup and the rum. Cover tightly and leave for a few days. Serve with whipped cream.

PRICKLY PEARS (*Fichi d'India*) *Apulia*

4–6 servings:

2 lb. prickly (cactus) pears	sugar

Prickly pears are cooked as a compote in southern Italy. The prickly pear vendor peels the pears and they are taken home in a plastic bag. If buying pears that are not skinned, use rubber gloves to perform the operation. Prickly pears are extremely good.

Cook the pears whole in enough water to cover, adding sugar to taste, until tender. Serve plain or with cream. They can also be cooked in red wine, or iced and eaten raw.

STRAWBERRIES SOAKED IN WINE (*Fragole al vino*) *Lazio*

2–3 servings:

1 lb. strawberries	whipped cream
2 cups (2½) sweet white wine	fine sugar

Hull the strawberries and soak them in wine. Drain and place them in a glass bowl. Cover with whipped cream and sugar and place in a refrigerator for 2 hours before serving.

In Sicily Marsala is used with strawberries instead of white wine.

SLICED ORANGES IN MARSALA (*Fette di arance al marsala*) *Sicily*
ILLUSTRATED PAGE 136

4–6 servings:

6 large blood oranges
sugar to taste
½ cup (⅔) sweet Marsala

2–3 tablespoons (2½–3¾) of any sweet
liqueur

Carefully peel the oranges, discarding all the pith. Cut them into slices, discarding the first and last slice of each orange as this will have too much pith. Sprinkle generously with sugar, add the Marsala and liqueur, mix well and chill.

CHESTNUTS (*Castagne*)

Chestnuts are good in Italy. They are much appreciated and used in sweet dishes as well as being roasted and dried. When the chestnut season is at its height, an Italian will offer the unexpected guest a bowl of hot roasted chestnuts with a glass of wine, both highly acceptable.

Chestnuts are also dried and ground into a fine flour, and in Tuscany they are made into a heavy cake called *Castagnaccio alla fiorentina* or *Castagnaccio alla toscana*, which is sold on the streets of Florence in the autumn.

CHESTNUTS COOKED IN WHITE WINE (*Busecchina*) *Lombardy*

3–4 servings:

1 lb. dried chestnuts
1½ cups (2¼) dry or sweet white wine
pinch salt

2 tablespoons (2½) sugar
½ pint (1¼ cups) cream

If a sweet wine is used, lessen the quantity of sugar.

Soak the chestnuts overnight in the wine plus sufficient water to cover. Next day put them into a pan with their liquid, salt and sugar, bring gently to the boil, lower the heat and simmer until tender, 20–30 minutes. Most of the liquid will be absorbed. Cool, chill and serve with cream.

MONT BLANC CHESTNUT PUREE WITH CREAM (*Monte-bianco*) *Lombardy*

6–8 servings:

2 lb. chestnuts
1 quart (5 cups) milk
1 small piece vanilla
8 oz. (1 cup) granulated sugar
½ cup (⅔) water

2–3 tablespoons (2½–3¾) brandy or
Strega liqueur
1½ cups (2¼) whipping cream
1 tablespoon (1¼) fine sugar

Cut a cross on the flat side of the chestnuts with a sharp knife and either bake them in a hot oven (400°F., mark 6) for 15–20 minutes, or boil them in water until they peel easily.

Pull off the skins while the chestnuts are still hot. Put them into a pan with the milk and vanilla and cook over a moderate heat until very soft.

While the chestnuts are cooking, make a syrup. Put the granulated sugar with the water into a pan and stir over a moderate heat until it is dissolved. Raise the heat, and without stirring cook the syrup until it thickens and reaches the soft-boil stage, this takes 6–10 minutes. Let this cool.

Drain the chestnuts and take out the vanilla (this can be washed and used again). Rub the chestnuts through a fine sieve. Combine the purée, syrup and brandy and beat until smooth. Cool. Put the purée through a potato masher and let it fall lightly into a pyramid or mountain shape onto the serving platter. Whip the cream until stiff, add the fine sugar, beat until the cream is very stiff, and spread it over the top of the chestnut cone so that it covers the peak, leaving the base comparatively free.

Failing fresh chestnuts, commercially-prepared chestnut purée can be treated in the same way.

LEMON WATER ICE (*Granita di limone*) *Sicily*
ILLUSTRATED PAGE 136

When *granita* is served in Italian cafes, it is the sign that summer has arrived. It is served at all times of the day and often it is eaten together with bread or a *brioche* (*granita con pane*) at breakfast time.

4–6 servings:

$1\frac{1}{2}$ **cups strained lemon juice**　　**1 cup sugar**
grated rind 1 lemon　　　　　　　**3 cups water**

Combine the juice and the rind. Put the sugar and water into a pan and cook over a moderate heat until the sugar dissolves, stirring all the time. Bring the syrup to a boil and, as soon as it bubbles, cook for exactly 5 minutes. Take it from the heat and cool. Stir the syrup, lemon juice and rind together, pour into an ice-cube tray and freeze without stirring until granular. Serve in sorbet glasses or tumblers.

It is immaterial what size measuring cups are used in this and the following two recipes, providing the same size is used throughout.

COFFEE WATER ICE (*Granita di caffè*) *Sicily*
ILLUSTRATED PAGE 136

4–6 servings:

1 cup sugar　　　　　　　　　　**3 cups freshly-made strong black coffee**
1 cup water

(See note on measuring cups above.)
Dissolve the sugar in the water over a low heat, stirring all the time. Bring this to the boil and boil rapidly for exactly 5 minutes. Cool, combine with the coffee and pour into a freezer tray. Freeze without stirring until granular. Serve in sorbet glasses or tumblers.

STRAWBERRY WATER ICE (*Granita di fragole*) *Sicily*
ILLUSTRATED PAGE 136

6 servings:

2 quarts (10 cups) fresh strawberries **1 cup water**
1 cup sugar **juice 1 small lemon**

(See page 169, note on measuring cups.)

Wash, hull and rub the berries through a sieve, or purée in a blender. Dissolve the sugar in the water, then bring it to the boil and boil for just 5 minutes. Cool. Combine with the strawberry purée and lemon juice, stir and freeze until the mixture is granular. If a less granular mixture is preferred, stir occasionally.

EGG PUNCH OR CAUDLE (*Zabaione* or *Zabaglione*) *Piedmont*

The latter spelling of this sweet dish is regarded today in Italy as archaic. The usual proportions for *zabaione* are, for each egg yolk, 1 tablespoon ($1\frac{1}{4}$) of sugar, and 2 ($2\frac{1}{2}$) of Marsala.

6 servings:

6 egg yolks **12 tablespoons (15) Marsala**
6 tablespoons ($7\frac{1}{2}$) fine sugar

Whisk the eggs until a pale lemon colour, add the sugar and beat or whisk until thick. Trickle in the Marsala, whisking all the time. Pour into the top of a double boiler and cook over ALMOST boiling water, whisking all the time, until the mixture thickens sufficiently to form small mounds. On no account allow the water under the pan to come to the boil or let the bottom of the pan touch the water. Scrape round the sides of the pan continuously. Immediately the cream is thick, take it from the heat and pour into shallow glasses and serve either hot or warm.

ICED EGG PUNCH OR CAUDLE (*Zabaione gelato*) *Sicily*

5–6 servings:

4 egg yolks **1 cup ($1\frac{1}{4}$) sweet Marsala**
4 oz. ($\frac{1}{2}$ cup) sugar **$\frac{1}{2}$ cup ($\frac{2}{3}$) cream, whipped**
1 long strip lemon peel

Beat the yolks, add the sugar and peel, and beat until thick. Discard the peel. Gradually add the Marsala, beating all the time. Pour the mixture into the top of a double boiler and cook over ALMOST boiling water (see preceding recipe), stirring all the time until the custard is so thick it stands in peaks. Take from the heat and whisk until it is cold. Whip the cream until stiff and fold it into the custard. Pour into tall, chilled glasses and leave in a refrigerator for several hours. Serve with wine biscuits.

WHITE WINE EGGNOG (*Bibita Valdostana*) *Valdostana*

4 servings:

4 cups (5) dry white wine   **6 oz. ($\frac{3}{4}$ cup) fine white sugar**
4 eggs

Beat the eggs, add the sugar and beat until frothy. Add the wine, beat for a few minutes and drink at once. Instead of beating, all the ingredients can be mixed in a blender.

In the Val d'Aosta it is usual to serve the *bibita* in a wooden mug called a *grolla*.

MACARONI COOKED IN MILK (*Maccheroni con latte*) *Southern Italy*

4–6 servings:

$\frac{1}{4}$ lb. macaroni   **1–2 teaspoons ($1\frac{1}{4}$–$2\frac{1}{2}$) finely-grated**
2 pints (5 cups) milk   **orange peel**
2–3 tablespoons ($2\frac{1}{2}$–$3\frac{3}{4}$) sugar

Have ready a large pan of bubbling boiling water. Add the macaroni and cook it until *al dente* (see page 83). Drain off the water. Return the macaroni to the pan and add the milk. Bring it gently to the boil, add the sugar and orange peel, and cook over a low heat until the macaroni is tender.

This is one of the rare sweet milk macaroni dishes of Italy. Either of two varieties of macaroni are usually used, the *zite* or *zitoni*. If orange peel is not available, use freshly-grated nutmeg or powdered cinnamon instead.

CHOCOLATE PUDDING (*Budino al cioccolato*) *Piedmont*

6 servings:

8 oz. (8 squares) bitter (bakers') cooking   **8 oz. (1 cup) sugar**
   chocolate, grated   **sweet almond oil**
2 pints ($2\frac{1}{2}$) milk   **sweetened whipped cream, about 1 cup**
pinch vanilla sugar   **($1\frac{1}{4}$)**
$1\frac{1}{2}$ oz. ($\frac{1}{4}$ cup) potato flour

Put the milk into a pan, sprinkle with vanilla sugar and warm gently. Combine the chocolate, potato flour and sugar in another pan. Put this on the stove over a low heat and very gradually add the warmed milk, stirring all the time. Bring to a slow boil, stirring continuously and cook until the mixture thickens. Beat well and then pour into a water-rinsed bowl. Leave until cool, beating it occasionally.

Grease a ring mould with the sweet almond oil and pour in the pudding mixture. Shake the pan to ensure the mixture is evenly distributed and leave to chill and firmly set. When the pudding is set, turn it out on to a round platter, pile whipped cream in the centre and garnish with small mounds of whipped cream round the sides.

RICOTTA CHEESE WITH COFFEE (*Ricotta al caffè*) *Sicily*

6 servings:

1½ lb. Ricotta cheese

4 oz. (½ cup) fine sugar

¼ cup (⅓) finely-ground coffee, preferably dark continental roast

¼ cup (⅓) rum

coarsely-grated bitter (bakers') chocolate

Beat the cheese until it is fluffy or press it through a fine sieve. Beat in first the sugar, add the coffee, then the rum. Put into glasses and chill for several hours. When serving, sprinkle with chocolate.

herbs and spices  aromi e spezie

The use of herbs varies in Italy from province to province, for what grows well in one area does not necessarily grow well in another, another factor which contributes to the variety in the flavour of Italian dishes. The following list contains the herbs and spices most frequently used in the Italian kitchen.

ANISE *Anice* These are seeds with a mild liquorice flavour used in sauces, sweet bread rolls and biscuits (cookies). Anise oil is also used to flavour pastries, and a liqueur is made from the seeds.

BASIL *Basilico* A green leaf herb (there are over fifty varieties) which prefers a warm climate and does not grow well in temperate countries. It is the basis of the Genovese *pesto*, and is included in tomato sauces, salad dressings, soups, stews, vegetables, and used with fish, poultry and other meat dishes. The leaves should not be chopped with a knife but torn apart with the fingers. Most Italian homes have basil growing either in the garden or in pots on terraces and verandas.

BAY LEAVES *Foglie di alloro* These are used in fish, meat and vegetable stocks, stews and soups and even in sweet custards; in marinades; and with spit-roasts, when a bay leaf is placed between the pieces of meat, poultry or fish. They are also placed between figs when packed in boxes to discourage weevils. Many people prefer to use fresh bay leaves, but others consider their flavour too pungent and prefer to keep them a day or two. Dried bay leaves have little or no flavour.

BORAGE *Borraggine* This grows wild and profusely in the Mediterranean region. Ligurians use it in a ravioli stuffing; it is cooked and served like spinach; or the leaves are dipped in batter and fried. It can be used in salads if the leaves, which are hairy, are first finely chopped. Use borage as soon as it is picked as it wilts quickly.

CAPERS *Capperi* These are not usually regarded as a herb. Capers are the buds of a pretty plant which grows in warm areas on old walls and ruins; but they are also extensively cultivated. For the market they are carefully graded and their price varies accordingly. On their home ground they are sold loose, salted or pickled. They are used in fish dishes, sauces, pickles, with salt cod, and with veal and lamb.

CHERVIL *Cerfoglio* The flavour of chervil is reminiscent of aniseed and it grows well in a temperate climate. It must be used fresh and added to a dish just before serving, for its flavour is too delicate to withstand long cooking. It is particularly good with eggs, salads and garnishes.

CHICORY *Cicoria* or *Radiccho* Herb chicory is meant here, not its close relative *chichorium endiva*, endive. The chicory herb, which grows wild, is a perennial with a clear bright flower and is much used in Italian cooking to add certain bitterness, particularly to salads. Probably the best, certainly the most esteemed, of the chicories is the lovely *cicoria di Treviso* with its pink and white leaves. But there are many other varieties, all with a completely different appearance, many very colourful.

FENNEL *Finocchio* The herb fennel is used both as a green herb, and for its seeds. It grows easily in most gardens. The flavour of fennel varies according to its type: wild fennel is slightly bitter, and sweet or Roman fennel has a somewhat aniseed flavour, and is generally preferred in Italian cooking. It is used with fish, particularly with red mullet, in fish stocks, soups and stews. Fennel is often added to a mayonnaise, and served with pork. Snails are flavoured with the green seeds of wild fennel.

GARLIC *Aglio* Garlic plays an important part in the flavouring of Italian food throughout the country, but it would be wrong to suggest that it is used everywhere with abandon. It adds to fish, meat and vegetables a zest, increasing flavour and reducing the fattiness of foods. There are several varieties of garlic, some with bulbs covered with white skins, others with pink or mauve skins. Some garlic have small cloves, others large. Also the number of cloves to a bulb varies enormously.

GINGER *Zenzero* This is used in large quantities in Basilicata and is simply called 'strong' by the local population.

MARJORAM *Maggiorana* This sweet and scented herb is related to thyme with which it can be mixed or even replace. It is used in omelettes, sauces, stews and salads and with clams, turtle, onions and poultry. However, like chervil, its flavour is not long lasting and it should not be added to a dish until shortly before it is to be served. There are several varieties of marjoram (see oregano).

MINT *Menta* This is not used a great deal in Italian cooking, but when it is, usually in stews, lamb dishes, salads, with fish and broad beans.

NUTMEG *Noce moscata* Every Italian kitchen has its nutmegs which are always freshly grated directly into the dish they are to flavour. A small grater should be kept exclusively for them.

OREGANO *Origano* Technically the same plant which is called wild marjoram. When it grows wild in cold climates it has what is called a 'green taste' and is less peppery than that grown in southern Italy but is far more pungent. It is particularly important in Italian cooking and is used dried more often than fresh. It is used with tomatoes, cheese, beans, soups, stews, ragouts, *pizze* etc. (see marjoram).

PARSLEY *Prezzemolo* Italian cooks add freshly-chopped parsley into their pans as instinctively as they add salt. In Italy both the flat or plain-leafed parsley, and the so-called Hamburg parsley (which is grown as a root vegetable although botanically it is also a true parsley) is used. The leaves of Hamburg parsley are used in the usual ways, and the fleshy white tap-root is cooked, or grated and added raw to salads. Its flavour is a cross between celeriac and parsnip. There is also Neapolitan parsley which is grown in southern Italy for its stems, which are eaten in much the same way as celery.

RED PEPPER *Pepe forte* This is made from the seeds of red or chilli peppers dried and crushed and is used to flavour stews, sauces, soups etc.

ROSEMARY *Rosmarino* This grows profusely in the Mediterranean countries but it will also grow in temperate climes, and is one of Italy's most popular herbs. It is used with fish, grilled or roasted meat (especially lamb and kid), with chicken, rabbit, and in Umbria with pork.

SAFFRON *Zafferano* This is considered an essential for a *risotto alla milanese* to give its traditional colouring; it is also used in 'white' and bland dishes both for colour and its faint flavour.

SAGE *Salvia* This is a powerful herb to be used with discretion. For cooking, the narrow-leafed sage with blue flowers is probably the best. It is used in Italy mainly with small birds, eel and veal.

TARRAGON *Dragoncello* Tarragon is not greatly favoured in Italy except around Siena where it grows.

THYME *Timo* This herb is used fairly generally, especially in soups, stews, sauces, salads, meat, poultry and game dishes.

cheeses  *formaggi*

ASIAGO A hard paste cheese made from skimmed and unskimmed cows' milk originally produced in Asiago in Venezia and in the Friuli mountains, but it is now also made in Lombardy. It is a most palatable cheese but is a little sharp, and is characterized by small holes fairly evenly scattered throughout its granular paste. Used fresh as a table cheese; hard for grating.

BEL PAESE This literally means 'beautiful country'. It is one of the best known of the Italian table cheeses, and the trade name of one of a group of uncooked soft, mild, fast-ripened Italian cheeses. The first Bel Paese was made in Melzo, near Milan, and it literally put this small town on the map for on the lid of each box there was and still is a map of Italy with Melzo marked larger than Rome. It is a bland cheese with a slightly salty flavour produced all through the year. It is an excellent melting cheese.

BITTO A hard, rather fat Lombardy cheese of the Emmentaler group with small 'eyes', made from cows' and ewes' milk or goats' and cows' milk mixed. It is sometimes eaten fresh when it is soft and mild, but it is usually allowed to ripen for two years before eating, by which time it becomes sharper in flavour and firm with tiny spots of moisture. When fully matured it is grated.

BUTIRRI A variety of Caciocavallo made in Calabria and Campania. A large knob of butter is embedded in the cheese which is shaped like an elongated fir cone, so that when cut each segment contains both cheese and butter.

CACIOCAVALLO A cheese of southern Italy and in particular Sicily, spindle-shaped with a pointed end and a neck and head at the top. Translators have had much amusement with the name of this cheese which, in effect, means 'cheese on horseback', *cacio a cavallo*. Many have decided that it was originally made from mares' milk but, sadly for this theory, a mare is a *cavalla* and not a *cavallo*. There is no generally accepted explanation for its curious name but one is that the cheese, which is always tied in pairs, is hung over a pole to cure and so made to look as though astride a saddle. In Naples they have a

176

theory that the name comes from *cacio col cavallo*, a cheese which is stamped with the effigy of the wild horse shown on the arms of the city of Naples.

It is a cheese with a pleasant, sharpish flavour usually made with cows' milk but buffaloes', goats' or ewes' milk is often added. It is now produced in most parts of the country. When used as a table cheese, it is matured from two to four months; but for grating purposes, it needs maturing up to twelve months. It has a smooth texture when fresh and both travels and keeps well which makes it an exportable cheese.

CACIOTTA A mild cheese made from ewes' milk in Tuscany, cows' milk in Umbria, and goats' milk in Capri. In the Marches they combine cows' and goats' milk. It is a pleasing cheese without being exciting.

CANESTRATO A salty, strong, yellow cheese made from ewes' milk and one of the most popular cheeses in Sicily. It is moulded in baskets and hardens sufficiently to be grated.

CASO FORTE The oddest of cheeses which is served not at the end of a meal but at the beginning, acting as an appetizer to stimulate the taste buds. Its aroma is strong but it has a pleasantly sharp flavour and its recipe has been handed down, so they say, for generations in Statigliano in the Naples region.

CASTELMAGNO One of the blue or green cheeses similar to Gorgonzola, made in Piedmont some fifty miles from Turin. It is strong and herb-flavoured, sharp and salty.

CASU MARZU This comes from Sardinia. The translation of the name is 'rotten cheese' but it is considered by connoisseurs as delicious.

CRESCENZA A winter cheese with a delicate flavour which has been described as 'table cheese, butter and cream' all in one mouthful. The best is said to come from Melzo, near Milan.

DOLCELATTE A mild and creamy cheese of the Gorgonzola variety. Its name means 'sweet milk' and it is also somewhat oddly called 'parsley in cream'.

ERBO A green cheese of the Gorgonzola type.

FIOR D'ALPE. Mainly made in Lodi near Milan from cows' milk. It is creamy, soft, with an elastic texture, and a pleasant buttery-herb flavour. It is produced throughout the year.

FIOR DI LATTE Literally translated this means 'flower of the milk'. An unsalted cheese which, when fresh, is extremely good and 'squeaks in the mouth' when eaten.

FIORE MOLLE A slightly salty, soft cheese from Lazio, around Rome. It is a bright creamy colour and is often heightened by a little saffron.

FONTINA One of Italy's great cheeses. The true and original Fontina d'Aosta comes from a rigidly defined zone, the Valley of Aosta, in northern Italy near the Swiss border. In appearance the cheese resembles Swiss Gruyère in that it has a brown crust and comes in wheels twelve to fifteen inches in diameter and three to four inches thick. The colour of the cheese is ivory, the texture fairly firm and broken here and there with tiny holes or eyes. For many cheese lovers Fontina is a cheese-maker's dream come true. It combines the nutty sweetness of Emmental with the tangy flavour of Gruyère. At room temperature it never liquefies but neither does it remain quite solid, being creamy.

Fontina d'Aosta has many imitators, known by such names as Fontal and Fantina. Its name is protected by law in Italy. It is essential for the Piedmont *fonduta*.

FORMAGGIO FIORE or FIORE SARDO (Flower of Sardinia) This is the Sardinian version of Pecorino. It is white in colour, with a hardish texture and a sharpish flavour. When fresh it is good for table use; when old, i.e. three months, it is better for grating. It is preferred by the Sardinians to Parmesan cheese.

GORGONZOLA Probably the best known of the Lombard cheeses and, indeed, of all Italian cheeses. It was originally made in the village of Gorgonzola but today it is produced in and around Milan. It is stored in damp but cool caves to develop its characteristic mould. Gorgonzola travels and keeps well and thus enjoys an international reputation. It is uniquely creamy, soft and buttery and with a sharp flavour. There is both *piccante* and *dolce* (sweet) Gorgonzola. Both types belong to the blue-streaked cheeses. There is also a white Gorgonzola slightly bitter in flavour which is much appreciated.

GRANA CHEESES This is the generic name of a group of Italian cheeses and refers to the closely grained texture of the cheese which is interspersed with tiny pinpoint holes. There are two main types both commercially called Parmesan outside of Italy, but known as Parmigiano e Reggiano and Grana Padano within the country.

GRANA, LODI A fine-grained Lombardy cheese equivalent to Parmesan or granular cheese, but somewhat coarser and stronger in flavour. It is also rather more yellow and is pitted with holes, but its flavour, though sharper, does resemble Parmesan.

MASCHERPONE or MASCARPONE A Lombardy cheese which is more like a clotted cream than a cheese and is served with chocolate cake, strawberries or with bread. Butter-coloured, it is made from fresh cream and tastes like thick, firm-whipped cream. It is generally considered a winter cheese, but is available up to late spring in some areas. Originally it was sold in muslin and wrapped in small packages, but today it comes in larger quantities. It is often mixed with rum and sugar and served as a sweet dish. There is also Mascherpone Passato, rather like a Taleggio; and a smoked Mascherpone.

MOZZARELLA A cheese which originated in the South, particularly in Campania, where it is still produced in vast quantities. It is a soft curd, solid but slightly rubbery cheese, with a smooth texture and snow-white in colour. It should be made of buffalo milk and still is in many parts of the South. It must be eaten fresh and is (usually) sold wrapped in paper, dripping with its own whey. It has become so popular in Italy that it is being made throughout the country, but since there is a decline in the number of buffaloes, more and more Mozzarella is made with cows' milk. Although good, this does not have quite the delicate, mild but fine flavour of the buffaloes' milk product. It is at its best absolutely fresh. Once it has been cut, its whey flows, therefore left-over cheese is best used in cooking. In Naples it is used in *pizze*. There is also a smoked, tan-coloured Mozzarella.

PAGLIARINI A cows' milk cheese from Piedmont, slightly sharp in flavour and sold on straw mats, hence its name.

PANNERONE A creamy cheese with a decidedly sharp flavour, made in the same manner as Gorgonzola except that it is not stored in caves to develop a mould.

PARMESAN One of the finest cheeses in the world, made in Italy for more than nine hundred years, some claim two thousand years. The full and correct name is Parmigiano e Reggiano, and it comes from a small area of the country comprising Parma, from which it gets its name; Reggio-Emilia, where most of the cheese is made; Modena; and certain sections of Bologna. It is made from mid-April to precisely November 11. Good Parmesan is golden-yellow, solid and compact and can be eaten fresh when (although sharp but never acid) it is delicious. However, it is best known as a grating cheese which has the quality of bringing out the essence of every other ingredient with which it is matched. It has never been duplicated outside of Italy and belongs to a group of cheeses known by the generic name of *Grana* (see page 178) or grain, which refers to their grainy texture. It is not cheap, even in Italy, where it comes in three ages: old, *vecchio*; two years, *vecchione*; three years and over, *stravecchione*. As a cooking cheese it has no equal, it does not toughen when cooked, nor melt rapidly, nor make strings.

PECORINO The generic name for all Italian cheeses made from sheeps' milk. Not all Pecorino cheeses have the same flavour, nor are all uniformly good; but generally they are good cheeses. There are many variants and most Italians have their favourite Pecorino. For some it is the Pecorino Romano, from Moliterna, of the Roman countryside, which is most favoured, especially in Lazio. This is a hard, dry, yet curiously tender and smooth cheese. Norcia in Umbria has a particularly piquant version with a ribbed dark rind. Sardinia has a very sharp Pecorino, Sardo. Siena has its version with a mottled red rind; Lucca, in Tuscany, has a charcoal-coloured rind, other areas have a variety with a coal-black rind. A young Pecorino, *pecorino da tavola*, is used as a table cheese, but hardened it becomes a grating cheese.

Most Pecorino cheeses come as round-shaped cakes weighing between three to five pounds, but there are other shapes some of which are very small. Siena produces her Pecorino in a variety of odd shapes. The rind is usually hard and the paste yellow in colour, although this again varies, for in Umbria much of the fresh Pecorino has a soft white rind and comes in round balls.

PROVATURA A soft, white buffaloes' milk cheese made in the countryside around Rome but becoming rare. It is sold in the shape of a large egg and must be eaten fresh and chilled.

PROVOLA A speciality of Campania which should be made with buffaloes' milk and eaten fresh. It can be aged by being slightly smoked. It is becoming a rare cheese, which is a pity for it has a good flavour.

PROVOLONE A cheese similar to Provola, which it has largely replaced. Previously made from buffaloes' milk, it is now usually made from cows' milk. It comes in many shapes and sizes, some very amusing, i.e. pigs, little men, melons, pears, cylinders and sausages etc.; which are hung on string or the 'hangman's rope'. Probably the most popular shape is the large oval, entwined with cord which leaves its characteristic marking on the shiny rind. When young, this cheese is delicate and even creamy, but the older cheeses are tangy, somewhat sharp and even spicy in flavour.

RAGUSANO A Sicilian hard cheese used as a table cheese up to six months, and later as a grating cheese. It has a sweetish, delicate flavour when fresh, but is sharp when ready for grating.

RICOTTA A white curd cheese made throughout Italy but particularly in the South. The name Ricotta means twice-cooked, for this cheese is produced by cooking the whey from other cheeses, such as Provolone, Pecorino and Mozzarella. Its most usual form is a soft, unsalted, white curd cheese, but it possesses a distinctive flavour. Fresh Ricotta is used in a great many well-known Italian dishes, such as the Sicilian *cassata*; also as a stuffing or a sauce for ravioli, lasagne, spaghetti etc. It can be eaten with sugar and fruit; in Tuscany it is served sprinkled with brandy and sugar. There are salted Ricottas, such as those made in the Marches, preserved between aromatic leaves; and there is *ricotta salata* which is sometimes known as 'Ricotta with rind'. In Sicily, smoked Ricotta is produced in the mountains.

ROBIOLA A cheese from northern Italy, particularly from the alpine country. Its name comes from the red covering in which it was originally encased. It is a soft, almost runny cheese, rich and can be fairly strong in flavour but it varies from place to place. Pressed into square and round shapes, it is eaten both fresh and aged. Some connoisseurs say it has something of the flavour of truffles.

ROBIOLINI A cheese made in both Piedmont and Lombardy, the latter claiming they produce the best. It is a smooth cheese with a distinctive flavour.

SARDO or SARDO ROMANO See FORMAGGIO FIORE

SCAMORZA or SCAMOZZA A soft, mild Mozzarella type of cheese made originally in Abruzzi from cows' milk. It should be eaten fresh, but it is also used in cooking.

STRACCHINO A generic name given to a group of soft, whole milk cheeses, particularly in Lombardy, to which Taleggio and Gorgonzola belong. The name is said to be derived from the word *stanco*, which means tired, for it was considered this particular type of cheese was best made with milk taken from tired cows, i.e. those who had enjoyed a long period of grazing in good pastures. It has a smooth, soft texture, a creamy colour and, although exceptionally mild, it does have a very special flavour.

TALEGGIO A fat, soft cheese of the Stracchino type, white to straw-coloured, with a thin, soft pinkish rind. It has a slight aromatic flavour and when ripened it is used as a table cheese, but it must be eaten fresh.

TOMINI A rather special little Piedmontese cheese made from goats' milk and preserved in pepper.

wines   vini

To drink wine in Italy is, and always has been, a way of life; for wine has been abundant in this area for centuries, long before the Romans. Today there is no region in the country which does not have its own wines produced from its own vineyards. An excellent and equable climate enables Italy to be the largest wine-producing country in the world, producing wines of character and distinction.

Grapes grow everywhere in Italy. Vineyards stretch for miles and they vary from the neat, scientifically-controlled rows of vines to those which are trained over garden fences and trellis work, or are strung between trees in smallholdings.

Obviously the great wines of Italy are produced in the large vineyards. The wines of the gardens and smallholdings are meant for local consumption, a *vino di casa*, or wines to quench the thirst. Much of this latter is both pleasing to the palate and light on the pocket, although sometimes it can be rather raw. Buying local wine in Italy is a gamble but one which nearly always comes off. Many albergoes, trattorias and ristorantes produce their own wines, pleasant and uncomplicated, which they sell in carafes. It is worthwhile remembering that many a nameless wine produced in areas of finer wines is often as good as the named one.

With so many vineyards it is not surprising to discover that the Italians have plenty of choice in their grapes, and consequently each region produces varying types of wines: red, white and rosé; dry, sweet, semi-sweet and sparkling wines; and vermouths.

To compare Italian wines with French is not fair to either country; conditions in the two countries are so different, that obviously different wines are produced. Not only is there a difference of soil, there is far more sun in Italy, methods of viticulture and vinification are dissimilar, and in general so are the grapes.

Although the classification of wines in Italy is firmly established, it is not possible here to go into details of the Italian wine laws. Briefly, there are three categories or denominations describing the origin of wines: 1. *Semplice* DOS (unblended); 2. *Controllata* DOC (controlled); and 3. *Controllata e garantita* DOCG (controlled and guaranteed).

Apart from State control, dedicated Italian wine producers, whether producing classified wines or not, have been organizing meetings, tastings etc., to promote their wines. Travellers interested in Italian wines can visit important wine cellars and vine-yards almost at any time. Anyone really interested in Italian wines should visit Siena and go over the Enotieca Italica Permanente (Wine Library or Museum) housed in a former Medici palace. There is no entrance fee, the wines of all regions are beautifully displayed in ancient cellars, and there are several tasting rooms, a fine dining room, and a staff both keen and knowledgeable. Wines can be bought and drunk on the spot or sent to any part of the world, and experts are on hand to give advice. The library also produces some literature on wines. For the traveller, the *strada del vino*, a map of the best wine areas of the country, is invaluable. Anyone with a car can visit all the important vineyards in any given area.

While classification is important, it must be remembered that it is not yet complete. Many good wines are waiting in the long queue for classification, while others are still working to reach the required standard. Not yet on the list of denominations, for example, is a favourite wine of mine produced from grapes of the hillsides of lovely Ravello, along the Amalfi coast. This is the curiously named Vino Episcopio which has been made since 1860, and was originally produced in the cellars of the Bishop's Palace, hence the name. It is now being made with loving care by the third generation of the Pasquale family. Matured in oak casks, it ages well. Just because it has no denomination, it would be a pity to miss this, and other such wines.

Although I would like to list every wine which has its classification, this is not possible here; there are too many Italian wines to attempt this other than in a book, which Cyril Ray has so admirably done in *The Wines of Italy* (McGraw-Hill, 1966). All I can do here is to indicate the best-known wines in the various regions.

PIEDMONT This most westerly region of northern Italy produces Barbaresco, a good dry red wine which receives its name from the place where it is produced

There are the Barberas, the commonest wine in Piedmont. Barolo, called in Italy the 'King of Wines', is a red wine which matures well; the Piedmontese open their bottles the evening before it is to be drunk. Piedmont is also the home of Asti Spumante, Italy's classic sparkling wine which is best served with sweet dishes, with fruit, or between meals. Brachetto, a rare red wine, comes both dry and sparkling. Also there is Cortese, a dry white, sparkling wine, and a semi-sweet version called Gavi. Gattinara is a red wine with a reputation and it is often chosen to be served with Piedmont's famous white truffles. A less renowned wine from the same area is Ghemme which is extremely good. Vermouth was first produced in Piedmont, but it is now produced throughout the country. There are three types: sweet red, dry white, and sweet white, the last a golden-yellow colour.

LOMBARDY An important province for wine which produces that fine red wine trinity: Grumello, Inferno and Sassella. The wines of Lombardy, which over the centuries have been praised by Pliny, Virgil, Roman Emperors and, somewhat nearer to our times Leonardo da Vinci, are not easy to classify because of their diversity, each village boasting its own production.

TRENTINO-ALTO ADIGE Here there are a number of red wines, including Lago di Caldaro, with a slight almond flavour described as 'good for those with stomach trouble'.

What an odd way to describe a good wine. There are several Rieslings, and a full-bodied Traminer, white with a slightly bitter taste. Teroldego is a particularly good red wine for serving with game and with meat dishes.

VENETO This region produces some of the country's best wines. There is the pleasing Bardolino, generally dry; a flinty dry Bianco di Conegliano; and another trinity, Recioto, red, white and rosé, but the red is not produced in large quantities. This region also produces Soave, one of the fine white wines of Italy. Probably the best known of the Veneto wines outside of Italy is the red Valpolicella.

FRIULI VENEZIA GIULIA This region produces wines mainly with non-Italian grapes: white wines with a pleasing flavour such as Sauvignon, and some good red wines, such as Tocai, not to be confused with the Hungarian Tokay.

LIGURIA This is the smallest region of Italy and, as far as wine production is concerned, it is shrinking, since land once devoted to viticulture has been taken over for growing flowers, particularly carnations. The most famous of the Ligurian wines come from the five 'lands'—*cinque terre*—which border the sea. Best known is Cinqueterre Bianco, a dry white wine. The genuine sweet wine produced in Liguria is rarely found outside the province.

EMILIA-ROMAGNA In this, the Italian gourmets' paradise, we find the Lambrusco wines which are red and sparkling; the Lambrusco di Sorbara is considered one of the most straightforward wines of Italy. Some of the sweet Lambrusca wines can only be served with the sweet course or between meals. A well-known red wine is the slightly flinty Sangiovese Romagnolo.

TUSCANY This is the home of Chianti, a wine that stands for all Italian wines in the minds of many foreigners. It is now strictly controlled, and only that produced in an area between Siena and Florence may call itself Chianti Classico. The black cockerel or rooster on the label round the neck is their sign. In the near future the famous full-bellied Chianti *fiaschi* is to be changed; sadly the bottles cost more than the wine. Do not, however, turn down those Chianti wines labelled *tipo*, they can also be good. A wine called Vino Santo, which is rather sweet, is not as one might think an altar wine. A particularly pleasant white wine of Tuscany is Vernaccia di San Grimignano.

UMBRIA Wines have been produced for centuries in this central province, especially in Orvieto where a visit to the caves under the city is an experience. They are pleasing but not outstanding wines.

MARCHES What little wine is produced in this coastal region is good, but the best undoubtedly is Verdicchio dei Castelli di Jesi, a fine white wine produced in amphora-shaped bottles.

LAZIO This province with Rome as its centre produces a fair number of well-known wines, the legendary Est! Est!! Est!!! and the several Frascati wines.

ABRUZZI AND MOLISE This rugged, mountainous region has only a narrow coastal plain on which to cultivate grapes, mostly for the table, but a few wines, red, white and rosé, are produced.

CAMPANIA A number of well-known wines are produced in this province dominated by Naples; the Capri red and white; Episcopio, red, white and rosé; and Falerno, red and white. The latter is produced from the falanghina grape and is a descendant of the famous Falernum wines of the Romans. Lacrima Christi del Vesuvio Bianco (The Tears of Christ) is an agreeable white wine, providing it is a true Lacrima; there is also a red and a rosé with a not unpleasant scorched flavour.

APULIA This eastern region of southern Italy produces the largest quantity of wine in Italy, much of which is so strong it is used for blending, and not only in Italy. Two such strong wines are the Aleatico di Puglia and the Barletta. Pleasant wines are the Castel del Monte, red, white and rosé and the Rosato del Salento which is used for special occasions.

CALABRIA This is the toe of Italy and has many exuberant wines which reflect the exuberant quality of the people of this region. Norman Douglas praised Cirò (his praise is reproduced on every bottle for all to read) which is a robust red wine and goes well with cheese, although I have had it served with a main meat course. Sweet Greco de Gerace is a fine dessert wine. Pliny, we read, favoured Balbino d'Altromonte, which is still famous today. It has a somewhat liqueurish flavour.

SICILY This island is a paradise for grape growers and some strong and powerful wines are produced. I am not sure how to take the words of one writer who described them as 'wines which flash like a knife, and leave an unprepared drinker more dead than alive'. Faro is one of the best wines of this island, a red which ages well; Malvasia is a pleasant golden dessert wine; and Etna a red and a white wine both with a volcanic flavour. Mamertino is an ancient wine and was served, it is recorded, at a banquet held to honour Caesar during his third consulship. Marsala, a fortified wine both brut and sweet, created by the brothers Woodhouse (there is still Woodhouse Marsala, although the firm is now Italian), owes much of its fame to Lord Nelson, and at one time it was popular in Britain. It has the virtue that it does not deteriorate once the bottle has been opened. Sicily's other two famous wines are the Moscato di Pantelleria and Moscato di Siracusa, both sweet wines, but the second is so rare it is almost disappearing.

SARDINIA. This is another island which produces a good quantity of wine. Cannonau, a grape which produces a slightly sweet red and rosé wine is used. There is Girò, a dessert wine served with sweet dishes; there are two or three kinds of Malvasia; white Moscato del Campidano, one of the best of the Sardinian wines and a source of energy; and finally Nuragus, probably the oldest white wine on the island, a trifle sharp and often used for blending. The Vernaccia, which has something of the character of sherry, is drunk on the island both before and after meals.

WINE AT TABLE   (*Il vino a tavola*)

HORS D'OEUVRE   Choose white wines, low in alcohol, which are preferably stimulating.

SOUP   A dry white wine or rosé is best with soup.

PASTA   Choose a light red or rosé wine for pasta with a heavy meat or tomato sauce. Where the sauce is simple, butter and cheese for example, a white wine is preferable.

RICE   The same advice as for pasta; heavy risottos take a red wine, light ones a white.

FISH   Choose a young white wine with a light bouquet to serve with plain boiled fish with a light sauce (even mayonnaise). Heavier fish dishes take an older, rather more alcoholic wine.

MEAT COURSE   Serve a white or rosé wine with fried food. The choice of wine with a roast depends on the type of meat: chicken and veal take a light red wine, nevertheless with a full bouquet; veal can also take a smooth, moderately full-bodied red wine; beef and other red meat are best served with full-bodied, austere red wines.

SALADS   No wine at all.

CHEESE   Ideally each cheese, if serving a selection, should accompany its own wine; but the general rule is to match a strong, robust cheese with an equally robust wine; a lighter cheese with a lighter wine. With fresh Parmesan, drink a dry sparkling wine.

FRUIT   A sweet, somewhat heavy wine is generally used, like the Vino Santo from Tuscany, or any of the wines which are labelled Moscato di . . . and, of course, Est! Est!! Est!!! With citrus fruit, no wine at all.

COOKING WITH WINE IN ITALY

With plenty of good, often cheap wine available it is natural that Italians should use considerable quantities in cooking. Red wine is used with meat and game, white with chicken, rabbit and fish, and Marsala or other sweet wines in sweet dishes, fruit cups and fruit salads etc.

Wine must be added with discretion to any dish, for it is added not to produce its own flavour, but to bring out the flavour of the foods with which it is cooked. In Italy, generally speaking, when wine is added to a dish it is always allowed to evaporate or be reduced by cooking before other ingredients are added.

A wine for cooking must be of reasonable quality, and drinkable. If it is not fit to drink, then it is not fit for cooking. On the other hand, no one cooks with vintage wine, since the very qualities which make it a vintage wine are lost immediately it is applied to heat.

coffee ❦ *caffè*

The Italians were among the first to propagate the habit of coffee drinking. It was the Venetian Ambassador to Turkey, Gian Francesco Morosini, reporting to his superiors on the Turkish habit of drinking coffee, who undoubtedly started the Italians doing the same. For not long after this report (1585), coffee drinking in *botteghe*, small shops, became a habit, a number of these establishments starting up in Venice. About eighty years later, a Sicilian called Procope started the first coffee house in Paris. The idea spread and coffee houses became the rage everywhere in Europe.

It should not be thought that there is only espresso coffee in Italy but certainly it is the most popular. This type of coffee is made in a large electric urn in which steam under pressure is forced through the powdered coffee.

If you want a small black coffee when in Italy, ask for *un caffè* or *un espresso* or *caffè normale*; it varies according to the locality. If a double or a larger coffee than the thimble-ful is required, ask for *caffè doppio* or *caffè alto*; coffee which is half milk and half coffee is *un cappuccino*; with a little milk only—i.e. a dash—it is a *caffè macchiato*; *caffè corretto col cognac* is a coffee well laced with brandy. Coffee can also be had with other alcohol, *grappa* for example.

In the home coffee is made either with a home-style espresso machine or a drip coffee pot. In the former the powdered coffee is placed in a wire basket or container. The bottom of the coffee pot is almost filled with water, the coffee-container screwed on the top and over this is placed another container which will take the final coffee, forced up by heat through a funnel. These are popular in northern Italy.

The *napoletana*, which works on the drip style, is universally used in the South. Here again there are three containers, one with a spout, one without, and a wire container for the coffee. This container takes just enough coffee to give the desired strength, according to the size of the pot, and this does not vary. To make the coffee, water is put into the spoutless container, and on to this is screwed the container with the coffee. On top of this is placed the spouted container, the spout pointing downwards. Then the water is brought to the boil over a low heat. When it indicates that the water has boiled, the *napoletana* is turned over, or reversed, so that the water in the lower container, now on top, slowly drips through the coffee grounds into the lower container with the spout. The resulting coffee will be strong, slightly bitter but extremely good. This can be drunk black or, as it is so often served in Italy, with milk, *caffèlatte*.

comparative cookery terms and measures

It is not simple to convert with absolute accuracy measurements for the kitchen. Generally speaking, absolute accuracy is not required, except when making cakes or pastries. Throughout this book both British and American measurements have been used and, as far as possible, ingredients have been measured in cups and tablespoons for easy conversion.

Fortunately for the cook, British and American solid weights are equivalent; but this does not always mean that the British housewife can readily understand American measurements or *vice versa*. In the United States the average housewife has her set of measuring spoons and cups. In Britain this is never so general, although most housewives do have a measuring cup or jug.

The British measuring cup used in this book is the British Standard Institute's Cup which gives a ½-pint measure, the equivalent to 10 fluid ounces (it is the size of the average British breakfastcup or tumbler). The American standard cup is equal to the American ½ pint, which is equivalent to 8 fluid ounces.

All spoon measurements are level unless otherwise specified.

Throughout this book British measurements are given first; the American equivalent follows, where necessary, in brackets.

CONVERSION OF METRIC MEASURES INTO BRITISH AND AMERICAN MEASURES

Exact measurements are, of course, not possible, and if applied in the kitchen would require all housewife-cooks to be also mathematicians, which most of us are not. The best, therefore, is the nearest approximation.

EXACT MEASUREMENTS

1 kilogram (kg) = 2.2 lb.   1 litre (l.) = 1.8 pints

APPROXIMATE MEASUREMENTS USED

1 lb. = 0.5 kg. or 500 grams	1 gallon = 4.5 litres
8 oz. = 240 grams	1 quart = 1.125 litres (1$\frac{1}{8}$ litres)
4 oz. = 120 grams	1 pint = 0.5 litres
1 oz. = 30 grams	$\frac{1}{2}$ pint = 0.25 litres
	$\frac{1}{4}$ pint = 0.125 litres ($\frac{1}{8}$ litre)

OVEN TEMPERATURE CHART

Electric Oven Setting Approximate Temperature	Gas Thermostat	Oven Description
250°F. (130°C.)*	$\frac{1}{4}$	very cool
275°F. (140°C.)	$\frac{1}{2}$	very cool
300°F. (150°C.)	1,2	cool
325°F. (160°C.)	3	warm
350°F. (180°C)	4	moderate
375°F. (190°C.)	5	fairly hot
400°F. (200°C.)	6	fairly hot
425°F. (220°C.)	7	hot
450°F. (230°C.)	8	very hot
475°F. (240°C.)	9	very hot

* Degree Celsius (centigrade) scale markings

THE INTERNATIONAL WINE AND FOOD SOCIETY

The International Wine and Food Society was founded in 1933 by André L. Simon, C.B.E., as a world-wide non-profit-making society.

The first of its various aims has been to bring together and serve all who believe that a right understanding of wine and food is an essential part of personal contentment and health; and that an intelligent approach to the pleasures and problems of the table offers far greater rewards than the mere satisfaction of appetite.

For information about the Society apply to the Secretary,
Marble Arch House, 44 Edgware Road, London W2

# select bibliography

Collecting material for this book I have naturally consulted a large number of books mainly local regional ones of which there are too many to be given at length here. I have also used the many culinary guide booklets issued by the Italian Tourist Board with pleasure and benefit, and consulted a number of Italian culinary magazines, such as *La Cucina Italiana* and *Nuova Cucina*. Of particular importance were:

Artusi, Pellegrino, *L'Arte di Mangiar Bene*, (50th edition), Casa Editrice Marzocco, Florence, 1950.

Boni, Ada, *Italian Regional Cooking*, Thomas Nelson & Sons, London, 1969.

Carnacina, Luigi, *Great Italian Cooking*, Paul Hamlyn Books, London, 1969.

Clair, Colin, *Kitchen and Table*, Abelard-Schuman, New York, 1964.

Contoli, Corrado, *Cucina Romagnola*, Edizioni Calderini, Bologna, 1963.

Hale, William Harlan, etc., *The Horizon Cookbook*, Doubleday & Company, New York, 1970.

Jarratt, Vernon and Enrica, 230 *modi di cucinare la pasta*, Arnoldo Mondadori, Milan 1969.

'Lisa Bondi', *Uova E Pesci*, Istituto Geografico De Agostini, Novara, 1969.

'Lisa Bondi', *Verdure*, Istituto Geografico De Agostini, Novara, 1970.

Paglia, Gianni, *Cucina Bolognese*, Edizioni Calderini, Bologna, 1959.

Ray, Cyril, *The Wines of Italy*, McGraw-Hill Book Company, London, 1966.

Root, Waverley, and the editors of Time Life, *The Cooking of Italy*, Time-Life Books, New York, 1968.

Guida Gastronomica d'Italia, Touring Club Italiano, Milan, 1951.

Il Cucchiaio d'Argento, (3rd edition), Domus Editoriale, Milan, 1951.

index

ITALIAN